The New Testament
with Imagination

The New Testament
with Imagination

A FRESH APPROACH
TO ITS WRITINGS AND THEMES

William Loader

WILLIAM B. EERDMANS PUBLISHING COMPANY

GRAND RAPIDS, MICHIGAN / CAMBRIDGE, U.K.

Published 2007 by

Wm. B. Eerdmans Publishing Co.

2140 Oak Industrial Drive N.E., Grand Rapids, Michigan 49505 /

P.O. Box 163, Cambridge CB3 9PU U.K.

Printed in the United States of America

11 10 09 08 07   7 6 5 4 3 2 1

Library of Congress Cataloging-in-Publication Data

Loader, William R. G., 1944-

The New Testament with imagination: a fresh approach

to its writings and themes / William Loader.

p.   cm.

Includes bibliographical references and index.

ISBN 978-0-8028-2746-3 (pbk.: alk. paper)

1. Bible. N.T. — Introductions. 2. Bible. N.T. — Theology.

I. Title.

BS2330.3.L63   2007

225.6′1 — dc22

2007003161

www.eerdmans.com

Contents

Acknowledgments

This book owes its inspiration to thousands of people whom I have met beyond the university setting over four decades of teaching, who have enjoyed camping in the New Testament. Most of them are not professionals and have not had the opportunity of formal theological education, but they have been enthusiastic and eager to explore. We have had some great times together. Some have had formal theological education but found themselves spending most of the time in camp, poring over detailed maps and loaded with information, rarely getting out to explore the highlights. This book reflects their challenges and their need to find out where to go and to get there within a short space of time.

The great New Testament scholar, Ernst Käsemann, once remarked to me, that if he had his time over again, he would concentrate on bringing people to the places that matter most, instead of focussing too much on extraneous detail. This book owes its inspiration also to his challenge.

I greatly appreciate those who read and commented on earlier drafts: in particular, Revd Dr Lee Levett-Olsen, Principal of Coolamon College, Revd Dr John Dunnill, my New Testament colleague at Murdoch University, and from local Perth congregations, Christine Fawell, and Neville and Karen Barber.

It is my pleasure to acknowledge the support of William B. Eerdmans Jr., whose publishing makes scholarship accessible and helps produce good maps and guides to help people find their way.

Introduction

There are many ways of reading the New Testament and many different ways of introducing it. This book offers a new way: through imagination and through sampling key passages.

It invites you to imagine yourself as someone waking up one morning in Capernaum at the time of Jesus and later making the pilgrimage to Passover, then as a woman travelling with your congregation's worries from Corinth to Paul at Ephesus, then as a scribe observing Matthew, the scribe, and finally as an older Samaritan woman in the circle where an older man wrote 1 John. There are no wild flights of imagination, no making up of stories, but just reflections of what we already know, but seen from a likely perspective within the scene.

The book also invites you to read some of the most important passages in the New Testament and to reflect on them. Its aim is not to overwhelm you with all you need to know, but to take you to where some of the richest fare is served. It is as much an introduction to the leading ideas as it is to details of time and place. It tries to avoid the dryness of abstract ideas and lists of information by inviting you to feel what was going on in key texts and sense the energy and excitement of the authors. It keeps bringing you directly to the New Testament itself.

My hope is that people reading this book will come away from it with a greater sense of the human encounters which lie behind the New Testament and what mattered most to its writers. In a technical sense it is a theological introduction, but it invites your engagement not so much with ideas as with the stories of people and their reflections.

History always entails imagination; otherwise we have no idea what happened in the past. The vehicle of imagination can take us into the ancient world more directly than long descriptions. So this introduction invites you to make that journey and then to sit and listen to what those people wrote. In the process they might also meet us in new ways and we might find with them a deeper common faith.

Each of the five chapters begins with an exercise in imagination. Then follow four sets of passages, each with reflective comment. I have selected these passages with a view to providing you with a path on entry into major issues and insights for understanding the New Testament. The passages and the attempts to imagine our way into the context where they were written belong together. Together they form five chapters on five significant aspects of the New Testament. The first two focus on Jesus. The third focuses on Paul and the letters. The fourth focuses on the first three gospels and the fifth on the gospel of John and its community.

We begin at the beginning: with Jesus in Capernaum.

CHAPTER ONE

Jesus and Capernaum: Hope and Change

Waking Up in Capernaum

What would be the first thing you would smell when you woke up, if you were living in Capernaum in the time of Jesus? Perhaps it might be the straw which made up the bed on which you were lying. Was it the smoke from the oil lamp which an early riser had already lit? If winds were from the south you might smell the tang of dried fish from the works across the lake near Magadan. Or it could be the smell of the fishing nets as the men were coming home from a night out trawling their nets.

Winters would be quite cool. But in summers you could look forward to very warm days. It doesn't take long for Capernaum to wake up. Soon you hear the clatter of carts bringing in vegetables and fruit for the market from surrounding villages. If you lived close to the lake, you might freshen your face in its sparkling water. The smell of baking bread would make breakfast something to look forward to. And what might await you in the day?

The same people might cross your path as yesterday: women fetching water, farm managers looking to hire some day help for the harvest, men hanging around the market hoping for such opportunities, people buying produce, old men sitting on benches deep in conversation, and perhaps, here and there, people with severe physical disabilities crouched at entries, hoping for crumbs of generosity.

It is unlikely you would see soldiers, although some days there would

1

be surprises: strangers passing through on their way east or west, crossing the borders to Philip's territory and Bethsaida or coming from there on their way to the bigger cities like Tiberias and maybe even on their way to the Great Sea, the Mediterranean, and ports from which to embark on great ships to Rome and Alexandria. You would have heard something of the language they spoke and perhaps you already knew enough Greek to say, "Hello," but all your townspeople speak Aramaic, a language like Hebrew and the languages spoken in Syria to the north.

You live not far from the border, so you would see the special arrangements which existed to collect tolls as people passed across. Would you have a known a Levi or a Matthew there? You might have heard the disturbance which recently took place, when Levi abandoned his post. Some people were glad there was one less toll collector or tax collector as they are sometimes called. Some were clearly "on the take."

They at least had enough money to create a social life for themselves in the way that had become fashionable. You might gain entry to one of their parties one day. Slouched around low tables they made merry with lots of food and drink. There were women. You have heard stories about what goes on. They could be loud affairs, but occasionally the company must have entertained itself with serious conversation.

These are a far cry from the very private gatherings at the more respectable end of town, where very devout men meet for study and discussion. They usually wore small tassels on the edges of their garments to symbolise their devotion to keeping the commands of the Bible. They were very careful about being clean in a ritual sense, especially before eating. So they had ritual baths where they immersed themselves. They also used stone vessels to store water for purification because people believed stone jars could not be contaminated. Even many ordinary people used stone vessels for this reason.

For some, their special gatherings included sharing in a special meal of bread and wine which they saw as a kind of celebration in advance of what was to come. They were praying for the day when God would restore Israel to its rightful place as God's special people in the promised land. That would be a time of great feasting. For some, it included a wonderfully wide vision of all the nations of the world joining in the celebration.

You are not likely to join in one of those meals without first establishing yourself as one of them. But you would see them often enough, praying aloud at the times of sacrifice in the temple in Jerusalem to the south.

When you went with others to the gathering on Saturdays, the sabbath, to hear readings from scripture and someone talk about them, they would be there. Often they would have a lot to say.

People around you seem happy, but there is also a lot of resentment. Those men waiting around for work at the market are clearly quite desperate. You wonder how their families make ends meet. The other day you heard the scandal that the wife of one of them had turned to prostitution to survive. People had nowhere to go. There was some help organised by the people who ran the synagogue, but it depended on gifts and donations. There were no government welfare agencies.

Apart from the officials of Herod Antipas, the ruler, who were mainly based in the bigger cities, local officials tended to be the leaders of the synagogue along with any priests in the area. They would sort out disputes and deal with crimes using the ancient biblical laws in the way they saw fit. Some people feared them. The few men who could write, the scribes, also exercised strong influence.

But most people were more afraid of the rich, especially those with big houses and big landholdings. There was a steady stream of people coming to their door and waiting around in the large public areas in the front of their houses. Most people ended up having to work for such people. In return, the best of the rich people made sure they survived. Yet even these so-called rich people were not really rich. They were just doing well at the top of the mass of the population who lived at a very basic level.

The truly rich lived in the big cities and owned great wealth. They had networks of farms and farm managers and had learned how to ensure their profits. Nevertheless they, in turn, paid significant sums in taxation to Herod Antipas. They could pass on those costs down the line, so that the people who felt the pinch most were the poor who had little prospect of work.

Some had drifted to the towns in hope of work, but mostly found little. Some would have been so impoverished and undernourished that they had no hope and thought no thoughts of hope. So people around you may seem happy, but inside and underneath the pleasantries is a lot of pain.

For those still sufficiently nourished to be able to reflect a little on their situation, this could become a spiritual problem. Constant exposure to stories of Israel's past kept the hope for some alive that life could change. God was a factor in hoping for new possibilities. Heroes like Moses and Joshua and David inspired some to think that there was an alternative to

3

what they were currently experiencing. Why should they be subject to Herod Antipas and through him to Rome? Why couldn't they be free? Hadn't God liberated their ancestors from slavery in Egypt? Hadn't David established a wonderful kingdom in the land of Israel?

People with enough food and enough time to think such thoughts faced important choices. One was to be resigned to the present woes. Nothing could change. It was too hard. You heard stories as a child about the freedom fighters in the time of Herod's father. One day your father showed you the caves where the rebels held out before they were trapped and burned to death. Occasionally you hear about bandits, making ends meet by robbery and sudden attacks on the unsuspecting. Apparently not all of them are criminals. But there's no revolt in your town.

You do hear about hopes for change from time to time, but it is mostly in the synagogue. You pray prayers that God will come and rule Israel again. Some people hope that God will send another king like David. Like David he will be God's anointed (Hebrew: Messiah; Greek: Christ) and will drive out the Romans and establish a kingdom of peace. Others hope for a new prophet and some insist that nothing will happen unless people learn to be much more obedient to God's laws. They make it their purpose to encourage people to greater obedience. One of the travellers coming up from the south told you once about the special community on the western shores of the Dead Sea, formed to concentrate on becoming more holy. They have a wonderful collection of writings, including holy scriptures but much besides.

More recently you have heard of another movement which has been attracting attention. A priest's son, called John, has been attracting large crowds not far from the Dead Sea, in the Jordan valley, announcing that God is soon to act and warning people to get ready by turning to God and letting themselves be dipped in the Jordan River. Perhaps it was an unsympathetic observer who called him John the Dipper (or Baptizer), but the name established itself and we know him as John the Baptizer or Baptist. He is certainly strange in his dress and apparently he lives in the wild, off natural honey and locusts, which some deem a treat.

You have heard arguments about John even in Capernaum. Some think he has gone too far in declaring that if people follow his instructions God will forgive their sins. The local priest seems to think that this is a challenge to the temple which has ultimate responsibility for such things. Others think it very odd that John makes everyone dip and makes no distinctions. It must be hard to take if you are a person of some standing.

None of this is comparable, however, to the major new events that have been happening right here in Capernaum. The man who originally came from Nazareth, Jesus (you would call him Jeshua or Joshua), has been causing quite a stir. It was his fault that Levi abandoned his post as a toll collector. Apparently two fishing families have also been disrupted. But these are just incidental to the sensational stories which are circulating about him.

He has performed acts of healing, including a leper and a madman from farther east who used to live in the cemetery. Some of the stories are probably exaggerated — people love stories — but there is obviously something to it. But even the miracles are not so important compared with what he has been saying. If anything, they make you want to sit up and take notice.

Yesterday you were in the marketplace when you heard him speaking to the old men. Lots of others had gathered around and even some women who had been making their purchases for the day. He was saying things like: "Don't worry so much about murder; look, rather, at murderous and hateful attitudes towards people. And don't worry so much about adultery; look, rather, at adulterous attitudes." He was looking at the men. They needed to stop blaming the women. He went on to imply that we ought to be looking at what goes on inside people which results in actions, good or bad, and not just at the actions, themselves. He even suggested people should not hate their enemies.

You could tell he had been with John the Baptist, because he had a similar attitude to living a simple lifestyle. He took it even further by challenging people to abandon their work and families and live with him in a kind of roving commune. Not everyone in Capernaum likes what they are hearing and seeing. No one really complains about miracles, although the old and wise say they have heard such claims before and speak of charlatans.

Some suspicions have been raised by the company he keeps. Women have joined the group. This is unusual and some wonder what this means. At least one of the women was held to be quite mad. Worse still, Jesus frequents gatherings of toll collectors. It is a good way of getting a meal for him and his companions, but it is hard for some to reconcile with messages of goodness. His generous acceptance of such company is perplexing. It seems the opposite of those who make their meals private and exclusive. This is all the more interesting, because he seems on the other hand to have so much in common with the latter. Like them he quite regularly speaks about the future and pictures it as a great meal, but in contrast to them he speaks of a meal open to all, for which people would come together from all directions.

This takes us to the heart of what has made Jesus so attractive. He talks about hope. You were there in the crowd when he declared he had good news to tell and proceeded to say that things were going to change for the poor and hungry. It was like what you had heard about John the Baptist, but this time with a major focus on the positive side. It addressed the deep pain people were feeling and it resonated with their faith that God really did care and that things would change, and change soon.

Some people really do believe it. It has certainly given hope to people who felt they had no hope and especially to those considered hopeless by others. In that sense a number of things have been happening which show that change for the better is already well under way. He speaks about God's coming reign, but in the next breath can say that God's reign has begun, at least for some people. The people considered to be possessed by demons have certainly had a kind of liberation.

A lot of the good news is much more than promise. There are good news stories of healing, of changed behaviour, of new networks of support for outcasts, and of a new sense of community. He has engendered a following, not only among those who travel with him, but also with many others in town who are changing their lifestyles and attitudes. He's doing great things for people who normally have little time for faith and little respect for themselves. He's changing people. Where will it lead?

A selection of passages to which this section alludes: Levi/Matthew: Mark 2:13-17; Matthew 9:9-13; Luke 5:27-32; tassels: Numbers 15:38-39; Mark 6:56; purity concerns: Mark 7:1-23; Matthew 23:25-26; John 2:6; the great feast: Isaiah 25:1-9; 2:1-4; Matthew 8:11-12; Luke 14:16-24; Mark 14:25; poverty and unemployment: Matthew 20:1-16; hope for change: Luke 1:46-55, 67-79; Acts 1:6; 5:36-37; Luke 10:30; John the Baptizer: Mark 1:1-11; Matthew 11:16-19; Luke 7:31-35; Mark 11:27-33; Matthew 21:28-32; Jesus calls disciples: Mark 1:16-20; 10:17-22; Jesus heals leper and "madman": Mark 1:39-45; 5:1-20; teaching: Matthew 5:21-30; Mark 7:21-23; Matthew 5:43-48; women: Luke 7:36-50; Mark 14:3-9; Luke 8:1-3; 10:38-42; Mark 11:20; 15:40-41; the reign/kingdom of God: Mark 1:14-15; Matthew 12:28; Luke 6:20-21; 11:20; 17:20-21.

1A. Luke 4:14-30:
The Beginning of Jesus' Ministry according to Luke

This is the first of a number of passages from the New Testament which we shall look at in this book. They are significant sample passages which will lead to the some of the major themes of the New Testament. They will also provide us an opportunity to reflect on the writings of the New Testament themselves, how they came about and how best to read them. These sections assume you have first read the passages. My comments are designed to supplement your reading.

Luke and His Sources

Luke is writing his account of Jesus (The Gospel according to Luke) and the early church (The Book of Acts) probably some time in the 80's, about 30-40 years after Jesus. In his introductory comments in 1:1-4 he tells us that he is not the first to write such an account. Others have done so beforehand. He is doing so not because he disapproves of what others have done, but because he has new information and also wants to draw together the various information and sources at his disposal. He wants to write an "orderly account," assembling all his information in a way that communicates the significance of Jesus in a way that will help people be confident in their faith.

He follows the style of many writers in his day by beginning his account with a very elaborate sentence and by dedicating his work to a sponsor, Theophilus, who may have been a real person or may just be a name chosen for the formal opening (a good choice — it means "friend of God"!). But Luke wrote so that his gospel would be widely read and become influential. In this he has obviously been successful.

We are able to identify one of Luke's sources: The Gospel of Mark, written probably about 15 years earlier in the late 60's or early 70's. Matthew, Mark, and Luke overlap in many ways. All but just over 30 verses of Mark are to be found in Matthew and Luke. After examining the material they have in common and noticing where one version obviously improves the other in style and content, most scholars have concluded that not only Luke but also Matthew used Mark as their main source. So they started with Mark as their base. With great care they each revised it in their own way, reorganised it in parts, and added other new material. The result was two new gospels: Matthew and Luke. They appear to have worked independently and not known each other's work.

Luke and Matthew do, however, share some material in common which they did not derive from Mark. We are now able to draw all that material together and identify it as belonging to another single source which appears to have been a gospel which consisted mainly of Jesus' sayings. Because some the earliest work on this source was done in German it has become the custom to refer to this source by the German word meaning "source," namely, "Quelle," shortened simply to "Q." Much of the material in the Sermon on the Mount belongs to that source. In addition Matthew and Luke each knew sayings and anecdotes about Jesus which appear on in their gospels. So only Luke has the parables of the Good Samaritan and the Prodigal Son, for instance. And only Matthew has the story of the Wise Men and the parable of the Hired Labourers. The chart in Appendix A shows the most common understanding of the dating of the writings and the way they relate to each other.

Writing a gospel was not easy. For Luke and Matthew it was not just a matter of copying Mark. Where were they to fit in all the other material? It was made harder and at the same time easier by the fact that no one seemed to have a life story of Jesus which recorded when the various episodes reported in the stories took place. Obviously the arrest, trial, and death took place at the end and the baptism at the beginning, but apart from that nothing is clear. When we look closely at Mark, we find that he has incorporated collections of stories and sayings which came about for a variety of reasons. The collection of parables about seeds in Mark 4 probably came about because people remembered these parables as all having to do with seeds. Mark 2:1–3:6 contains five stories about Jesus in conflict. It is not hard to imagine people drawing together such stories, perhaps for purposes of teaching. We see this also elsewhere in Mark.

It means that we cannot assume that Mark is using a diary of Jesus' life to shape the order in which he tells the story. Rather he is having to produce an order himself that enables the story as a whole to have the greatest impact. At some points he appears to have deliberately placed two stories side to side to create such an impact. For instance, following a conversation where the disciples show themselves to be particularly lacking in understanding and blind to what Jesus was saying (8:16-21), Mark places a story about Jesus healing a blind man (8:22-26). One can hardly miss the point!

We also find that both Matthew and Luke appear to assume that the order of events and sayings is not fixed. They feel free to change it to make their version of the story as a whole work more effectively. Both of them give special attention to the way they begin their gospels, each adding two additional chapters. They also give special attention to how they describe the beginning of Jesus' public ministry. Appendix B shows these differences in outline.

Approaching the Text

This brings us back to the passage which we are examining in this section, because it is Luke's account of the beginning of Jesus' ministry. Luke puts the story of Jesus' visit to his own home synagogue right at the beginning. He found this story down in chapter 6 of Mark, but he brings it up from there and expands it, perhaps with other traditions which he has at his disposal. As a result, when he gets down to that part of Mark in following Mark's order, he leaves out that episode because he has used it here at the beginning.

So when we approach any text in the first three gospels we need to bear the broader setting in mind of how the gospels relate to one another, what the order within them reflects, and, in the case of material occurring in more than one, where it comes from or how it is reused. It is also useful to reflect on how a story or saying might have been told and retold and why. That must to some degree be left to our imagination, but occasionally we may see signs which help us reconstruct what was probably the case.

When we approach a text, we usually come with our own agenda. Mine, in this instance, is to focus on those aspects of the text which will help us reflect further on the material of this first chapter of this book. The material about conflict which begins halfway through 4:22 relates more especially to our chapter two. But it is important even so to listen to the text in its own terms and especially important to listen to it in its context. We therefore turn to story as we have it in Luke.

Jesus in the Synagogue at Nazareth

The story in the synagogue at Nazareth itself tells us something incidentally about how people encountered such writings, including Luke's writing. They would not normally do so by taking Luke's gospel, for instance, onto their lap and reading it silently in a quiet room, as we might. Rather for most people the only encounter they would have with Luke's gospel would be when it was read aloud in a gathering, just as Jesus reads a segment of Isaiah aloud in the synagogue in our passage. So things like reading glasses, small print, paragraphs, and chapter headings played no role for them. Instead a skilled reader would speak the words of Luke's gospel out aloud. That reader would have to work with lines of letters which came one after another with no breaks to indicate where words began or ended. It was a skilled task indeed.

When you write things to be read in this way, you can't depend on bold or italics for emphasis or on paragraphs to indicate change of focus. You have to incorporate all the special emphases and indicators into what the reader will read aloud, so that hearers will gain a sense of what is important and what is not, and where the focus changes. People who learned to write usually also learned how to write in a way that worked well for the listeners. It included giving careful attention to how you said things but also to the order in which you said them. This was an important part of what people studied in schools of the time.

So Luke has made a deliberate decision to begin his account of Jesus' public ministry by making Jesus' visit to his hometown synagogue the first episode to be told. It gives important signals for what follows. Luke must have felt that by doing it this way he could help his hearers know from the beginning what mattered most for Jesus. In some ways the story is a mini-version of the whole story of Jesus which follows in the gospel and also of the story of the church which comes in Luke's volume two, namely the Book of Acts. It begins with a positive response to Jesus, but when Jesus speaks of God's love for outsiders, it swings around to a negative response: people try to kill Jesus. That is what happens in the gospel. It also happens in Luke's story of the church. Initially people respond to the church's preaching in thousands, but soon, especially as the church expands to include people who are not Jews (Gentiles), there is strong opposition and rejection. Luke is giving us a foretaste of what is to come.

In our first chapter of this book we have been imagining being alive at the time of Jesus. As Luke tells his story 50 years later, he still reflects some the main emphases of Jesus. Luke probably knew that Jesus saw himself through the eyes of the prophet who wrote Isaiah 61:1. At least that is how some the first believers saw Jesus. It may be the one of the reasons why they spoke of "the good news." Either Jesus himself or some of the first follow-ers to think further about Jesus read Isaiah 61 and said: that fits! The Spirit anointed Jesus to proclaim good news to the poor. Some may have also thought of Isaiah 52:7, which speaks of someone proclaiming as "good news" the hope that God would soon reign. These two passages echo im-portant themes in the story of Jesus: the Spirit anointing Jesus, good news for the poor, kingdom of God.

So Luke tells a story of Jesus identifying himself and his role by using Isaiah 61:1. It is unlikely that Luke made up the story from scratch and looked up the Isaiah scroll to copy the words. It looks much more like Luke combines the story from Mark with another one which contained a refer-ence to Jesus' public reading of Isaiah 61, a detail not in Mark 6:1-6. It prob-ably existed as something that was told and retold. We see this reflected in the fact that the quotation is rather inexact. It follows the Greek transla-tion of the Hebrew in which Isaiah was originally written and now in-cludes a line from Isaiah 58:6 as well. It appears to have been a well loved passage in Isaiah. Perhaps already the Hebrew existed in different versions, as sometimes happens when we repeat stories many times.

Hopes for Liberation

In Luke's gospel the hopes of the people included liberation. "Redemption" is the religious word which people have sometimes used to translate the word for liberation. It was in part about freedom from being dominated by foreign powers, especially the Romans and those who represented them at the local level, the sons of Herod the Great. That would be very good news for the people, who saw themselves as poor and oppressed. Some of them might have known that "good news" was a favourite term of Roman propa-ganda, as Rome claimed that it was "the good news" for the world. People who had a nose for politics would sense the challenge when Jesus pro-claimed "good news," especially people in touch with the wider Roman world and its ways. This would include many of the hearers of the gospels. Roman propaganda also claimed that emperors were sons of God who brought peace to the world. Luke's Christmas story would make people sit up and listen: here is a different peace from a different kind of Son of God!

Luke is not only speaking about future change. He is already claiming that some good news has already happened. He sees this in acts of healing and where people were liberated from powers which oppressed them as individuals. In his world people said that these powers were demons. So the rest of the quotation from Isaiah also fits: Jesus engaged in healing. After 4:14-30 Luke goes on to report such acts of healing. It is an ideal place to take up the stories at the beginning of Mark's gospel which show Jesus in action and to add in some of his own. By the time we reach 7:17 Luke has been able to illustrate nearly every item in Jesus' "job description" from Isaiah 61. As a result, when John the Baptist sends his disciples to ask Jesus if he really is the one John was hoping for, Jesus can answer with a fairly comprehensive list: "Go and tell John what you have seen and heard: the blind receive their sight, the lame walk, the lepers are cleansed, the deaf hear, the dead are raised, the poor have good news brought to them" (7:22).

Notice that at the end it includes good news for the poor. The hope for future change remains alive. In the middle of this section of Luke between the visit to the synagogue in 4:14-30 and the response to John in 7:22, we have a second major occasion of Jesus' preaching (6:20-49). It begins with Jesus' words: "Blessed are you who are poor; for yours is the kingdom of God" and goes on in similar vein to say: "Blessed are you who hunger now, for you shall be full." These head up a collection of sayings which Luke has drawn from "Q." It works well that Luke has placed them here because it means that Luke's hearers, who have just listened to the story in the synagogue at Nazareth, actually hear Jesus proclaiming hope to the poor. And just a few minutes later they will hear the words of 7:22, which repeat the theme.

In Luke's story there are memories of Jesus as a proclaimer of good news that God's kingdom would come. The people saw themselves as the poor and Jesus offered both hope, but also practical experience of change in the here and now. In chapter two we shall see that Luke also reflected on memories passed on to him about negative responses to Jesus.

Luke and the Historical Jesus

Notice that throughout this discussion of Luke 4:14-30, I have been discussing two different things: Luke's gospel and the historical Jesus. We can be much clearer about Luke's gospel and what its author appears to be doing than we can about what the historical Jesus was doing. They are 50 or more years apart. It is almost impossible to get back to exactly what Jesus said. Too many exciting things happened in those 50 years. On top of that

Jesus spoke Aramaic, not Greek, and we only have the gospels and they are written in Greek. On the other hand, this is always the case in trying to reconstruct or imagine history and we are as well resourced for doing so as for any other figure in the ancient world.

While we cannot be sure of exact wording, most scholars would argue that there is enough of an impression left behind in the extensive material we have for us to have a fair idea of Jesus' main emphases and activities, at least the way the earliest Christians remembered them. As with most reconstructions there are some areas which are firmer than others, just as there are some areas where most scholars will agree and others where there is extensive debate and little hope of solutions. Along the firmer end of the spectrum are some of the key themes of this passage: Jesus' baptism by John and Jesus' message of the kingdom of God for the poor with future and present dimensions.

1B. Matthew 20:1-16:
The Parable of the Labourers in the Vineyard

How Parables Work

This passage in Matthew's gospel contains one of Jesus' parables. A parable was a story or a picture which functioned a little like a joke. In jokes we tell stories which end up either with a punch line or an event or detail which makes the joke funny. Some people can hear a joke and not get it. When they do get it, we sometimes say: "the penny dropped" or "it clicked" or something similar. In other words the point is not immediately obvious. That is part of what makes jokes fun. Parables also work like this. Someone tells a story or conjures up an image, but we are left to make the connection. Sometimes the point will be simple. Sometimes a story or image may match what we know in a number of ways. Parables, like jokes, draw us in and string us along, hoping to lead us into a new insight.

We have to imagine what it must have been like when Jesus told parables. Sometimes the point is fairly clear. Sometimes it is not clear at all and does not even seem to have clear among the first people who retold it. We see this when we find a parable followed by explanations, even different explanations. Sometimes people place sayings of Jesus directly after parables as a way of interpreting them.

That seems to be happening in our passage. The saying, "The last will be first and the first will be last" (20:16), is one such saying. Matthew has a version of the same saying just before the parable, in 19:30. Thus Matthew surrounds the parable with this saying, offering it one way in 19:30 ("many who are first will be last and the last will be first") and then playfully reversing it after the parable ("the last will be first and the first will be last"). In Matthew's gospel at this point the focus is on leadership in the community. The effect of Matthew's careful placement of this saying is to warn people who are leaders that they should not assume that they are the most important people.

The Parable and Jesus

The parable itself stands on its own and very probably goes right back to Jesus himself. We can imagine that people remembered it easily. It has a simple form, like many parables. There are two main actions: hiring the labourers and paying for them. All you needed to remember was the timing: 6 am, 9 am, 12 noon, 3 pm and 5 pm and then the surprise payment. The parable reflects daily life, as do many of Jesus' parables, but often with a surprising twist which is meant to make you think. Jesus often drew on such scenes of daily life, from farming or commerce, but frequently also from biblical images, such as vineyards and harvest.

Jesus' parables sometimes give us a glimpse of daily life in Galilee and surrounds. One form of agriculture was to grow grapes for wine, a staple drink. At the time of harvesting the grapes you needed extra help. The parable also tells about unemployed people who waited in the marketplace hoping to get work. Perhaps it reflects a situation where some of these people were once farmers who had been forced off their farms through debt. Jesus often talks about debt. He also often talks about masters or bosses. Some of them are quite ruthless. This one obviously has little sympathy for those who had been waiting around all day. Even then people could accuse unemployed people of just being idle.

In the story the master seems to be in complete control, perhaps even arrogant and unfair in the way he acts. Many in Jesus' day will have had such experience at the hands of these men. They were the local version of what was happening to the community as a whole. Powerful people threw their weight around, from Rome at the top, to Rome's representatives, the local rulers of Galilee, to the rich landowners, who sometimes lived far away and managed their estates through agents who could be cruel and oppressive. This master might have been just like some of these agents.

Yet ordinary people were trapped. If you were not a landowner yourself, you had to work for someone else as a tenant on a farm or at the bottom of the social heap as a day labourer like the men of this parable. You became dependent on your bosses for almost everything. There was no social insurance. If you got sick or had family troubles, your best chance was that you might get some support from one of these richer people, to whom you would then be obliged in loyalty for the rest of your life. No wonder people cried out for change and longed for freedom, especially those who were well enough and sufficiently nourished and informed to know that things needn't carry on like this. To such people Jesus' words about the prospect of the kingdom of God sounded promising.

The parable also tells us something about what people might earn or at least what they would need as a daily wage. The story mentions a "denarius," a silver coin. Many modern English translations simplify the story by translating "denarius" by a description of its practical value: the daily wage. The story is outrageous and offensive. How dare a master treat people like this! It is quite unfair! Why should those who worked for just one hour get the same wage as those who worked all day or at least three times as much?!

Jesus appears to have been fond of using shocking stories which seemed outrageous. It was a way of getting people involved. Can we imagine why he told such a story? To begin with, the story is both realistic and unrealistic. That, too, was typical of Jesus. You begin with the familiar and then you stretch it in a way that is slightly absurd. It was probably somewhat stretching the imagination to ask people to believe that the master spent so much of his day recruiting. This alerts the hearer to look beyond the surface meaning of the story. But what was its point? What might it have meant in the setting of Jesus' ministry?

The Point of the Parable

It may not be possible to answer these questions with certainty or at all. It does not usually help to examine each detail of Jesus' parables and to try to match them up with Jesus or his world, such as saying that the master means God. It is not a very good match! People have found their own stories in the parable. Some have tried to match all five recruitment drives with initiatives of God, with the final one being the call to the prophet Mohammed. Jesus' parables do not usually suit such elaborate interpretations, commonly called allegories.

How then might the story say anything relevant in Jesus' context? One very plausible answer begins with the following information. Jesus often seems to use parables to defend his own behaviour against people who criticize him. One of the major criticisms which we will explore more fully in the next chapter is that Jesus welcomed people who were sinners, such as toll collectors, prostitutes, and others whom many of Jesus' critics saw as unworthy of God's goodness. How could Jesus claim that God welcomed these people with forgiveness and love, when the religious people had spent their lives serving God?! Has the penny dropped?

God's action is like the master's action and yet it is the opposite. It doesn't all match up neatly, but there's enough similarity for some of Jesus' hearers to say: aha, I know what you mean. Part of why the parable works is that while the master is callous, he does nevertheless give everyone what they need for a day, a day's wage. Seen from the perspective of human need there was something good in that. That aspect makes the connection possible.

This detail reminds us of Jesus' focus on God's goodness, as Jesus talked about it. It was there for everyone. It was not about rewards or how well one kept rules, but about responding to people's needs. In this sense the parable is similar to the parable of the prodigal son, whom the father welcomes home because he cares about him in contrast to the elder brother who complains that this is unfair. Jesus uses both parables to defend his radical openness in relating to people of all sorts and to give voice to his teaching that this is how we should think about God.

1C. Matthew 5:17-48:
Jesus and the Scripture according to Matthew

Matthew and the Sermon on the Mount

Our passage belongs in what we commonly call the Sermon on the Mount (5:1–7:29). The Sermon on the Mount forms the first major event in Jesus' public ministry as Matthew tells the story. Matthew, writing probably about 15 years after Mark, uses Mark as the base for his gospel but significantly expands it. Like Luke, he adds in two chapters about Jesus' birth. Then in chapter 3 he returns to Mark's story to tell of John the Baptist and Jesus' baptism and in the following chapter he expands the account of Jesus' temptation, using a version which Luke also knew, from the source we call Q. Most of the additional material in Matthew 3–4 beyond Mark comes from this source. See Appendix B for detail.

Then in the rest of chapter 4 Matthew returns to Mark, but has further expansions. From Mark 1:16-20 he brings the account of the call of Simon and Andrew and James and John (4:18-22), and then we are ready to launch into the account of Jesus' public ministry. Instead, however, of following Mark at this point and telling of Jesus' entry into a synagogue where he healed a demon-possessed man (1:21-28), Matthew rearranges the material. Like Luke, he has obviously given great care to how he should begin the account of Jesus' public ministry. We saw that Luke makes an opening scene in which Jesus uses Isaiah 61 to present his mission. Matthew is also aware that he could be free to change the order of events, because the order had been something which Mark had largely had to construct for himself.

Matthew begins in 4:23 by using the summary statement he found down in Mark 1:39. He uses it again in 9:35. In between 4:23 and 9:35 there are two large blocks of material: 5:1–7:29, the Sermon on the Mount, and 8:1–9:34, a sample collection of Jesus' deeds. Together 4:23–9:35 is like a mini-gospel. So Matthew begins his account of Jesus' ministry by showing us Jesus in word and action. It is a neat scheme.

When we look closely at the Sermon on the Mount (5:1–7:29), we see that its order matches what we find in Luke 6:20-49. The material comes not from Mark, but from Q. In Matthew's version of Q it had been considerably expanded and Matthew may have drawn together into these chapters other material from Q, which we find scattered through Luke. In a similar way the block of material about Jesus' deeds (8:1–9:34) is also a collection of stories, most of them from Mark, some of them from Q. On the chart you can see how Matthew has drawn all this material together, sometimes following Mark, sometimes taking stories from later in Mark.

Immediately after the summary in 4:23, which Matthew drew from Mark 1:39, in 4:24-25 and 5:1 Matthew uses another piece which belongs to a summary in Mark, namely 3:7-13. It also refers to Jesus' teaching and healing activity and mentions at the end that Jesus went up a mountain and there appointed twelve disciples. Matthew gives us the list of the twelve disciples much later (10:2-4), but he makes very creative use of the detail about Jesus going up a mountain. He uses it here to give us a picture of Jesus going up a mountain in order to teach the disciples. The result is "The Sermon on *the Mount*." The equivalent shorter version in Luke is given on a plain (6:17). Matthew has redrawn the picture so that now Jesus teaches on a mountain. Jews of his congregations would immediately think of Moses on the mountain. Jesus is like a new and greater Moses. Already in the previous chapters this theme has been echoing.

Jesus' teaching opens in 5:1-12 with the so-called beatitudes, which we found in an earlier form in Luke 6. Here they have been expanded, partly from the psalms, and rewritten so that they bring a message of comfort and encouragement to the people of Matthew's day. Not only will there be hope for the poor and hungry, as in Luke and originally in Jesus, but now those who are in solidarity with the poor and who hunger and thirst for justice, not just for themselves but for others, will be blessed.

The eight beatitudes in 5:1-10 all have a matching form, which makes them very memorable. The first and the last have the theme of the kingdom of heaven (Matthew's preferred term for the kingdom of God, meaning God's reign — on earth and not just in heaven!). At the end of each group of four comes a reference to righteousness or justice, which means something like compassion and goodness in Matthew and is a major theme as we shall see. Matthew is making it clear right from the start: Jesus' message is about God's reign and God's reign is about goodness and compassion. In the following verses, 5:13-16, Matthew shows Jesus calling people to be salt and light like a city on a hill. These were familiar images of Israel, the people of God.

The Warning about Scripture: 5:17-20

Now, with this background, we come to our passage, 5:17-48. It falls into two main parts: a warning in 5:17-20 and some examples in 5:21-48. The warning is against those who accuse Jesus and Christians of undermining or setting aside scripture (the law and the prophets). It may also be a warning against Christians who think they should set scripture aside. Nothing could be further from the truth. Jesus does not set scripture aside. He helps us to take it more seriously. In the typical language of exaggeration he asserts that not even a stroke of a letter is to be changed. Anyone wanting to do such a thing has no place in God's kingdom, or, at least, the lowest place — because Matthew was probably aware that some Christians did teach that parts of the scripture should be set aside. The final part of the warning (5:20) shows where the emphasis really lay: on goodness or compassion.

Illustrations of How to Interpret the Commandments: 5:21-48

Jesus then goes on to offer six illustrations of how a serious approach to scriptures interprets the commandments. With the words, "You have heard that it was said to those of old," Jesus reminds people of the commandments. He is not setting them aside — that would be hardly to be expected after the warnings of 5:17-20. Rather he is saying: do you really understand the implications, or do you just hear the command at a surface level? So Jesus shifts the focus from murder to anger which expresses itself in hate. The issue is not the feeling of anger but what we do with it.

Jesus has creative ways of getting his message across. We have seen that already with the reference to strokes of letters in scripture. Here we find it in the form of his instruction, because it reads like rules for punishment. It certainly uses that language, but that is to make an impact. We miss the point if we try to calculate why the punishment gets progressively more severe and how the punishment fits the alleged crime — which words for "fool" are more serious than others. It is very much like the next example where Jesus suggests people gouge out their eyes or cut off their hands. This is the language of exaggeration designed to make us sit up and listen. Similarly the instruction that we should make the long trip back to Galilee and sort out our relationships before making an offering in the Jerusalem temple is to startle us to think. People matter. Relationships matter. How we handle anger matters. When it expresses itself destructively in attitudes and actions of hate, we have parted company with God. The sixth example makes a similar point. We are not to hate our enemies, but like God, we are to love and never give up loving, even those who hate us.

In a similar way Jesus moves the focus from acts of adultery to adulterous attitudes. Again the problem is not sexual feelings, which are, in themselves, natural, but what we do with them. Adultery means having sexual intercourse with the wife of another man and was usually understood as a sin of one man against another man. Here the emphasis typically moves beyond that to look at the attitudes which produce that kind of behaviour and we might want to expand that to apply just as much to women as to men and or see women as just as much wronged as men. The point is similar to the other examples considered: people matter and our attitudes towards them matter.

The example about divorce refers to Deuteronomy 24 where there is only an incidental reference to a certificate divorce. Its aim was to enable the woman (usually men divorced women) to marry again. That passage cites the bizarre situation of a woman being divorced once and then either widowed or divorced from a second husband and then returning to the first husband. Such a return was forbidden. This reflected the widespread belief that sexual intercourse with someone other than your husband made you unclean for your husband and so the marriage must cease. This lies behind the words, "except for unchastity or sexual immorality," meaning except in cases of adultery. So the view of Jesus was: no divorce except where it has to happen because of adultery. A person divorced on illegitimate grounds cannot marry again because the first marriage is still intact and so they would be committing adultery.

In the world of Jesus' day, his stance seems to have been countering a very lax approach to marriage and divorce. It also reflected the cultural assumptions of the time. Already in New Testament times people found themselves having to weigh more factors in making such decisions, including some basic principles which were deeply rooted in Jesus' own teaching. If the focus is always what is good for people and what will bring the best healing and hope for the future, then we may miss the true emphasis of Jesus' teaching if we take his sayings about divorce as rigid law. Sometimes the more compassionate option is to recognise that a marriage has broken down and a new beginning is the way forward. Similarly, Jesus' message of grace and reconciliation challenges the old cultural assumption that adultery should automatically lead to the termination of a marriage. Reconciliation and forgiveness is possible.

The sayings about making oaths can easily become a set of rigid rules. Some have taken Jesus' saying very literally and refused to take an oath in any circumstance. This does not appear to be the way many early Christians understood it. Paul often uses the form of an oath to make important statements. Overall the emphasis is on not using oaths in a manipulative way. If something is true, it is true. There should be no need to back it up in this way. Straight communication is part of loving one's neighbour — and one's enemy.

Similarly it is easy to turn the statements about retaliation into rules. It is better to see these statements in the context of the passage as a whole. Their focus is on how I relate to someone acting against me. They are telling me never to hate back. This is about loving our enemy. So it is very close to the final example about hating enemies. It is not about my need sometimes to act to stop destructive behaviour towards others, or even towards myself. We do sometimes need to intervene to stop harm being done. The all important thing is the attitude which informs our behaviour. This is the golden thread running through Jesus' teaching in this passage. It relates to the theme of righteousness or goodness, which is what these examples are illustrating.

The examples reach a climax in the words of Jesus: "Be perfect, as your heavenly Father is perfect" (5:48). That sounds impossibly unrealistic and some have used this statement to dismiss the teaching of the Sermon on the Mount as impossible idealism or just something to make us feel guilty and keep us in need of God. Matthew does not seem to read it that way. "Perfect" is also the word for mature and suggests something healthy and wholesome. Its equivalent in Q is: "Be compassionate, as your Father is compassionate" (Luke 6:36). Matthew, too, has just been referring to the God of compassion. So the call is not to a quantitative, statistical perfection, but to a relationship with God, which acknowledges God as God, as the centre and source of life and so letting oneself be filled with God's life and love. The goal can be nothing less than that.

These themes and attitudes find their echo elsewhere in the teaching of Jesus. In the Sermon on the Mount, 7:12 returns to the theme of the law and the prophets to declare that in essence their fundamental principle is that we treat others as we want people to treat us. The shift from deeds to include attitudes also finds an echo in the words of Jesus, that it is what comes from within the human mind that makes us clean or unclean in God's eyes. Jesus helped people to see themselves as a whole, not just to look at themselves externally or to look at behaviours. The fruit of the tree is a sure sign of what is going on, but the tree itself deserves our attention as well.

1D. Mark 10: Leadership, Family, Wealth

In Mark 10 we have a number of very interesting and challenging stories about Jesus. As usual we need to read these in their setting. One of the themes of the second half of Mark 10 is leadership.

Leadership

This is a theme which comes up already in Mark 9. We see it especially from 9:31 onwards. There for the second time Jesus announces that he will be arrested and killed and then rise again. On the first occasion, 8:31, Peter responds by telling Jesus he should not be thinking like that. Peter had just acclaimed Jesus the Messiah. He wasn't meant to be defeated and die. Jesus rounds on him sharply and tells him that he does not understand God's ways.

A similar thing happens the second time Jesus predicts his suffering and death (9:31). Mark goes on immediately to say that the disciples were preoccupied with which of them was going to be the greatest. They had very different priorities. Jesus saw his greatness as giving his life for others in love, even when it meant facing rejection and death. The disciples, like Peter, want to think about success and a different kind of greatness. Jesus then takes a child and declares that greatness is something very different.

A similar conversation takes place in Mark 10, on the third occasion when Jesus predicts his suffering (10:33-35). Again the disciples seem to be walking a very different track. This time it is James and John who illustrate the clash in values about greatness and leadership. They want the top jobs in Jesus' kingdom (10:35-40). The other disciples were annoyed when they heard this (10:41), possibly because they feared they would miss out. Jesus was also disappointed. He was disappointed because the disciples were failing to understand greatness and failing to understand him and his mission.

In 10:42 he points to popular understandings of what it means to be great: to have power over other people. Jesus challenges this idea. His notion of greatness is to be a caring person (10:43-44). He then returns to his predictions about himself to illustrate his point. He did not come to be served, but to serve, even to the extent of giving up his life to benefit others (10:45).

Mark ends the chapter by telling of the healing of blind Bartimaeus (10:46-52). While it is a story in its own right, Mark is also using it symbolically to contrast with the blindness of the disciples. He is fond of doing that sort of thing. Once previously when the disciples were shown to be blind (8:14-21) Mark immediately tells another story about healing a man who was blind (8:22-26).

There is no doubt that Mark is underlining one of the distinctive approaches of Jesus about what it means to be a good or great human being. Jesus himself embodies the approach. It doesn't mean serving in the sense of always doing what other people want you to do, being a doormat. On the contrary, it means always acting in God's name in love and compassion for others, even when they reject it and even when they want you to do something else. Sometimes it will mean conflict.

In the account of Jesus' death we can see how the values clash. Jesus is, indeed, king and wears a crown, but he is enthroned on a cross and wears a crown of thorns. This turns upside down the popular notions of greatness. Mark wants to tell us again what Jesus himself taught: greatness is not might and power, but love, even to the extent of suffering and humiliation. It is a very different model of looking at human life and at leadership. It also leads us to a very different way of looking at God. In one of his most famous parables Jesus gives us an image of God as a father running down the road to embrace a lost son. It was like he was saying: why can't you think of God like that? Don't think of God in terms of what human beings think of as greatness. Try to see God as compassionate.

So leadership is a key theme in much of Mark and also already in Mark 9. It looks very much like Mark, or perhaps someone before him, has gathered together a number of stories that have special relevance for how congregations and communities of faith should work. The first eight chapters of Mark focus more on Jesus' public ministry. They reach a climax with Peter acclaiming Jesus the Christ in 8:29. But, as we saw, there are immediately some things to be sorted out. In Mark 9–10 we hear stories which would have helped Christians sort out their thinking about what matters.

When we look at the earlier parts of Mark 10, we see they deal with marriage, children, and wealth. The latter part of Mark 9 deals with rival preachers and what to do when things go wrong: the need for discipline in the church.

Marriage and Divorce

Mark 10:2-12 brings us back to the theme of divorce which we discussed in the section on Matthew 5. Here it belongs within a discussion in which Jesus says some important things about marriage. The coming together of a man and a woman, including their sexual union, is something very positive and belongs to the way God made creation. Jesus quotes the relevant passages from Genesis to make this point (1:27; 2:24). This is about companionship. It is not just about having children, although that is part of it. The coming together is something good itself. So Jesus resists those who want to break up marriages. To do so and then to marry someone else abandons God's intention. So Jesus was putting a block against such lack of respect for marriage. He was not addressing the situation where a marriage had seriously broken down and where the only realistic way out was to acknowledge this and start again. When we, today, face such situations our commitment to care and compassion, which we have learned from Jesus, will sometimes mean acknowledging divorce as the only way forward. But we need to see that Jesus' teaching makes marriage very important and that means doing everything to try to make it work as it was meant to.

Children

10:13-16 is the wonderful passage about Jesus welcoming the children. We usually take for granted that children matter, but this is not always the case. In Mark's day older children, especially boys, were sometimes in danger from men who wanted to sexually abuse them. Every generation has known forms of abuse of children. Such abuse is much wider than sexual exploitation. It includes treating children cruelly, ridiculing or humiliating them, not listening to them. They are not things or possessions. They are persons to be loved and respected and taken seriously. That needs to be reflected in the way we relate to children within families and also within the church, including in worship and educational settings.

Wealth

10:17-22 is the famous story of Jesus and the rich man. Frequently people refer to him as the "rich young ruler." He is not young in Mark, but only in

Matthew; nor is he a ruler, except in Luke. This is a good example of how people merge the gospel stories together. The man wants eternal life, to share in God's life in this world and the next. Jesus' response is no different from what other teachers of his day would have said: keep the commandments! Jesus gives this answer with some interesting emphases. Notice how he turns the attention away from himself towards God by stopping the man calling him good. It was not that Jesus was saying he was bad. It was rather a matter of putting God into the centre of attention.

The man tells Jesus he has kept the commandments. Many others would have been able to say that, too. This was good. Jesus looks at the fellow with approval and affection, but there is also sadness. Something is missing. It was not that he had missed one of the commandments. The list of commandments in the story comes from Jesus, not from the man. What was missing? Jesus exposes what was missing by challenging the man to give his goods to the poor. What was missing was what lies behind the commandments: compassion for others. Without that the commandments are just rules to be kept, not guidelines for the God-like life of love. If you want to share God's life, eternal life, then you have to understand that. The rich man did not understand and went away sad. To follow Jesus means to follow Jesus' way of understanding the commandments. When we looked at Matthew 5, we saw that Jesus kept bringing the commandments back to attitudes. He was speaking about a way of being.

Jesus' challenge exposed the big gap in the man's approach. Jesus did not ask everyone to give up their possessions. Some did, like Peter and Andrew and James and John. For others the radical compassion for the needy would be best expressed by their staying where they were and using their skills and their possessions effectively in their local community. Many who responded to Jesus did just that.

Inevitably this challenging story set people thinking about possessions. Mark brings us snippets of such conversations in the verses which follow. Obsession with material possession can block people from what matters most — and block out those who need help! This is certainly the case in today's world. But even then the disciples feared Jesus was asking the impossible. So it is interesting that Jesus points them again to God's grace.

As we struggle with the seduction of wealth and the disastrous effects of our greed on the plight of millions of people in the world, the gospel does not tell us not to worry and to ignore the issue. It promises that when we face the issue fairly and openly, God is in there with us and we need not be crushed by the overwhelming nature of the problem. We are not being asked to save the world or solve world poverty all on our own, but we are being asked to take it seriously — because, as Jesus keeps reminding us: people matter. What we say and do needs to be good news for the poor in our world if we truly mean to follow Jesus.

Mark 10 serves us well for sorting out priorities — in leadership, in congregation and faith communities, in families, and in our world. In each area there is a clear thread binding the themes together: God cares about all people; no one is worthless; greatness is about love, not about might, success, and wealth in the world terms. To follow Jesus is to walk the path of compassion — even when sometimes it is unpopular or even downright dangerous. The cross becomes its symbol, turning popular notions of greatness (and of God) upside down.

CHAPTER TWO

Jesus and Conflict: Death and Resurrection

Springtime in Jerusalem

Let's imagine ourselves again back in Galilee at the time of Jesus. It is springtime and people are getting ready for the long trip south to Jerusalem. Soon it will be the Passover festival and thousands of people will flock to the great city. There they will roast their lambs, prepare herbs and spices, and cups of wine, for the Passover meal. Not everyone can make it. Men are supposed to try to come each year, but this is unrealistic for many. Nevertheless many go down from Galilee. The journey with family members is probably just as important as the actual stay in the city.

What a time for catching up on news! You have been hearing a lot about Jesus from Nazareth. Apparently for some, the good news stories have been a little soured and some people have started complaining. No one complained when Levi left his post at the customs centre. But there have been complaints about others who have left their families and businesses and joined Jesus on the road. You knew about James and John. How will their father, Zebedee, cope now? But then he has employees. Some people apparently thought Jesus' good news for the poor would mean a miraculous turn around in poverty. That hasn't happened. People are still poor and some have lost their enthusiasm for Jesus' movement.

But with others this is far from the case. Lots of stories are circulating about people who have found their feet again. Healing is not just about limbs and bodies. It is also about minds and hearts. Some of the most disreputable people on the local scene have suddenly turned into generous people. They form groups of people who care for one another and try to reach out into the community. But Jesus keeps being interrupted by the complainers.

Someone was telling you about an occasion when Jesus was having a meal with such folk and some of the respected religious people stood by muttering to themselves that this was inappropriate, even contrary to God's will. We have always been taught to avoid bad company and here he is mixing with some quite shady characters, both men and women. Apparently they began pestering his disciples. Shouldn't your teacher bear in mind that these people have little regard for God's laws? They are probably serving him food that has not been tithed in accordance with what scripture requires. Apparently Jesus' responses have infuriated some of them. On one occasion he said a doctor needs to attend to the sick, not the well.

Nearly all the stories you are hearing about good things Jesus has done seem to be tainted by controversy. One of the leaders in the local synagogue was outraged that Jesus healed a man with a shrivelled hand on the sabbath, when it would have been so easy just to wait till the next day. On another occasion Jesus refused to reprimand his disciples for picking heads of wheat and chewing them as they strolled through the fields of grain on the sabbath. Apparently he didn't think such things mattered. People were more important to God than keeping rules. "The sabbath was made for people," he said, "not people for the sabbath." It was not that he disregarded the sabbath, let alone scripture. It seemed that he approached it with a different stance.

You keep hearing stories about him from your fellow travellers on the way. Apparently he also told stories and often used word pictures and parables. Once he pointed to what happens when people sow seed in their fields to make the point that what appears insignificant can lead to great things. Perhaps in this he was talking about himself. He was sometimes on stony ground. Some of his followers may have wondered whether after the early successes, things were on a downhill slope. Jesus was apparently defiantly hopeful. Don't worry about the birds! Don't worry about the rocky ground! Don't worry about the weeds! Think of the seed that falls in the good soil. It certainly set some people thinking about what they could do to make themselves into good soil in which the seed could grow.

On another occasion he spoke about a family feud. One son wanted to get his hands on the money which he would inherit when his father died.

His father was still alive! The father gave him the money and the son went abroad to enjoy himself. A number of your friends have gone abroad like that to see the world. So it all sounded rather familiar. But he ended up in dire straits and had to work on a pig farm in Gentile territory. That's a terrible humiliation for a Jewish boy, especially because pigs are forbidden food and seen as unclean. The young fellow finally set off home with his head bowed in shame to plead for some sympathy from his father. His dad had never given up on him. He got wind that he was coming and when he saw him down the road he couldn't help himself. Instead of playing dignified father, he dropped what he was doing and ran down with outstretched arms to meet him.

It was a wonderful story. Jesus was trying to say that we should think about God like that. But then the story, like many of Jesus' own experiences, turned sour. The older brother resented what his brother had done and complained about his dad's behaviour. This was a thinly veiled allusion to those who were complaining about Jesus' willingness to reach out to people who were obviously bad.

The conflicts were hotting up. Apparently some have even accused Jesus of being a sinner himself, and drinking too much alcohol. They had much more sympathy for John the Baptist, who kept strict rules about food and drink. But both Jesus and John behaved as outsiders. Both offered God's forgiveness freely. There was nothing wrong with that, but normally it was something that belonged in the realm of the priests. Jesus and John were freelance preachers and might just get out of control. That was the fear.

If you are travelling to Jerusalem with the groups that have less time, you are probably going to go through Samaria. That can pose a problem. It is not that they speak a different language. They are also Jews speaking Aramaic like you, but their accent is different. The Judeans also have a different accent. They would say that they speak properly and you Galileans have a funny way of speaking — and there are the usual snobby jokes about Galileans. Can anything good come out of Galilee? A number of Jewish families moved up into Galilee a century or so back. Jesus' family was one of them. You get on reasonably well with Judeans. It's a bit more serious with Samaritans. They are Jews, too, but you have been taught that they are not pure Jews and their faith is not true Jewish faith. So there are tensions. Just hope that that there are no conflicts along the way!

Jesus appears to have had some impact here, too. There is a story about a woman who had a conversation with him at a well — not exactly the best location for a holy man to be, but then it seems rather typical from what you have heard. There is also the story he is alleged to have told about a Samaritan being like God. Some must have found it outrageous. You have been taught that you should look to the priests to learn about God. The last people who could teach you anything about God were Samaritans. Jesus seems to have been deliberately subversive. He won't be popular in priestly circles, that's for sure.

As you approach Jerusalem you come across more and more people. Some of them have come great distances. Some speak different languages, especially Greek, which was like English in today's world. Thousands of Jews lived in the surrounding countries, from Rome in the west to modern-day Iraq in the east, from modern-day Turkey in the north to Ethiopia in the south. Even some Gentiles try to make it for the festivals. They were great occasions. Jerusalem was jam-packed. It was great for the local economy. One of the two main tithes which all Jews were obliged to keep entailed bringing money to Jerusalem and spending it there. It helped the city. It was also a good way to ensure one had holiday money. The other main tithe consisted of giving the priest a tenth of all local produce. You could do that at home.

The demand in Jerusalem for accommodation was huge. Many people camped down in the surrounding countryside and especially over the valley from the city on and around the Mount of Olives. Crowd control was also a problem. It was so easy for things to get out of hand. Passover festivals were notorious for disturbances. The Roman prefect Pilate stationed troops in the city to keep things in order. The temple authorities must have found it a worrying time. The last thing they wanted was disturbances, especially if it meant soldiers. It was something of a balancing act to make sure the festival went well and at the same time to restrain hotheads in the crowd to keep Pilate and his troops at bay. The city had suffered already far too much at the hands of its conquerors. The worst scenario would be that the Romans might close the temple down or destroy it.

Your chance of meeting up with Jesus during the festival must seem to you very slim as you make your way up into the hill country where Jerusalem lies. Some travellers seem to think that he took the alternative route and is coming up through Jericho. You might be fortunate to be there when he arrives. It probably turns out that you miss him. There are just too many people pouring into the city. But those who were around at the time say that he came in sitting on a donkey, like many others, but that some of the bystanders became very excited and waved branches.

Some people have been speaking about him as the Messiah, God's anointed. It would have been very dangerous to do so. Later you will hear a story about Peter, one of Jesus' closest companions, who hailed Jesus as the Messiah. The story illustrates the problem very well. Jesus apparently replied that he was going to be killed. Peter protested, because that was not meant to happen to a Messiah. A Messiah was meant to win victories and hopefully drive the foreign invaders from the land, like a new King David. In most of the stories you hear about Jesus he speaks of the kingdom of God, or God's reign. Messiah (Christ) was such a dangerous term which could so easily be misunderstood. Later his followers had no doubt: he was the Christ. People therefore called them Christ-people, Christians.

Your chances of seeing what went on in the outer courts of the temple were probably also rather slim. The area was huge, as large as six football fields. People crowded in there, partly on their way to the inner courts, but partly also because it was the place where you exchange money and also buy animals for sacrifices of various kinds — and lambs for the Passover meals. Gifts of money for temple had to be in the currency of Tyre, so that meant lots of moneychangers. In one section of the outer courts Jesus apparently started to disrupt all this activity, tipping over some of the tables and scaring away some of the animals. It must have been over in just a few moments before the crowd controllers had time to act, but people soon heard about it.

Then and now, people have wondered what Jesus was up to. Nothing indicates that it was a problem of the rate of exchange, or that people were profiteering from the sale of the animals. Jesus shooed off the buyers as well. Perhaps he was upset by the commercialisation. More likely he was angered by the temple leadership and all its activities, which he was known to criticise elsewhere for its greed and disregard of people. Jesus' act was like the actions of prophets of old, who also declared God's judgement on the temple authorities and predicted its destruction.

Was it possible to be in Jerusalem at the time and not know what was going on? Apparently it was. The temple authorities deliberately tried to handle things behind the scenes. It is not clear that they would have been much bothered by the complaints from Galilee, but they would have been very worried about disturbances in Jerusalem. Jesus did have a following. They are unlikely to have known very much about him, except that he seemed to belong to a series of homegrown enthusiasts who promised change and regularly ran into conflict with authorities. They were the last people one wanted to have in Jerusalem during a festival.

We can see that the authorities put Jesus in this general category of popular messiahs. They would have heard of his actions in the temple and perhaps of the celebrations of his arrival. We can imagine that their first strategy would have been to take him aside and talk to him sternly about not causing any more trouble. But it seems as though that was not nearly enough. Life was cheap. The better solution was to squash the movement altogether by executing the leader. It would not be difficult to secure Roman assistance, because they, too, would have seen the wisdom in the more radical approach.

Later people will report the secret manoeuvres. You will hear how Judas, one of the close circle of Jesus, contrived to tell the authorities about Jesus' whereabouts. You will hear how the authorities arrested Jesus across the valley on the Mount of Olives side. He had spent some time there with his closest disciples and had prayed in great distress because he sensed his life was now in danger. You will hear various stories about what happened next. Apparently there was a hearing before some of the key authorities who interrogated Jesus about his attitude towards the temple and the claims he made about himself. There, the category, "Messiah," must have played a role. Jesus seems to have responded in ways which the authorities took as grounds for carrying out their plan.

At the very least you might have seen the crucifixes on the way out of town. Perhaps you were present when the cruel Pilate dealt summarily with the case. He, too, put Jesus in a category. The accusation nailed to the cross made that plain: "King of the Jews." This was a mockery of Jesus' claims. The two on either side belonged to the same category as Jesus in Pilate's assessment, as did Barabbas. In a police state where life is cheap, enemies of the state are to be executed, preferably in a manner which discourages others. No one really cared about the finer points. Just get rid of them!

Of course, Jesus could have compromised and pulled back from his radical ways. He might have saved himself if he had shown himself loyal to the temple and stopped encouraging large crowds. He could have removed any threat to Rome's interests by parading as a philosopher, concerned only with the moral improvement of individuals. The vision of good news for the poor and hungry could have been watered down to some sustained instruction about sharing and kindness. Instead he chose to go right to the heart of the religious and political establishment with his message. He was on a collision course. Everything he stood for was at stake.

At his last meal with his close inner circle, he chose to give grace a special meaning. Breaking the bread in the usual manner he added: this is me. The message was clear. He had given himself for others throughout his life and he was not about to stop doing so. At the end of the meal he did something similar with a cup of wine, inviting them to share it. It represented his life poured out for people. Jesus identified himself with the vision of the future when people would gather together in peace and goodness and he made it his life's agenda even to the extent of going all the way to death.

This self-giving was so powerful that his followers had no hesitation in declaring that this was none other than God's self-giving, that Jesus was in the very highest sense God's agent, indeed God's son. While the charge laid against him was false, because he was not making himself a Messiah to threaten the state, there was a sense in which it was terribly true. He was, indeed, God's Messiah and Anointed, but of a very different kind than most expected.

In the same way, to some Jesus' death seemed like a disaster, another example of callous politics, of intolerance of change, of suppression of dissent, of the silencing of radical compassion. That was all, of course, true. Yet paradoxically, Jesus' death also unleashed a flood of compassion which transformed people's lives. You had heard stories of what happened during Jesus' life. Now you will hear similar stories after his death.

Jesus' death was not the end. The news will have spread quite quickly that people had seen Jesus alive just three days after he was executed. There were visions, stories of an empty tomb, and personal encounters, which brought Jesus' followers together again as never before. They returned to meeting together, remembering Jesus' stories and deeds, reflecting on the horrendous events of that Passover weekend, and reaffirming the vision of Jesus that now included not just the gathering of all peoples in peace, but also the gathering of all with Jesus himself.

Sometimes they spoke of the overwhelming presence of God's Spirit in their new communities. Sometimes they spoke of the Spirit of Jesus himself as a living presence with them already in the present. Those who joined the movement were baptised, a sign of belonging, but also of hope. You could hardly miss coming across the renewed Jesus movement in Jerusalem. Back in Galilee, his home turf, you will see much more.

A selection of passages to which this section alludes: Passover: Exodus 12:1-28; discipleship and families: Mark 1:16-20; 2:13-14; Matthew 10:37-39; Mark 10:17-31; controversies: Mark 2:15-17; 3:1-6; 2:23-28; Matthew 11:16-19; Luke 7:31-35; parables: Mark 4:1-34; Luke 15:1-32; Samaritans and Galileans; John 4:1-42; Luke 10:25-37; 9:51-55; Matthew 26:69-75; tithes: Numbers 18:8-32; Deuteronomy 14:22-29; Matthew 23:23; Luke 11:42; Jesus' entry into Jerusalem: Mark 11:1-11; John 12:12-19; Jesus and Peter: Mark 8:27-38; John 6:14-15; Christians: Acts 11:26; temple incident: Mark 11:15-17; John 2:13-22; the arrest of Jesus: John 11:45-57; Mark 14:1-2, 10-11, 32-50; Jesus on trial: Mark 14:53-65; Luke 22:66-71; Mark 15:1-15; mockery and crucifixion: Mark 15:16-41; the Last Meal: Mark 14:22-25; Luke 22:15-20; resurrection: Mark 16:1-8; 1 Corinthians 15:1-5; John 20:1-23.

2A. Luke 15

This chapter in Luke contains two of the best-known parables of Jesus and between them a third which also has special value. Most famous of all is the third and longest parable, commonly called the Parable of the Prodigal Son (15:11-32). The other which is very famous is the Parable of the Lost Sheep (15:3-7). Between them is the Parable of the Lost Coin (15:8-10).

The Parables in Context

It is important to see how these parables fit into their context. Luke commences this chapter with a report that Pharisees and scribes were grumbling about Jesus' behaviour. What was their problem? Jesus was in contact with toll collectors and sinners, welcoming them and even eating with them. To share a meal in those days meant to express a level of acceptance. Meals were ways of welcoming people. According to his critics Jesus should have been avoiding such bad company. To them it was very inappropriate that Jesus mixed with such people.

Their worries probably arose from the concern that such people were in fact sinners. Some of them may have been cheats who pocketed too much for themselves when they collected tolls as people crossed the borders from Herod Antipas' kingdom to that of his brother Philip. They may have included people who engaged in loose moral behaviour. It is very likely that prostitutes were a regular feature of their parties. They were almost certainly also people who did not make any real attempt to keep the commandments relating to such things as tithing food and ensuring tithed food was not ritually contaminated. If you spent your life trying to live a holy life according to scripture it was an insult when someone like Jesus seemed to want to ignore all those efforts and declare riff-raff to be just as loved by God as you are. Surely God disapproved of such behaviour and so should we. So we should steer clear of all such people.

Jesus saw things differently. It was not that he pretended these people were not sinners. Jesus called a spade a spade. But Jesus' approach was not to abandon bad people to protect himself and keep himself uncontaminated. Rather he believed that God still loved and valued even those people who had gone off the rails and made a mess of their lives and, often, also the lives of others. God wanted those people to be his people as well as the others who were making a big effort, the good or righteous people. God did not want to cut anyone off.

So Jesus felt free to associate with such people. No one would have objected if he had turned up to their parties and told them they must change their ways. His critics might have cheered. The trouble for them was that Jesus appeared to value them as people even before they made amends and changed their ways. It was this friendship that eventually led to some of them changing.

Criticism can be quite stinging. It is easy to run away to avoid unpopularity. Jesus did not do that. He knew that to do so would be to abandon those people and it would be to abandon what he saw as God's way. Instead he told some stories that had their own way of dealing with the problem. The parable about the sheep appeals to common sense. Surely a shepherd will go out and find a lost sheep. Everyone would have agreed. Then why couldn't people think of God like that? The Old Testament sometimes speaks of God as being like a shepherd. So people probably got the point. Luke, or someone before him, appears to have added a line to the parable about joy over sinners repenting (15:7). That might well be an outcome, but originally the parable seems to be focusing on the action of the shepherd.

The next parable likens God to a woman looking for a lost coin, a denarius. That's about as much as people needed to live for a day, so it is a fair amount of money. It is also an appeal to common sense. Of course she will hunt high and low for it. Again the story invites people to say: oh, I get it. You mean we need to think about God like that and see what you are doing in that light? Exactly. Notice that here God is like a woman. It is always good to be reminded that God is not a male or a female. But sometimes we forget that and speak of God only in male terms.

The Parable of the Prodigal Son

The final parable is the longest. It is also an appeal to common experience. It was not at all unusual for young people to want to travel and see a bit of the world. It did not happen nearly as much as in our day, but it did happen from time to time, especially where people had the money to do so. The younger son is rather selfish and his behaviour in wanting his father's money before he even dies would be a shocking example of disrespect in those days. Perhaps some people knew of such experiences and the heartbreak which could accompany them. It is a disaster story. This selfish boy wasted all the money and then ended up with the pigs. For Jews pigs were unclean animals, so he had sunk as low as he could go.

The story assumes meanwhile that the father has heard nothing from his son. These were not the days of email. We are told that the son decided in desperation to go back home, perhaps again motivated by selfishness. Would he really mean he was sorry? In the story the father knows nothing of this until one day he sees his son coming in the distance. What would he do? According to some expectations of the day about proper behaviour the father should conduct himself with dignity and hold himself back. This father followed his heart and ran down the road to embrace his son — not even knowing whether the son was wanting to come good nor knowing what he had been up to. He was his son and he loved him. That was all that mattered.

This is an interesting story because most of Jesus' audience could identify with the father's response. It was natural and human. It was from the heart. Some might have been critical that the father lost his dignity and control at that moment. Those who sensed Jesus was saying something about himself and God would get the message: why can't we think about God like that? God loves like a parent loves — even before we decide to change our ways. That changes us.

Some other elements in the story might have helped people click on to its meaning. The feast would remind people that Jesus was criticised for feasting with unworthy people. The response of the elder brother would certainly help people make the connection. That brother's response is like the response of Jesus' critics. What justice is there if you make a feast for this wayward selfish son, when, as elder brother, I have stayed at home and worked hard for the family? It is a very fair story, because it shows the elder brother is not a bad person and he has a point. But it encourages him in the story to have a different set of values and to be glad about seeing his brother. It is unfair if you count up what each brother deserves. But unfairness is irrelevant if the concern is about welcoming back the son into the family.

The story we considered in chapter one about the men hired at different times of the day, yet all paid the same wages, is making a similar point. That, too, is unfair, unless we see that the focus was meeting what people needed to live on: a denarius a day. Jesus wanted people to think about God like that.

One of the most dramatic of all the stories about Jesus is that of the toll collector, Zacchaeus of Jericho. He scaled a tree to see Jesus. Here too there were critics that Jesus mixed with such types. Zacchaeus invites Jesus to a meal and Jesus is not afraid to accept. Zacchaeus changes. He revises his finances, pays restitution to the people he has wronged at the rate set by scripture, and declares he will use his money to benefit the poor. The offer of an accepting and loving relation in God's name sets Zacchaeus free to change. Jesus calls that salvation: he has been made whole and his use of money shows it!

Meals and Their Meanings

Meals were a common theme in Jesus' ministry because they were so important in those days for expressing togetherness, much more than in ours. They were also important because they were a favourite image for talking about our future with God. Using such passages as Isaiah 25 and related imagery, people looked to future salvation as a great feast with bread and wine and lots of food. It was one of Jesus' favourite images. He told a parable about an invitation to a great feast to which guests had been invited. When the host sent out word, as was the usual practice, to say that the meal was ready, those invited refused to come, making up all kinds of excuses. So the host told his agents to go out and find anyone else they could in the surrounding roads and bring them in. This was a hardly subtle reference to what had been happening in Jesus' ministry. He had been inviting people to respond to God, but those who should have been coming refused and so Jesus turned to the outsiders.

So Jesus' meals with outsiders also had a wider meaning. These occasions were a little bit like the great feast of the future, when all different people would come together to feast together in peace in the presence of God. It was like Jesus was acting out in the present what was promised for the future. Other people did similar things. Jesus' own critics met for such meals of bread and wine to celebrate that they were the special ones whom God had chosen to join the great feast of the future. For Jesus all were welcome to the feast. So he feasted with all sorts of people.

We see this trouble also in Mark 2:15-17, where Jesus eats openly with toll collectors and sinners. Mark tells the story immediately after reporting the call of Levi, the toll collector, so that it is easy to link the two stories, as Luke does, and imagine it is Levi who plays host. Jesus refuses to give in to the criticism, but responds with what was probably a known image of his time: the sick need a doctor, not the well. The point is that Jesus saw himself acting in God's interest and God is interested in helping people to become well. God does not withdraw love from the needy. That makes no sense. So Jesus declares: I did not come to call the righteous, but the sinners.

Similarly both Matthew and Luke pass on the words of Jesus preserved in Q, according to which Jesus complained about the inconsistency of his critics. They thought John was mad because he ate so strictly and sparingly and they think he is a glutton and a drunkard because he is a friend of toll collectors and sinners.

The meal was an important image for Jesus' ministry. As we shall see, his last meal with his disciples was one of these meals, in which he virtually said: you see, I have been broken and poured out for this. It became the basis of our celebration of Holy Communion. Jesus' open meals and his willingness to eat with all people reflected his belief that God's love reached out to all with no exceptions. That would land him in trouble. It would also cause trouble. But Jesus persisted.

2B. Mark 2:23-28 and 2:1–3:6

Controversy dogs Jesus in his ministry. We have already seen that people complained about the company he kept. Here they complain about the way he treats the sabbath day. This story belongs in a set of five stories in

Mark 2:1–3:6 which all deal with controversy between Jesus and his critics. It is very likely that in the years before Mark wrote his gospel people had gathered these stories together from various incidents in the life of Jesus because of their common theme. Much of Mark's gospel seems to be using collections like this.

Now the collection has a neat shape: the first and the last stories tell of Jesus healing someone with paralysis. The second and fourth deal with controversy about eating. In the middle is a story about fasting. That gives the group of five a neat symmetry on the surface. But deeper down in each story there is also a consistent conflict going on. Before turning to our passage, we can briefly look at the other four stories to see this conflict working its way out.

The Paralysed Man and Forgiveness

In the first dramatic story — and people loved storytelling those days, too! — the roof comes off and a paralysed man lands in front of Jesus while he is teaching in a crowded house. Jesus heals him by declaring to him that his sins are forgiven. Nothing in the story suggests that all paralysis is caused by sin or that all sin causes paralysis. In this instance it is typical that we hear nothing about the man's background, how he came to be paralysed, what the relation might have been between his sin or sins and his paralysis. People of those days found it easy to believe that there could be a connection. All the emphasis falls on the outcome: the man can walk again and shows that dramatically by taking up his bed and walking. The story has been trimmed right down to the essentials. When he retells the story Matthew trims it down even further by leaving out the detail about the roof.

The story found its way into this collection because of what follows the words of Jesus. Some scribes (experts in interpreting scripture) complained. What right did Jesus have to forgive sins? That's God's prerogative! Jesus was insulting God. They misunderstand what Jesus is saying. Jesus' words were: "Your sins are forgiven" — obviously by God! Then 2:10 explains: Jesus has been authorised to do this on God's behalf. The scribes might have said that only the priests in the temple could do so on God's behalf, but scripture, which governs the practices of the temple, nowhere suggests that this is so.

The same problem arose earlier with John the Baptist, who also declared God's forgiveness as people submitted themselves to God by undergoing baptism in the Jordan river. The critics were unhappy at this informal new rite and those who feared the temple would be undermined opposed John. On the other hand, nothing John did was contrary to the biblical law and people were increasingly using rites of washing to symbolise inner cleansing in those days. Jesus is very aware that he is facing criticism from the same direction, so that later when challenged about his authority he quite deliberately responds by saying: "What about John's authority?" Jesus and John were both doing the same sort of thing.

But Jesus' first response is different. It is a kind of riddle: which is easier to say, "Your sins are forgiven," or to say, "Rise, take up your bed and walk"? It is clever, because at one level it is much easier to tell someone they are forgiven than to tell a paralysed person to walk. But for the critics it is the other way round. Yet they would never have objected to Jesus saying the man should get up and walk. Jesus' answer exposes them for having their priorities all wrong. They are worried about God. Jesus says: God does not want to be worried about or looked after, because God is "worried about" or cares most about people. Forgiveness is part of that loving and of course God wants Jesus to pass that message on. Matthew, when he tells the story, will say that it is also a message we all need to pass on.

Controversies over Eating and Fasting

In the section which looked at the Parable of the Prodigal Son, we also looked at the next controversy in the group of five in 2:1–3:6, namely 2:15-17, where Jesus eats with toll collectors. The underlying conflict is similar. The critics are worried that Jesus is offending God by keeping bad company. Jesus obviously does not see God like that. Rather God is more like a doctor whose concern is with people and their well-being. So God and God's agents are going to be found where the need is. People matter most to God.

The third controversy is interesting because it highlights a difference between Jesus and John. In the section on the Parable of the Prodigal Son we also looked at a passage where Jesus contrasted himself and John the Baptist over their approach to food and meals. That difference comes to the surface again in 2:18-22. John and Jesus both declare God's generosity and forgiveness, but their lifestyles contrast dramatically. The explanation given here is that John belongs to those who grieve about the need for change. Jesus believes that the change is already beginning to happen. So John grieves about change and Jesus celebrates that it is starting to happen in the here and now. Jesus uses the image of a wedding. For John the wedding day has not come. For Jesus it has come and it is time to celebrate and feast. It also reflects Jesus' approach to people. John calls to all and offers them forgiveness if they promise to change. Jesus welcomes all and believes they will change.

The two approaches are not really compatible, like old and new cloth in a single garment or like new wine in old wineskins. Yet later the church would also turn to fasting because there is still a lot of change to happen. The major difference remains, however. Jesus brings a new approach with a new authority. This emphasis comes right at the heart of the group of five incidents, taking a central position. Mark's hearers would probably have recalled to words in 1:22 that Jesus taught with authority and not as the scribes and 1:27 that people were amazed about his new teaching.

Sabbath in the Wheat Field

Next comes the controversy about the disciples. The sabbath day (Saturday) was special. Keeping the sabbath day was one of the ten commandments. No one was to work. People were to rest. Those who worried about offending God or who believed that God wanted them to be very exact and careful about keeping the commandments — and why not? — tried to define very carefully what one could not do on the sabbath.

This story shows the disciples walking through fields of grain and apparently casually picking heads of grain and eating them. Nothing says they had walked too far (there were restrictions on how far one could walk). Nothing suggests they were constructing a path — making their way simply means walking along. Nothing suggests they were stealing — it was acceptable to do what they were doing. But they were doing it on the sabbath and the critics assert that by plucking heads of grain they were working. Perhaps the storytellers who passed on the incident mean us to sense that this was really quite silly. Certainly it would not have been the view of all Jews of the day, including interpreters of scripture, that they were doing anything wrong. But the critics come through as worried about God. Was God worried about such things?

The simplest answer Jesus gives comes in 2:27. The sabbath was made for people, not people for the sabbath. This is saying: God did not set up the sabbath day as another set of rules to test whether people would be obedient. God gave the sabbath day for the sake of people and is not going to worry if people are doing something that does not harm them or anyone else on the sabbath. People were not made for rules. Rules were made for people. To God people matter most. That doesn't mean abandoning commandments, but it means reading them in the light of what Jesus says is God's intention. So there was nothing wrong with what the disciples were doing. There was something wrong with the way the critics thought about God.

The story also includes some other answers, which may also go back to Jesus, although they could possibly come from further reflection by those who told the story and wanted to back it up with more support. The incident referred to in 2:24-25 refers to 1 Samuel 21:1-7. It is about David asking to eat the special bread in the holy shrine which he was not allowed to eat according to biblical law. David and his men were hungry. They did eat the bread. So sometimes it is acceptable to set aside the law to meet human need. We do so when we may have to speed to bring someone to a hospital, though that can usually be avoided.

In some ways the illustration does not work well. It is even incorrect in claiming the high priest at the time was Abiathar. He was high priest later. The incident did not take place on the sabbath day. It concerned food and hungry men, whereas the incident with the disciples says nothing about them being hungry. Perhaps the fact that it was David encouraged someone to make the comparison with Jesus. However, there is a similar stance: people matter most, not laws.

At the end of the story Mark reminds us of Jesus' authority. It is an authority to interpret the sabbath law and indeed to interpret all scripture so that we read it in the light of what he has been asserting are God's priorities. God is not like a man who is obsessed selfishly with himself and wants everyone else to be subordinate to him. God is not the kind of person, who, when you enter their house, you feel like the most important thing to them is not you as guest but their house — and don't you move the cushions! Rather God is generous and loving, like a loving mother or father, wanting what is good for people and wanting a relationship of love with them.

Sabbath in the Synagogue

The last incident of the five also takes place on the sabbath. Again the story-tellers have sharpened the conflict to the point of ridicule. How absurd to worry about helping a person on the sabbath! We need to be cautious not to think that all Pharisees were like this. We know they were not. But the story serves to contrast two diametrically opposed approaches to scripture, which keep coming up in every generation, including within Christianity. At one stage they often focused on the so-called Christian sabbath, Sunday.

Jesus' response identifies the options: is it lawful to do good or to do harm on the sabbath, to save life or to kill? People of the day may have remembered debates about what to do if attacked by an enemy on the sabbath. Do you fight back or do you let yourself be slaughtered because you don't want to work on the sabbath? Here the issue is healing. There was some debate about what was acceptable and what was not. Many would have supported Jesus' stance. Others would have disagreed. Some, like the leader of the synagogue in Luke's story of another healing by Jesus on the sabbath, would have preferred Jesus to leave the healing till the next day. Wouldn't that save all the fuss?

It sounds like Jesus did not worry much about such things, but was prepared to respond to people there and then. For him, as for God, people mattered most and other laws, which he continued to respect, took second place after loving one's neighbour as oneself. At the end of the five stories Mark tells us that this made the Pharisees and the Herodians so mad that they wanted to do away with Jesus. This is quite shocking after Jesus' words about killing or giving life. Mark will go on to report a number of incidents in which Jesus is at loggerheads with interpreters of scripture. Sometimes people's religious enthusiasm can become so intense that it is dangerous and destructive. As Jesus challenged common assumptions, he would run up against that kind of zeal and hatred, not from all, but certainly from some.

2C. The Last Meal: Mark 14:22-25; Matthew 26:26-29; Luke 22:15-20; 1 Corinthians 11:22-26

We have four accounts of the last meal of Jesus with his disciples. I call it the "Last Meal" rather than the "Last Supper," because in many parts of the world, including where I live, supper means a short snack before going to bed at night, not the evening meal. In the case of our passages, they are describing not a late night snack but an evening meal. You can find the four accounts set out in parallel columns on page 51 below.

Mark's Account in the Context of His Gospel

We shall look first at Mark and then at the others. First we look at the context in Mark's gospel. The account belongs to the meal scene. Already in 14:17 Mark mentions that Jesus and the twelve disciples had come together for a meal. There Jesus indicates that one of them will betray him. In the world of the story the disciples are shocked and wonder who it is. Jesus does not tell them. Mark does not tell us, although we already know because Mark has mentioned Judas' act of treachery in 14:10-11. This introduction to the meal makes it far from a pleasant evening out. Jesus is facing betrayal and death. This is the atmosphere of the meal.

If we look farther back in Mark we see from 14:12-16 that Jesus made plans for him and his disciples to celebrate the annual Passover meal, in which Jews recalled the great deliverance of their people from Egypt, eating a roast lamb with accompaniments which recall that fateful night. This tells us that according to Mark Jesus' meal with his disciples took place in the context of a Passover meal. The Passover celebration followed a certain pattern. We might expect to see that reflected in the way Mark describes the meal.

Just before the reference to the preparation for the Passover meal we have the reference to Judas' initiative to betray Jesus (14:10-11) and before that, by way of contrast, we have the story of the woman who anointed Jesus (14:3-9). Again, by contrast, just before that Mark tells us that the authorities planned to arrest Jesus and kill him (14:1-2).

Thus Mark's story of Jesus' last days consists of a series of contrasts, swinging from negative to positive and back. The story of the Last Meal is on the positive side. It follows, on the negative, the prediction of Jesus' betrayal. It is followed, also back on the negative side, by Jesus' prediction that the disciples would abandon him and Peter deny him.

People hearing Mark's gospel read at a single setting and those familiar with what went before, would also hear echoes of earlier events in Mark's story. The plot in 14:1-2 recalls the reaction to Jesus' provocative acts in the temple. Jesus and the temple authorities are on a collision course. Much earlier, in 7:1 and earlier still in 3:22, Mark reports conflicts with such authorities. In fact Mark indicates tension almost from the beginning, contrasting Jesus' authority and theirs (1:22) and showing them attacking Jesus on five different occasions (2:1–3:6), finally resolving already then to put him to death (3:6). The accusations of blasphemy in 2:7 already point forward to the accusations of the high priest at Jesus' trial in 14:64.

The Story and the Historical Jesus

Back in the time of Jesus, when some of these conflicts were first played out, the situation was probably quite complex. The Romans, that is, the prefect, Pilate, and his band of soldiers executed Jesus. They used their method of execution: crucifixion. When Mark portrays the temple authorities as having some involvement, this is likely to have been the case. The motives likely to have led to such action are explored in the opening section of this chapter where we seek to imagine our ways into the tension of those times. Life was cheap and the simplest way of silencing someone who seemed to be a troublemaker was to find some way of doing away with him. It still is in many parts of the world today.

While we might have the impression on hearing Mark that the conflict was a consistent one throughout Jesus' ministry, so that it included controversy over Jesus' approach to the Scriptures, even Mark does not mention this as an issue in the trial. Those issues do not seem to have been paramount in the final conflict. It was Jesus' own attack on the temple (or better, the temple authorities) and the apparent build-up of his popularity (and thus hints of messiahship) which seem to have sparked the final initiatives to do away with him.

The Sadducees

In Jesus' time there were many groups within the Jewish people who held strong views about what God intended for the people. The temple authorities, including the high priests and the senior families, based in Jerusalem belonged to the party sometimes called the Sadducees. Perhaps the name derives from the high priest Zadok. They saw themselves as entrusted with the defence of the faith and particularly the temple as well as ensuring it was properly administered. They resisted innovation by and large and took a conservative approach to the way they applied biblical law. They played a vital role in maintaining stability. At times they had to ward off Roman interference with reassurances that everything was in hand. They might join forces with the Romans to quell disturbances, as in the case of Jesus and some others of the period, but from different perspectives. The Romans were worried about ensuring Judea remained stable and peaceful for the sake of the empire. The temple authorities were worried about the freedom of their faith and assuring the Romans that everything was under control.

The Pharisees

Also closely associated with the temple was a largely lay movement called the Pharisees. Perhaps their name refers to their stance of preferring to remain separate from people who disregarded the Law. It may reflect what appears to have been one of their major emphases: holiness in everyday life. They even took some aspects of the Law which had to do with priests and applied it to their daily life. They, too, shared with the Sadducees a concern for the people. Many of them espoused the hope that one day God would liberate the people from their foreign controllers. Some were prepared to support armed uprising, as were some Sadducees. When the major revolt took place in 70 CE, the temple authorities stood against the Romans and it seemed that most Pharisees did not or at least were sufficiently away from the spotlight to be considered acceptable leaders in the aftermath of the debacle.

The Pharisees were much more innovative than the Sadducees in interpreting the biblical law, mostly in the direction of making it easier to apply to everyday life, sometimes with the result that it was stricter, sometimes with the result that it was more lenient than the traditional interpretation. They were building up a body of interpretation, called the oral tradition or even, the oral law. Much of it found its way into the Mishnah, the collection of rabbinic sayings and discussion on some more difficult sections of the Law, compiled in the late second century CE. It then became the core for a further collection of discussion, compiled in later centuries, called the Talmud. These are important sources for finding out what rabbinic Jews thought in these centuries and can be useful also for trying to reconstruct what earlier rabbis, including those of the time of Jesus and before, thought. There are difficulties, however, because we cannot always be confident that the reports are historically reliable.

There was probably a variety of stances among what we call the Pharisees. We should be very careful not to stereotype them. The evidence we have suggests that they were mostly far from what we have come to term "pharisaical," that is, pompous and self-righteous. Some of them probably were — Matthew would certainly say so — and some Christians still are. It was inherent to the Pharisees as a movement. In fact there were probably also differences among them about interpretation of the Law. The rabbinic literature assumes this to be the case.

The Essenes

There were also some who took quite extreme stances or who took on lifestyles which reflected that they belonged to yet a further group. These were the Essenes, who never appear by that name in the New Testament, but who may well figure in some of the gospel stories. Josephus, the Jewish historian, who in the late first century CE wrote compendious volumes about his people, about the great revolt of 70 CE, and an autobiography, tells us that the Essenes lived in separate groups. They had processes for initiation into the group. Some did not marry; others did. Philo of Alexandria, who wrote extensively in the first half of the first century, mostly expositions of the Law, also mentions the Essenes. The group who appear to have hidden the scrolls in the caves of the Dead Sea when the Romans came as part of their crushing of the revolt of 60-70 CE, and who lived on its shores, were probably a branch of the Essenes. They appear to have been a group which had connections with high levels in the temple priesthood, but who split off from the temple over what they considered an illegal high priest and temple practices. Their core group eventually withdrew to the Dead Sea and lived there in strict observance of the Law, hoping and praying for the liberation of Jerusalem.

Jesus and the Hopes of Israel

Into this turmoil of hopes and the sheer business of a Passover Jerusalem, filled with pilgrims from many parts of the world, Jesus came with his band of Galileans. He had been declaring a new order in which God would reign, justice would be done and peace restored. His acts of healing and exorcism promised new things to come. He shared the hopes of many of the other diverse groups, but differed from most in his methods. There were some obvious implications in his message which were not difficult to see. God's reign would replace the rule of the Romans and the temple authorities. Jesus envisaged a new relationship with God which would affect everything: the way people related to each other and the way society functioned.

He would have possibly done enough to be noticed, even before he arrived in Jerusalem. When he did arrive, the welcome some gave him, then his confronting act in the temple, put him firmly on the agenda of those wanting to keep the volatile pilgrim crowds of Passover Jerusalem calm. Many would share his hope. He would even have much in common with Barabbas and the two revolutionaries who would die on either side of him on the cross. The Romans obviously thought so and were in one respect right. But Jesus approached the common hope of liberation from the Romans quite differently and would have pictured the outcome differently. His were not the methods of violence. His was not the way of hating the enemy: liberation then slaughter of the oppressors.

The Last Meal: Timing

So Mark sets the scene for the Last Meal by alerting us to conflict. Historically the situation was, indeed, complex. What would it have been like on that last evening for Jesus and his disciples? We strike a difficulty before we talk of the meal itself in more detail. Mark and the other two gospels, Matthew and Luke, who follow Mark's outline, indicate that the Last Meal took place at the time of the Passover meal and belonged within that context. Luke identifies it directly as the occasion when Jesus ate the Passover meal with his disciples.

The difficulty is that John's gospel, while not reporting the details of the Last Meal, nevertheless makes it very clear that it happened not at the time of celebrating the Passover meal, but the night before. In fact, according to John, Jesus died at the time when the Passover lambs were being killed, ready to be prepared for eating that evening (18:28; 19:31, 42). All agree that Jesus died on a Friday and that the Last Meal was on a Thursday evening, but in the first three gospels the Passover (which like all days in Jewish timing, commenced at 6 pm and ran till 6 pm the next day) was the night of Thursday and the daytime of Friday, whereas for John, the Passover commenced 6 pm Friday and ran through the daylight of Saturday (the sabbath).

We may never know which of the two versions is correct. Was it symbolism that made John identify Jesus' death with the death of the lambs? Was it symbolism which made the first three gospels identify the Last Meal with the Passover meal, to celebrate Jesus' new act of liberation? I think it is likely that John's chronology is correct. The very short account of the meal itself, apart from in Luke, contains no specific allusions to the Passover ritual. Even if Mark's timing is right, this remains the case. The meal focuses entirely on Jesus. We shall look at it in that light.

The Last Meal: Jesus' Actions

Breaking bread and distributing it was a normal part of meal, usually at the beginning and often a form of giving thanks, as it is here. So at this point we are not led to expect anything extraordinary; nor are the disciples. What changes this is Jesus' statement: "This is my body." The words do not mean: here is my body, not my soul. Rather it is the equivalent of saying: this is me! It is also clear that Jesus still had a body and was present, so that something very creative is happening. He is sharing himself in an act of distributing bread. This has led some traditional interpreters to see a miracle being announced here: the bread also becomes at that moment Jesus' body and ceases to be bread. This understanding has been reinforced by the profound sense of Jesus' presence which thousands have experienced in celebrating the eucharist.

It is, however, more likely to have been a symbolic act than a miracle, but this is still a source of profound meaning. Here I am: I am giving myself to you. It is what Jesus had been doing throughout his ministry. As the disciples take the bread they are invited to take Christ himself into their lives. It was not to be reduced crudely to a reminder: when you eat this bread, remember me. It was a way of Jesus giving himself. For those who accepted the invitation to receive, this was a nonverbal act of receiving Jesus' sharing of himself. Later people would reflect on the broken bread and see in that otherwise very ordinary act a representation of Jesus' brokenness for others, especially in the light of the cross.

Similarly, Jesus' words over the cup reflect such sharing. This is my blood is again, not a literal statement about Jesus' blood. It was still pumping in his veins. It can be interpreted as a miracle: this also becomes my blood and you drink it. The literal sense of drinking Jesus' physical blood which has been miraculously transformed into blood from being wine, is unlikely to be the intention here. Even those who prefer a miraculous interpretation hold back from such a view. They do not expect to taste actual blood. The action works at a different level. Blood was more than blood cells white and red. It was already itself a symbol of life in biblical thought. To be offered Jesus' blood is to be offered his life. Once again this connects with Jesus' life poured out for others during his ministry and especially his life poured out on the cross, where, quite literally, his blood would flow.

The words are rich with meaning not only because of their connection with Jesus' life and death, but also because of their association with biblical images. One way of expressing the hope for change was to speak of God renewing the covenant with the people. The ritual of covenant renewal took place with a sacrifice and the sprinkling of blood, as Exodus 24 tells us. Jeremiah 31:31-34 also spoke of a renewed covenant, indeed a new covenant, although without mentioning blood.

Jesus is setting his life and ministry in the context of this wider hope. This should not surprise us, because throughout his ministry he used the image of the great feast and interpreted meals as carrying symbolic significance. They represented in the present the hope of what was to come when all peoples would gather in justice and peace. So the allusion here to covenant puts Jesus' Last Meal into this framework of thought. In a way Jesus is saying by this act with the cup: see I am celebrating this covenant hope and I am (and have been) giving myself for this hope.

Jesus' Final Meal

Matthew 26:26-29	Mark 14:22-25	Luke 22:14-20	1 Cor 11:22-26
26While they were eating, Jesus took a loaf of bread, and after blessing it he broke it, gave it to the disciples, and said, "Take, eat; this is my body." 27Then he took a cup, and after giving thanks he gave it to them, saying, "Drink from it, all of you; 28for this is my blood of the covenant, which is poured out for many for the forgiveness of sins. 29I tell you, I will never again drink of this fruit of the vine until that day when I drink it new with you in my Father's kingdom."	22While they were eating, he took a loaf of bread, and after blessing it he broke it, gave it to them, and said, "Take; this is my body." 23Then he took a cup, and after giving thanks he gave it to them, and all of them drank from it. 24He said to them, "This is my blood of the covenant, which is poured out for many. 25Truly I tell you, I will never again drink of the fruit of the vine until that day when I drink it new in the kingdom of God."	14When the hour came, he took his place at the table, and the apostles with him. 15He said to them, "I have eagerly desired to eat this Passover with you before I suffer; 16for I tell you, I will not eat it until it is fulfilled in the kingdom of God." 17Then he took a cup, and after giving thanks he said, "Take this and divide it among yourselves; 18for I tell you that from now on I will not drink of the fruit of the vine until the kingdom of God comes." 19Then taking a loaf of bread, having given thanks, he broke it and gave it to them, saying, "This is my body, which is given for you. Do this in remembrance of me." 20And the cup similarly after the meal, saying, "This cup that is poured out for you is the new covenant in my blood." (Other ancient authorities lack, in whole or in part, verses 19b-20 [which is given . . . in my blood].)	22For I received from the Lord what I also handed on to you, that the Lord Jesus on the night when he was betrayed took a loaf of bread, 24and having given thanks, he broke it and said, "This is my body that is for you. Do this in remembrance of me." 25Similarly also the cup after the meal, saying, "This cup is the new covenant in my blood. Do this, as often as you drink it, in remembrance of me." 26For as often as you eat this bread and drink the cup, you proclaim the Lord's death until he comes. *NRSV modified by W. Loader to ensure the translation is identical where the Greek of the gospels is identical*

The Last Meal: Two Versions

The matter is a little more complicated by the fact that we have two different versions of the meal. Matthew follows Mark's account very closely, making improvements here and there with the result that the two acts match each other more closely in form. Matthew adds to Jesus' statement about the blood the words "for the forgiveness of sins," an important theme in Matthew, perhaps prompted by his awareness that covenant may allude to this aspect of the promise in Jeremiah 31.

When we turn to Luke we can see influence both from Mark and from the version of the story we have in 1 Corinthians 11:22-26. Paul knew the story in a version which Luke knew independently of Paul some 20-30 years later. The main differences come in the wording. Mark and Matthew simply have: "This is my body." Paul and Luke have the additional words "which is for you" (Paul; 11:24) and "which is given for you" (Luke 22:19). This difference is not substantial.

With the statement about the cup and wine, however, the difference is more significant. Mark has two matching statements: "This is my body" and "This is my blood of the covenant poured out for many." Paul has as the second statement: "This cup is the new covenant in my blood," to which Luke has added: "poured out for you." Luke's addition looks like his adaptation of what Mark has: "poured out for many." In addition Paul has after both (and Luke after the first): "Do this for my remembrance."

The other interesting feature in both Luke and Paul is that they suggest that the sharing of the bread comes first, before the meal. The action with the cup comes only after the meal ("similarly after the meal": Luke 22:20; 1 Cor 11:25). Probably by Mark's time the two acts were done together, leading to the matching forms, whereas the earlier form of the tradition envisaged two acts separated by a meal.

The Last Meal: Hope

The words of the second statement differ between Mark/Matthew and Luke/Paul. If the focus on the cup is more likely to be closer to what Jesus said, then we can see that the emphasis is on the action not on the actual substance of the blood. "In my blood" refers to Jesus' life which he has expressed in his ministry and will express even in death. Jesus' act is a celebration of the new covenant. "New" is an allusion to Jeremiah, but it means much the same as in Mark. Jesus defiantly celebrates hope even in the face of his own death. He invites his disciples to join him.

Luke has carried across the words, "poured out for many," into the second statement. Possibly it alludes to Isaiah 53. Isaiah 53 portrays a figure called God's servant who is put through suffering which will bring benefit to others. It is a remarkable passage, which reverses a common notion that suffering only happens to bad people. It seems to have been a way of coming to terms with Israel's own suffering. It is suggesting that there is benefit in suffering for others. In a similar way the heroes who died keeping their faith in the light of the attempt by Antiochus IV Epiphanes in 167 BCE to suppress it were said to have benefited others by their goodness.

People soon saw the death of Jesus in a similar way. It was not just the death of the innocent, but an event which made waves and brought benefit to others. In some streams of early Christianity, for instance, in Paul's circles, it became the dominant way of explaining the death of Jesus. He died "for us." That benefit brought a surplus of goodness which flowed over to us. It brought forgiveness of sins. "He died for our sins." Soon people were developing all kinds of imagery, often related to the temple, to describe Jesus' death as a sacrifice. There were all different kinds of sacrifices, not all of them relating to sins. Covenant sacrifice which lies behind the words of the Last Meal was not such a sacrifice. But others were or came to be. So Jesus' death was seen as a sacrifice to deal with human sin. This has often been the main way that people have come to see the Last Meal of Jesus, so that the continuing celebration of that occasion, which we variously call the eucharist (= thanksgiving; communion, Lord's Supper), all become focused on saving us from our sins. This is, however, only one aspect of Christian reflection on the event. It is a pity that we too often lose the connection with the rest of Jesus' meals and the hope they represent.

In time the celebration of Jesus' final meal accumulated a rich texture of meaning. Focused on the past, it helps us remember Jesus and the forgiveness and hope he brought. Focused on the future, in it we share Jesus' vision of the feast of justice and peace. Focused on the present, it is one of the main points where we celebrate Jesus' presence with us and our presence together in fellowship with him as we open ourselves to receive him again into our lives as simply as we eat bread and drink wine. The broken and poured out life we recognise as God's life and we feed on this life for meaning and hope. It stands in stark contrast to the invitations to feed on visions of greed and power and selfishness. Holy Communion remains a central act for the community of faith, not to be ritualised to the point of losing any connection with life, not to be trivialised by the lack of dignity and respect that reduces it to mere ceremony. It remains a moment of profound meaning for many and those responsible for leadership need to ensure that it happens in a space and setting where people can engage its action without the distractions, such as disorganisation or where something or someone else, like the leader, becomes the centre of attention.

2D. Mark 16:1-8 and 1 Corinthians 15:1-11

When we read passages from Scripture in English, we are already some way down the road from where interpretation of Scripture really begins. It really begins with working out what was likely to have been the original text which the author wrote. Fortunately there are specialists who do this work, as there are specialists who then translate the text from the Greek. But the matters are not simple.

Finding a Good Text and Translation

Our passage from Mark illustrates the problem. Nearly all English translations end Mark 16 with verse 8. Most indicate, however, that some ancient manuscripts contained another 12 verses. The old Authorised Version contained these verses as part of Mark. We now have many more Greek manuscripts of Mark and much older ones than were available to the translators of the Authorised Version. The oldest manuscripts do not contain Mark 16:9-20, although it is common among later manuscripts. The overwhelming evidence points to 16:9-20 being added at some point to the original which finished at verse 8.

In the previous section we were looking at the Last Meal of Jesus. A similar problem arises there with the text of Luke's account. Some manuscripts do not contain the verses 22:19b and 20 ("'given for you. Do this in remembrance of me.' Likewise also the cup after the meal, saying, 'This cup is the new covenant in my blood poured out you'"). The best and oldest texts with only a few exceptions include these verses. This widely accepted longer text actually has Jesus sharing a cup twice, but the second time it is after the bread and like the accounts in Mark and Paul it accompanies each act by a word of Jesus. Perhaps a scribe decided it was a mistake to mention two cups of wine and so left out the second occasion.

We have over four thousand manuscripts of the New Testament, most of them from many centuries after the New Testament writings were first penned, but some are very early. Some fragments of papyrus copies of the gospels appear to come from as early as the first half of the second century. Beside the major variations, such as the ones we have mentioned, most variations are relatively minor, but there are many of them and the best translations note the important ones.

Translations are also very important. Ideally one should read the New Testament in its original language. Many are able to do this these days. Good commentaries reflect that kind of careful detailed reading of the Greek text. Next best are translations which try to remain as close to the ancient text as possible, such as the New Revised Standard Version. Others which handle the translation more freely may be more readable and may be just as good at capturing the meaning of a passage. It is good to consult more than one translation when working closely with the text and using only English. Good commentaries will usually draw attention to verses where translation poses difficulties and where the meaning is therefore uncertain.

The Resurrection Story

Returning to Mark 16, here we have the climax of Mark's gospel, the Easter story. Already in 8:31, 9:31, and 10:33 Jesus had indicated that he would face rejection and death, but would then rise again from the dead. Within Mark's story the disciples are shattered at Jesus' death and all run away. Peter even denies he belongs to Jesus. It is a disaster. Only the women remain close by. It is rather typical that Mark turns things upside down. In his world one would expect important men to be the heroes. Mark's heroes are not the typical heroes of the day. In this way Mark was also reflecting an emphasis of Jesus. Women, the poor, outcasts, sinners, were seeing things which the wise and especially the leading men were not.

These women come to the tomb to embalm Jesus' body. They didn't do so on the sabbath, because it was regarded as work. Counting the day of Jesus' death as day one, the sabbath as day two, then on the third day (or after three days, reckoned inclusively), they arrive at the tomb where Jesus' body was supposed to be. To their surprise the stone had been rolled away. This could look like someone had stolen the body except for what happens next. They enter the tomb and see a young man dressed in white clothes. It wasn't Jesus. It probably wasn't even a human being. Although Mark doesn't say so, it is likely he pictured the figure as an angel. They were usually dressed in white like that. The young man tells them what has happened: Jesus is not there. He has risen. He then tells them to go and tell the disciples and Peter that Jesus is going to Galilee, as he predicted (14:28-29). The women are so afraid. They run away. They say nothing.

This is very simple and strange story. If the women said nothing, how did the story ever get told? We have to assume that eventually they did speak up. The story appears to know more than it lets on. It suggests Peter and the disciples will see Jesus in Galilee. Perhaps this was one of the things that inspired someone to tell more of the story by adding 16:9-20.

Belief in Resurrection

The story also has a simple message: Jesus is alive. It assumes God has raised Jesus from the dead. How did people come to think that way and what did they mean? And how come they applied this to Jesus? Most of the Old Testament assumes that at death people die and that is that. At most there is something like a ghost or spirit of a person which continues to exist in the place of the dead, called Sheol. But it is hardly a real existence and not seen as something to look forward to.

When, however, people thought about the future of Israel, they looked to a time when God would judge and punish Israel's enemies by bringing misfortune upon them. The prophets turned this back on Israel itself, reminding them that God would also deal harshly with them if they did not follow the ways of justice and compassion. Some saw all misfortune as punishment and all good fortune as reward, but this did not make sense of much of life's experience. The Book of Job illustrates the problem. Sometimes the innocent suffer. Sometimes it cannot be seen as God's judgement. Sometimes it is just plain human cruelty and oppression. How can evil oppressors get away with it and prosper? How can people go on suffering and nothing changes? Where is God in all of this?

One answer came from those who had learned from surrounding cultures to think differently about the future. It combined with faith in God as good and just to produce the belief that one day nations would have to stand before God and face up to their wrongdoing. All kinds of speculation arose about how this might happen, but a common feature was judgement. God will surely judge the unjust and reward the good. For that to happen, people who had already died would need to be brought to life again. For them that meant coming back from the dead in some bodily form so that they could experience things. Most of them did not think of souls existing in any real sense without bodies.

The worse life became and the more hopeless Israel's future looked, the more they began to run to the hope that one day God would intervene and change things. Mostly they still thought of that happening within history. Jesus' vision of the coming of God's reign belongs to such hope. But this often came together with the belief that eventually God would at least reward the good. Many Jews of Jesus' time believed in such a future resurrection. The only passage where we find this clearly expressed in the Old Testament is Daniel, where in 12:1-3 it looks to the raising up of the righteous so that they would shine like stars.

Writers like the author of Daniel and many others in the following centuries envisaged this resurrection life not as a return to the old life, nor as a resurrection of their old corpses, but as something new where their buried body would be transformed to become a new kind of body, like that of angels. This is why Daniel speaks of something shining. Paul makes a special point of arguing that the resurrection body is a spiritual body, not a physical one in the sense of being the same as the one we have now (1 Cor 15:35-49).

People facing suffering looked to the hope of resurrection, just as the Book of Daniel held out this promise to Israel as it faced the persecutions and sufferings of the ruthless Antiochus IV Epiphanes who was trying to suppress Jewish faith in 167-164 BCE. Jesus saw his own future similarly, according to Mark. He knew he would face suffering and he believed God would raise him from the dead.

So when people declared: God has raised Jesus from the dead, it would not have been all that strange a thought to many people of the time. It would have been unusual to suggest that God had not also raised other dead people at the same time. There may even be some traces of a belief that Jesus was the first of many more which would come and that the final judgement day was at hand (1 Cor 15:20; Rom 8:29).

The story they told about Jesus fits the understanding of resurrection which many people held in those days. There was no body in the tomb because resurrection meant taking the corpse and transforming it into a resurrection body. Often people unaware of this background think of the resurrection of Jesus as being like his resuscitation so that he walked around as before. This would not have been the way the people of Jesus' day understood it. As we have already noted, Paul would say that the resurrection body is a spiritual body. He would not have meant it was invisible. All of the stories assume people could see the risen Jesus. Some even have him inviting people to touch him and then have him eating. But he can also vanish and pass through walls. They thought of Jesus' risen body as belonging to a different order of reality.

Interpreting Jesus' Resurrection

More important than how they saw Jesus was what they believed had happened. Time and time again in Acts, Luke tells us that the early preachers contrasted Jesus' rejection and his resurrection: you killed him; God raised him up! The message was clear. God did not abandon Jesus in his death, but raised him into resurrection life, thus showing him to be his faithful servant and son. Jesus was right. Acts shows us the disciples continuing to preach what Jesus preached and continuing to do what he did.

At one level the resurrection was a way of affirming everything which Jesus said and did as coming from God. It was like a big Yes from God at the conclusion of Jesus' life to all that he did and was. It was also much more than this. It became a fundamental story of hope. As Jesus loved to the end even through suffering and death and was raised, so we can have hope that the way of love leads to life. It was a story to join oneself to, a story to live by. Paul described baptism as a way of joining oneself to the story: letting oneself be symbolically put through death and burial and then rising to new life. It is a story to live by.

Still more, the first Christians declared that this was much more than Jesus' resurrection. It was in fact his elevation to God's presence. They took the language of hope for a royal messiah and applied it to Jesus. At first they appear to have dreamt of the day when Jesus would return to do what the Messiah was promised to do: to set up a kingdom of love and peace. So they now not only looked forward to the kingdom of God, but also to Jesus' return as their Lord and Messiah. One of their earliest prayers, preserved for us by Paul, still in the Aramaic language in which it was first formulated is the cry: *Marana tha!* "Our Lord, come!" (1 Cor 16:22). As time went on, they also pictured Jesus in God's presence praying for them or sitting enthroned beside God.

So the Easter story was always part of a much bigger story. It was about the story of Jesus' life and death. It showed that this was God's story. It was about future hope: there is more to come. And it was about much more than resurrection itself. It was about God saying Yes to Jesus, and raising him up to his presence. Some simply declared: God has made him Messiah and Lord, this Jesus whom you crucified (Acts 2:36). In this act God has adopted Jesus as his Son, just as in the ancient coronation rituals God was believed to adopt kings as viceroys (Ps 2:7).

Luke puts the stories into a framework of time which has set the pattern for the church's year. He suggests Jesus made appearances to people after his resurrection up until the 40th day, when he went up to heaven, not to return in the same way again. No other New Testament writer has this scheme. In fact it looks like something Luke created to hold the stories together, much as the gospel writers needed to do when handling all the stories about Jesus. Luke then has the Spirit given at the Harvest Festival time, Pentecost, fifty days after Passover. That is wonderful symbolism. But John's gospel suggests Jesus gave the Spirit to the disciples on the very day of the resurrection and even ascended to heaven that day, returning subsequently to make appearances to the disciples in various places. There are in fact many stories about the risen Jesus and it is hard to harmonise them. They all share the conviction that Jesus was no longer dead.

Paul's Account of the Resurrection

Our oldest account comes from Paul, who received it from others. It simply states that Christ died, was buried, was raised and appeared to Cephas (= Peter) and then to the Twelve and then to James and the apostles and to a large crowd and finally to Paul himself (1 Cor 15:1-8). This list of events reflects special occasions. It assumes that Jesus appeared and then disappeared, much as he did to Paul on the road to Damascus. That convinced Paul he was alive. Notice that that event happens well after Luke's forty days, another reason why most recognise Luke's scheme as an artificial structure.

Of special interest is Cephas (= Peter). Jesus' appearing first to Cephas would make him the leader and so he was. Mark, as we saw, seems to hint at this appearance to Peter and Luke knows a story according to which the apostles believe in the resurrection because he appeared to Simon (Peter). It is a remarkable turnaround: Peter denied Jesus but Jesus did not abandon Peter. That is a gospel in itself. Peter was apparently the leader already during Jesus' ministry. Perhaps this is why he was singled out.

Some people think the stories of the empty tomb are not historical but reflect what people thought must have happened. Others are confident they also have a claim to truth. Common to all of them are the women, in John only Mary Magdalene. Mark makes the women the only witnesses to the empty tomb and the message of angel. Mark, like Paul, assumes Easter faith has its primary origin in Peter's experience. In their gospels, Matthew and John, however, have Jesus appear to the women — John only to Mary. Some argue from this that a woman was the beginning of Easter faith. Certainly there is a defiance of traditional values in the way that the stories give prominence to women.

Resurrection Faith and New Beginnings

What might the first Christians have concluded from their affirmation that God had raised Jesus from the dead? It would certainly have meant: Jesus was right and we must continue doing what he did. That meant meeting for meals. They must have been very significant occasions where they sensed his presence but also began reflecting on his sufferings. For this they used Psalms like Psalm 22 to guide their thoughts and memories. They would have also shared Jesus' hope for the future, now expanded with the hope that he would come again as the Messiah. It is very likely that some interpreted his resurrection also as evidence that history was very soon to reach its climax. Still, 20 years later we find Paul believing that the final intervention of God would occur in his lifetime and that he would be among those to see Jesus return.

Another major development was the awareness of the Spirit. Promised as a gift for the "last days," according to the prophet Joel, the first believers celebrated the presence of the Spirit (Acts 2:17-21). Luke, as we noted, dated this to the Festival of Pentecost. Others report this as something which occurred much earlier. In any case they believed that the life of the new age to come, which would be a life in the Spirit, was already beginning to break into their lives in the present, much as Jesus had declared that the reign of God was already breaking into the present when people were set free from the powers that oppressed them. So they kept looking to the future but they also celebrated the present.

This means their special meals of bread and wine also had these dimensions. They looked forward; they looked back and they celebrated the present. Similarly new members were baptised into the community. As with John the Baptist's baptism this looked forward to a time when God's presence would flood the world. It hadn't happened yet, so they kept the symbol going. But baptism also was a way of looking back to Jesus and a way of celebrating belonging together with him in the present. It became a moment for celebrating the coming of the Spirit, as it had been for Jesus. Baptism was now "in the name of Jesus," which included a sense of belonging and also of acclaiming Jesus as "Lord."

"Lord" became a favourite word for Jesus in the early Christian communities. At one level it meant master and leader. At another level in Greek it was also the word used for God. That brought their thinking about Jesus and about God very close together. One of their early affirmations, looking like a hymn or poem, declares that one day God will give Jesus his own name (the name "Lord") (Phil 2:5-11). This would be about much more than naming. It was a simple way of saying: God will give Jesus the right to act on his behalf. That is, after all, what believers had claimed about Jesus from the beginning and what in a sense Jesus had also claimed about himself. So when Christians thought about God, they immediately thought about Jesus and when they thought about Jesus they thought about God. The coming years would be an explosion of creative ways of thinking these thoughts together. Perhaps the most famous of all was when people said that Jesus was God's word or communication and then proceeded to say that really Jesus was at the heart of God's being from the very beginning of creation (Col 1:15-20; John 1:1-5; Heb 1:1-3). Jesus is God's wisdom now for a short time made human and visible for all to see.

The bigger the understanding of Jesus' significance, the wider the reach of the gospel. After some hesitation the first Christians saw no barriers to the good news which Jesus proclaimed. It was not only for Jews but for all people. God's communication and wisdom was the wisdom which everyone needed. This created a revolution. The movement expanded in all directions, but not without stresses and strains. Some Jews, in particular, saw the claims made about Jesus as going far too far and threatening to depose God from the centre of faith. Others worried about the implications of the expansion for Israel's special place. And then there was the problem of whether one could really do all this and remain faithful to the scripture. Would it lead to compromises? Would it go off the rails? Christians had to face many of these problems and one key figure at the centre of such controversies was Paul.

CHAPTER THREE

Paul amid the Turbulence of the Church

Letting Your Hair Down

We need to jump two decades to reach the new setting for imagining the New Testament. You find yourself on a ship on your way from Corinth to Ephesus. Probably it is now with a sense of relief. Preparations for such journeys were as hectic then as they are now. Your husband needed to complete some business arrangements in the city. The servants needed instructions about what to do in your absence. The fact that you can even make such a journey means you must have some wealth and so have your own household, but your life in the city is far from luxury. There is a huge gap between those with power who flaunt their wealth and the little you have.

You know your servants well. After all, it is your task to manage the internal affairs of the household, including ensuring supplies of food from the market. It is a world where men matter and take the prominent roles in public life, but you know that without their home managers many would never make it. It is good to be able to talk to others in the same position. You married around the age of 18 and as in most marriages your husband was going on 30. It is not always comfortable that the men think of their wives as daughters, but it was a common view.

You can now sit back and relax for the few days that it will take to make the crossing. The servant who looks after the children will ensure they get to school and won't tolerate any nonsense while you are away. At least the household is in order, good enough for the small group of Christians to make your house their meeting place. But your Christian group is another worry and that is why you are making your way to Ephesus. The plan is to speak with Paul directly. The good news of the gospel has done wonderful things for people, but somehow it all now seems under threat of falling apart.

You met Paul only a few years back when he made his first appearance in the synagogue meeting. It was impressive. You had heard about this man before, possibly as long as 15 years ago. Then people spoke of his exploits in stamping out the Jesus sect in Jerusalem. And here you are, one of its key members in Corinth! Reports had filtered out into the Jewish community in Corinth and elsewhere that there had been major problems among the Greek-speaking Jews in Jerusalem, because many had been converted to the sect.

While the Aramaic-speaking locals also had their problems, the conflict reached its greatest intensity with the Greek speakers. People who had courageously maintained their Jewish faith out in the wider world did not take lightly to finding it being undermined in the holy city. Crowds stoned one of the first Christians, Stephen, and Paul was among those who hounded most of the Greek-speaking Christians out of Jerusalem. The apparent disaster for these Christians turned out to be a resounding success. Wherever they went they spread their teaching about Jesus and soon there were little groups of Christians springing up everywhere.

Paul, or Saul, as people called him, using his informal name, set off to chase the Christians and then what happened is legendary. He was stunned by a vision of Jesus on the way to Damascus and changed sides. Perhaps he had already come to know so much about Jesus and his teaching that its potency overwhelmed him. It was an impressive reversal and hearing it from his own lips was very convincing. So you and your husband joined the Christians. The whole household, including servants and children, was baptised and you offered your place for meetings of the new believers. That became very important after the local synagogue stopped letting the Christians peddle their message there.

There is now a series of house churches in the city. But that's where the problems begin. You all have in common that you acclaim Jesus as Lord and tell the story of his death and resurrection as God's action to win the world to faith. But there were difficult decisions to be made and you have heard that in some places these became almost paralysing.

One of the problems was with the men. Your Jewish men are all circumcised. What happens when Gentiles join the faith? Scripture teaches clearly that they should be circumcised. That was God's instruction to Abraham. Quite early on many Christians became convinced that this should not be required of Gentiles. The debates were fierce. It depended on how you approached scripture. The circumcision party could point to chapter and verse. The others claimed that compassion should override such demands. By and large, the more liberal approach won the day.

You can just imagine what that meant for the many Gentiles who had already found Judaism attractive but baulked at full membership because they didn't want the operation. They streamed into the people of God via the Christian way. Over in Asia Minor (Turkey) inland from Ephesus, the issue is far from resolved. Perhaps you have heard this. Teachers have come into communities of believers which Paul founded in Galatia, persuading the people that Paul and others had not been giving sound biblical teaching and requiring all men who join the faith to be circumcised.

But some of the local problems in Corinth affect women as well as men. You, too, have had other teachers call by. Some of them have created a strong following. It is a great pity, but the result has been that factions have developed. Some people look to Paul, others to Apollos, a very eloquent and learned preacher, others to Peter, while others resist all of this and claim to belong only to Christ. Personality has become a problem. Not everyone warmed to Paul. Some compare his preaching style unfavourably with Apollos. More seriously, some find insulting the fact that he worked on the side at his trade to make ends meet instead of accepting support from the congregations. Some say he lacks faith. Still others insinuate that the money he is collecting for the poor in Palestine will end up in his own pocket. It is getting out of hand and Paul needs to be told what is happening. That is why it is important that you make this trip.

Things have become so bad that some have also written to Paul setting out a number of questions. Poor Paul will have his hands full just dealing with Corinth, let alone other communities. He has already written to you all once, warning about sexual immorality. But now there is the fellow who is living with his father's wife. You don't know all the details — neither do we! — but it could be his father's second wife. If she is a young widow, then the two of them are about the same age. That needs sorting out. Some Christians have gone so far as to take each other to court — not exactly good publicity for the new faith.

Others are so proud of their new spirituality that they have really pushed the limits. They see no problems in dining at the restaurants attached to the many pagan temples in the city. But can one do so without falling under their influence? Some get so carried away in the excitement of worship and praise, that anyone coming in from outside would think they are slightly mad. For some, speaking in tongues has become the key sign of spirituality. Some of the women have abandoned their normal way of dressing in worship and pray and worship just like men, with heads full uncovered — is that a problem?

Some women and some men have abandoned their marriages or stopped engaging in normal sexual relations. They see this as a sign that they have left such things behind, while others, perhaps even some of the same people, claim that visiting prostitutes has no effect on their spiritual life. It is a mess. And it doesn't end there. The poorer folk complain that when they turn up for worship, all the food is gone, and they just have what remains for communion. What are they celebrating if they can't share and care about each other? Too many people seem to be thinking only of themselves. That even affects the way they think of the future. They are not really interested in a transformed creation or a renewed humanity. For them, going to heaven when they die is all that matters and they look down on ideas of a future resurrection as rather primitive ideas which should be abandoned.

Sometimes you wonder whether it was not all so much easier before you joined the movement. But then that misses the point. You have found a living faith. You know that your relationship with God has changed forever. You can see the signs of love and compassion in your life, and in the lives of those around you. And there is something exciting about belonging to this new faith which is bringing hope to so many people. It makes you feel that you truly belong to God's people and that the faith you learned as a child in the synagogue is now blossoming into something which will be a blessing to all nations, just as God promised Abraham long ago. You treasure the scriptures in a new way.

Paul is busy. The room still holds the aroma of the oil lamps from the night before. Pacing up and down Paul has been formulating his letter to the Galatian Christians, pestered by those new missionaries who want to circumcise their men. One of Paul's faithful helpers sits there pen in hand scratching each word onto the small roll of papyrus. It gives Paul time to think before the next sentence.

If you had arrived earlier you might have seen him pacing up and down, sometimes formulating arguments with great care, other times almost bursting with passion and anger about what he has been hearing. These intruders who were discrediting him are about to undo his whole mission in the region. They might as well tell the people to go back to their old religions again. To insist on circumcision, on keeping sacred days, on observing laws about what you can eat and not eat, puts the focus in the wrong place. These things no longer matter. What matters is a relationship with God where we simply accept God's generous goodness and try to live in a way that is consistent with this. The living Christ, the Spirit of God, is the driving energy behind living according to God's will, not laws and commandments. It is outrageous to let these things interfere with our relationship with God and with each other.

That is, however, a sore point, because according to Paul, Peter, too, fell for this kind of approach. Under the influence of people who had come from James in Jerusalem, Peter and Paul's colleague, Barnabas, pulled out of sharing meals in common with Gentiles believers. It made Paul furious. It was a betrayal of the good news of God's grace which is freely there for all.

You will doubtless hear more from Paul about this. But will you hear the other side of the story? The conflict left Paul out on a limb because he was not prepared to compromise. For Peter and James, only some things could be surrendered, like circumcision. Other things could not. Again it was all about the approach to scripture. Which command do you keep and which can be abandoned? The people who argued that none should be abandoned seemed to have the most consistent approach, but already quite early most had agreed that this ran contrary to the new openness which they found in the gospel. Paul would spend the rest of his life fighting off criticisms from Christians who he thought would only go halfway with grace and refused to remove all the obstacles to unity of Jews and Gentiles.

The attacks were often very personal and reminded you of some of the things being said at Corinth. People who claimed to follow Peter were probably aware of the differences and saw Paul as too radical. It was not difficult to question whether Paul had the right to be a leader, anyway. He had persecuted the church and while people could celebrate his conversion, did that really give him the right to stand up to the apostles who had been with Jesus from the beginning? Could he really claim to be an apostle? Did his encounter with the risen Jesus justify such a claim?

It must have been difficult being plagued by such questions. Paul kept appealing to that event, then reporting how people like Peter and James and John did initially approve of his preaching. He claims they did so along with an agreement that Paul would bring a sum of money to Jerusalem for the poor. Paul took this very seriously. He organised collections wherever his mission went. He appears to have laid great store on the collection as a sign of the Gentiles also belonging to the people of God. Perhaps prophetic visions of Gentiles bringing gifts to Zion inspired his efforts. He certainly saw the practical side. To describe the collection he sometimes called it "fellowship/communion" or "ministry/service." Gathering money for the needy belonged to his call.

And now Paul must turn to your problems at Corinth. You can do little more than report what you know and ensure Paul receives the letter. It will not take long for Paul to respond. Just a few months later Timothy arrives and you all sit down eagerly awaiting the first reading. You could tick off in your mind the issues which you raised and which had gone forward in the letter.

Paul is his challenging self. He refuses to make himself the centre of attention. Vulnerable love is what we see in the cross. That is God's power and wisdom, not the rhetoric and bamboozling miracles of missionaries. Love is a constant theme and for Paul the main sign of the Spirit. Paul is uncomfortable with women abandoning traditional dress. He doesn't want them to change, but he still approves their roles in leadership. Against men who emphasised that women were created after men, a subordination which Paul does not deny, Paul responds: now, don't forget that all you men also came from women!

Against those who claimed that celibacy should be the norm for spiritual people, an option which Paul had chosen for himself, Paul finds himself needing to argue the case for marriage and sexual relations as part of God's good creation, at least in this life. Paul challenges the naiveté of those who push the limits of freedom with little regard for the consequences. Eating at temple restaurants is out, as is use of prostitutes.

You can now look forward to Paul coming over in person, as he promises in the letter. But when he does eventually come, all your worst nightmares come true. Instead of unity there is a major catastrophe. Someone grossly insults Paul. Paul leaves to go north, and instead of returning to Ephesus via Corinth, as he promised, he drops the second visit and instead writes one of his deeply personal and confronting letters.

The situation is rather fragile, but one outcome is that the person who affronted Paul is disciplined. Unrest continues, however, and soon you are sitting listening to another letter from Paul, this time a strange mixture of consolation and anger. Paul is obviously relieved at the news that Titus, who brought you the other letter, reports, but matters are far from settled. It had come to Paul's ears and probably to yours that those who had little respect for Paul saw his constant change of plans as a sign of instability. They still harped on about his failure to behave like the other apostles and to accept their monetary support. There were still innuendos about the collection.

It has also not helped that other visitors have arrived who parade their credentials in a way that is ammunition to Paul's opponents. They carry impressive references, boast authoritative links with the real apostles, and have a strong impact through their preaching and miracles. Paul's letter ends by confronting these issues directly, although not without a little rhetoric of his own. Tongue in cheek, he compiles his own list of achievements, which include courageous faith in the face of adversity and even a visionary experience. But with the latter he is clearly embarrassed to make such a boast and ends up declaring that the place where he feels most confident is not his great achievements, but his human frailty because it reminds him that God alone is the basis of his security and of his ministry.

You will have experienced the impact of this letter. It must have made an impression, at least on a good number of your people, because not long after Paul comes to Corinth and spends some months there. It must also have been a time of relative calm, because while Paul is with you, he writes his long letter to the congregations at Rome. He already knew some of the Roman Christians, but he was not the founder. Visiting another's patch was a matter of sensitivity.

Paul had a chance to take stock while he was with you. He was planning a visit to Rome and then to Spain. But first he was also planning the major visit to Jerusalem in which he would present the great collection, the symbol of his life's work. It was important that he set down clearly the gospel which he preached, so that he could settle once and for all the problems which kept arising. People in Jerusalem and people in Rome will have been very aware of his problems. Away from the heat of conflict which produced Galatians and the pain which flows through the correspondence with your people, he could deal afresh with the issues in a more systematic way.

Paul begins Romans with an expanded form of greeting in his usual manner. He does the usual assurance about prayers for them and mentions a coming visit. His sensitivity is very apparent, when in one breath he writes of wanting to impart something to the Romans and in the next backs off slightly to speak of mutual benefit which he could bring to them and they to him. Paul is still having to make a case for his way of preaching the gospel, as he does in other letters, because for him everything stands or falls on whether you really believe that God's goodness is so generous that all we need to do is respond in faith and live accordingly.

He starts the main part of the letter with what almost amounts to a role play. He declares how God is angry with what human beings have done. They have failed to recognise God in the world of nature around them. They have turned to idols. They have also deliberately distorted their own natures and have turned to homosexual intercourse. Alienated from God and from their own natures, they have also gone on to all kinds of other alienating acts.

If Paul ever read you his drafts in Corinth, you would immediately re-cognise what he was doing. He was conducting a typical attack on the pa-gan world of his day. It was common to link idolatry to sexual immorality. It was also common to single out homosexual acts as signs of perversion, because this was how people understood them. Jews like Paul did not con-template that some people might be homosexual by nature. His focus was on deliberate perversion. You would sense how your Jewish colleagues and their converts would say a loud, "Amen," to Paul's opening statement.

But then Paul subtly switches attention to hypocrisy. People who al-most enjoy attacking the pagan world are no better themselves if they, too, do wrong and abusive things. It is as though Paul's opening statement was designed to puff people up with self-righteous pride only so Paul could burst their bubble and bring them crashing back to reality. In effect Paul is wanting to bring everyone down to the same level and undercut any spe-cial claims made on the basis of being Jewish, having knowledge, or being circumcised. The really good people, whether like Abraham or like Gentiles, are good because their behaviour shows it. It can be tested. God who knows what is going on in people's lives will judge it. The upshot is that everyone needs God's transforming love. Everyone needs the love which God has shown in Christ.

By showing that all people need God and all people can find love and forgiveness and renewal, Paul is reinforcing his gospel which knows no dis-crimination and no favourites. Jews and Gentiles are all on the same level.

None of this behaviour of remaining separate! Paul is, however, sailing close to the wind. It almost sounds like he is dismissing any advantage in being a Jew altogether. You can just hear the accusations which you know already in Corinth: Paul has abandoned the scripture and betrayed Israel! Once again Paul backs off slightly. Using a favourite style of asking questions and then answering them, Paul poses the issue of whether being a Jew is of any value. He answers with a resounding Yes, pointing to the wonderful heritage of the scriptures. He also answers his own question about whether he has abandoned God's law with a resounding No. His answer is only partly true. He has, of course, abandoned parts of the Law, but he would argue not the main part.

Corinth's problems laid Paul open to the charge that his gospel obviously didn't work. It created chaos. It simply will not do to say all that matters is Christ. You must have the Law. Other people will go off the rails. Paul is not convinced. To those who think he is saying, forgiveness is so free, who cares about sin? Paul responds by explaining that becoming a Christian is not about getting onto a list of the saved. It is about a whole change of being, represented by being buried and raised with Christ in baptism.

For Paul, it is impossible to think about faith without thinking about an ongoing relationship. He turns the argument on its head. You will not change people by heaping commandments on their head, even if they are sound and biblical. All you will do is increase people's sense of guilt and make them even less capable of doing or being good. You will change people by offering them a new relationship in which they are confident of God's goodness. That will start a process going which will in turn begin reproducing that goodness in their lives, as they become more and more free to focus not on themselves but on others. This is what it means to walk by the Spirit and bear the fruit of the Spirit. When people do this, you will find that they more than fulfill what was trying to be achieved by the commandments. Paul goes on to argue that the Spirit continues to yearn until the day when the whole creation will be renewed.

While this will convince some that he is not abandoning the Law, but fulfilling it in a different and more adequate way, it still leaves the question about Israel. God chose Israel. Paul can hardly deny this. Yet Israel has not taken up the gospel. Does this not amount to an abandonment of Israel? Paul reminds the Gentiles not to think themselves superior. Perhaps he had to issue similar warnings in Corinth. But then Paul cannot bring himself to believe that God will abandon Israel, even if there is no sign of their coming to faith. Later generations would quite happily reach that conclusion. Instead, Paul declares that God will never abandon Israel. Paul is so infected by the love he has learned in Christ that he cannot imagine God will stop loving and shut the door forever.

Perhaps, just as Paul's last letter to you at Corinth helped settle matters there, Paul's letter to Rome may have settled anxieties there. Later we hear of Peter and Paul being in Rome together without any reports of dissent. Paul's journey to Jerusalem, however, was not so simple. His anxiety shows in his request to the Romans that they pray that the folk at Jerusalem will accept his collection. Why should they not? At Corinth you could give any number of reasons!

Unfortunately we know little of what happened beside what Acts reports long after the event. There we hear something rather strange. James and his elders meet Paul, but report that they have heard rumours that Paul persuades Jews not to observe the law of circumcision and the like. We would have to say that the rumours were in effect true! But Acts (and the welcoming party from Jerusalem) assumes they are not. They suggest that Paul can help dispel the suspicions by paying a large amount of money to the temple to enable some local Jews to complete one of the requirements of releasing themselves from an oath. In the story Paul obliges. Was this the collection money? You may know, but we do not know. Acts then tells the story of Paul's arrest and his appeal to the emperor in his right of Roman citizenship, which he will have inherited through his father, possibly as a slave set free in the household of the Paulus family.

Perhaps you knew many things that have been lost to us. Did Paul ever make it to Spain as he planned? We have a number of Paul's letters, probably more than you ever saw. Did the Philippians send you a copy of theirs? Two of the letters which Paul wrote to you have survived. We would love to know what happened to the rest. If you lived to a very great age, you might have been alive when Clement of Rome wrote to Corinth in 96 CE, but that is most unlikely. We have other letters which may come from people who greatly honoured Paul and wrote in his name. There is debate about whether they are his originally, especially because they seem to express themselves in ways that were not typical of Paul. They include two letters to Timothy and one to Titus, but also letters to the Colossians and the Ephesians, and a second to the Thessalonians.

Colossians and Ephesians continue many of the themes. Colossians rejects the imposition of supplementary demands, in a way that reminds us of Galatians, but connected to more speculative ways of thought. Ephesians celebrates the unity of Jews and Gentiles, but without addressing Israel's future. It stands firmly in Paul's tradition with its daring suggestion that biblical commandments are a wall which must be broken down, an enmity which must be set aside for the sake of inclusivity. Both also address household rules. Slaves should obey masters, children should obey parents, and wives should obey husbands.

You will be used to this, but how does it work out, now that in Christ distinctions between male and female, slave and free, Jew and Gentile, no longer count? There must be a lot of pressure on women to fall back into the traditional patterns of the day. You would be shocked to hear what comes later, when women are soon forbidden to speak in church altogether. Imagine what Prisca the preacher would have felt! Your own leadership would also have been called into question.

A selection of passages to which this section alludes: delegation from Corinth: 1 Corinthians 1:11; 16:17-18; Paul and Corinth: Acts 18:1-17; Paul and the first Christians: Galatians 1:13-14; Acts 6–7; 8:1-4; 9:18; 22:1-21; 26:1-18; Galatians 1:15-17; circumcision: Genesis 17:9-14; Galatians 1:1-10; Acts 15:1-35; Galatians 1:6-9; 5:2-12; teachers in Corinth: 1 Corinthians 1:10-17; 3:5-23; 9:1-23; correspondence with Corinth: 1 Corinthians 5:9; 7:1; issues at Corinth in 1 Corinthians: incest, 5:1-13; lawsuits, 6:6-11; temple restaurants, 8:1-13; 10:1–11:1; speaking in tongues, 13:1; 14:1-39; women at worship, 11:2-16; rejecting sex, 7:1-40; visiting prostitutes, 6:12-20; injustice at communion, 11:17-34; future resurrection, 15:1-58; love, 13:1-13; issues in Galatians: intruders, 1:6-9; 4:12-20; reversion to old practices, 4:1-10; Peter's failure, 2:11-14; personal attacks on Paul: 2 Corinthians 10:1-11; 11:1-15; 12:11-13; disastrous visit: 2 Corinthians 1:12–2:11; 7:2-16; defending apostleship: Galatians 1:11-24; 1 Corinthians 9:1-2; Paul and the promised collection: Galatians 2:10; 1 Corinthians 16:1-4; 2 Corinthians 8–9; 12:14-18; Romans 15:22-33; credentials: 2 Corinthians 3:1-3; 10:12-18; 11:16–12:10; Paul and Rome: Romans 1:8-15; 15:22-33; issues in Romans: God's saving goodness, 1:16-17; 3:21-31; human alienation and universal need, 1:18–3:20; countering criticism about sin, 3:1-8; 6:1-23; the Law and human failure, 7:1-25; liberation through the Spirit, 8:1-39; Israel not betrayed, 9–11; Paul and Jerusalem: Acts 21:17-26; Colossians on the world body of Christ: 1:12–2:3; Ephesians on unity of Jew and Gentile: 2:11-22; household rules: Colossians 3:18–4:1; Ephesians 5:21–6:9.

3A. Galatians 1–2

Galatians is one of Paul's letters, traditionally called an "epistle." "Epistle" sounds formal and is not the word we would use for letters which we write, let alone emails. But "epistle" is not so unsuitable for the letters which Paul wrote. They do have a rather formal character and they were written not as part of individual correspondence, but as communications to groups of people. They were to be read out loud in house churches and gatherings.

Writing Letters

Our letters also mostly still have a formal opening. We still tend to write, "Dear William," and conclude with "Yours sincerely" or something similar. In Paul's day the traditional elements were more extensive. People learned how to write letters just as they learned to write speeches. They learned more about these things than we do today and it shows. Paul's letters are full of special techniques which he has learned.

The way he begins his letters is always the same. Basically the greeting reads: "X to Y, Hi!" X is the sender. Y is the recipient. Hi is the greeting. Standard Greek letters used a word sounding like "Hi!": *chairein*. It meant something like: may you be happy, be glad, rejoice. Paul's greeting uses two words, grace *(charis,* looking a little like *chairein)* and peace. "Peace" (Hebrew: *shalom!)* was, and still is, the usual Jewish greeting. "Grace" means something like good favour, generosity, kindness, love. In a Jewish and Christian context, such greetings were usually linked with their source: the God who gives grace and peace. So Paul's form of the standard greeting follows a Jewish model, but it is also specifically Christian. The grace and peace are from "God our Father and our Lord Jesus Christ." While this greeting was a standard formal element in Paul's greetings, it was likely to have been much more than a form of words. In some ways it encapsulated the heart of the gospel and its continuing good news.

Other elements of Paul's greetings also show signs of careful thought. Usually they reflect concerns to be expressed more fully later in the letter. Thus Paul supplements his own name with a description: "an apostle not from human beings nor through a human being but through Jesus Christ and God the Father who raised him from the dead." In the rest of Galatians 1 we shall see that Paul makes a special point of explaining the basis on which he claims to be an apostle. It was obviously a matter of some dispute and of great importance for Paul.

In the greeting he also supplements his usual form of words with additional comments about Jesus Christ: he "gave himself for our sins to rescue us from the present evil age according to the will of our God and Father" (1:4). One of Paul's major themes will be this salvation. He will defend it against those who want to supplement it and those who, he thinks, are in danger of undermining it.

His greeting ends in a liturgical acclamation, which would have suited well its reading in the gathered congregation: "to whom be glory for ever and ever. Amen" (1:5). Usually after the greeting there follows either a statement of praise to God or a more extended expression of thanksgiving to God for the hearers, sometimes including assurance of prayers on their behalf and some indication of desire to see them again, before the author comes to the main purpose of letter. Galatians is unusual because, apart from the brief acclamation in 1:6, Paul goes directly to the substance of the letter and misses the traditional thanksgiving. Most people think it is because he feels so intensely about the problems he needs to confront — he may not be feeling particularly thankful for the way the Galatians are at the moment!

The Galatians and Their Problems

The Galatians, people of Galatia, are probably the peoples who settled in the middle of what is today Turkey. They were Celts (Galat and Celt are variants). Paul is probably writing to them about the same time as he is dealing with problems at Corinth, in the early 50's. It is, however, also possible that "Galatians" refers to all the people who lived in the Roman province which was named Galatia. In that case it could refer not to the ethnic Galatians in the centre but to congregations which Paul founded in the southern regions. It could also mean that the letter might be six or seven years earlier. While such details are uncertain, there is more than enough in the letter itself for us to be able to sense that this was a lively interchange and that there were important issues at stake.

Paul comes straight to the point in 1:6. Instead of thanking God for them, he confronts them with his surprise — or better, his disappointment and frustration. They are abandoning Paul's gospel. More important, they are thereby turning away from the gospel, and therefore from God! They are doing so because other Christians have come into their communities preaching a different version of the gospel. Paul takes a zero tolerance approach. Theirs is no gospel at all. He does not care how authoritative the preachers are. Even if angels were to preach such a gospel, it remains no gospel. Such people are accursed! This is strong language. Paul is hopping mad.

Paul and His Credentials

Only as we read on do we understand what the hearers would have known all along: Paul is referring to other Christian Jews who disagree with Paul's approach and demand that all converts must join the people of God in the way the scripture prescribes. That included circumcision, the cutting off of loose skin from around the tip of the penis. It also included keeping all the biblical commandments. Paul had conducted his mission to Gentiles on the basis that such things were no longer necessary. These people made Paul look like a renegade who undermined the Bible. It undid all his work.

As Paul continues we can hear some of the criticisms. Paul has watered down the biblical commandments just so he can win people to join his cause (1:10). His gospel is false and sells the scriptures short; he has no authority to do so (1:11). Paul refutes these charges, claiming instead that he got his authority from Christ himself (1:12). His opponents were probably claiming that the real apostles had given them authority. Paul refuses to play that game. Instead he reminds them of his conversion, which was also his call by God to proclaim the gospel to the Gentiles (1:13-16). Of course, as a persecutor he must have had a fair idea of what he had been fighting against, so when he changed sides, he knew what the issues were and what the gospel was.

He then reminds them that he did not run to the apostles to be told what to say, but went off to Damascus. It was only three years later that he went down to Jerusalem to meet Peter (Cephas) and stayed a fortnight with him. Apart from Peter he also met James, the brother of Jesus, who was growing in influence in Jerusalem and would eventually become the leading figure until his death in 62 CE. In 1:20 he emphasises that he is not lying. Why? Because he is trying to say that the Galatians should recognise that it was Jesus himself who authorised him to preach the way he does. It was not one of the apostles. Paul was an apostle in his own right. He then went off to Syria and Cilicia (south eastern Turkey) to preach and had little if anything to do with the movement as it was expanding in Judea (1:21-24). The point Paul is making here, too, is that he has no need to justify what he is doing by constantly seeking authority from the apostles. His opponents were probably claiming that they had done exactly that and this was why they had the right to disagree with Paul. Paul saw no such need.

Paul does in Galatians 2 explain that he did go back to Jerusalem, but only after some 14 years! On that occasion he shared privately with the important people what he had been preaching all those years, just to ensure that he had not been wasting his time (2:1-2). While Paul does not immediately say so, it is clear that there was no disagreement with his stance. Paul illustrates this by reporting that they did not insist that Titus, a Gentile convert, be circumcised (2:3). That was proof enough. However we see from the following verse that the issue was quite contentious and this will explain why Paul approached the matter privately at first. 2:4 shows that even then there were Christians disapproving of Paul's stance. They would have insisted on circumcision. Paul accuses them of just wanting to impose their controls (2:4-5).

It is not until 2:6 that Paul tells us what the important people actually said. His references to them are strangely ambiguous. Paul does not want to place them on a pedestal in a way that would undermine his own authority. God is not interested in human hierarchies. He probably needed to say this because his opponents were claiming that their stance had the backing of such important people. Paul is more interested in what he sees as the truth, not in people's claims to status.

Paul reports that the important people saw no deficiencies in Paul's preaching (they added nothing; 2:6). They acknowledged that Paul was entrusted with mission to the Gentiles as Peter was to Jews (2:7-8). In 2:9 Paul finally tells who these important people were: James, Peter, and John, held to be "the pillars" (Paul still shows he has reservations about such claims). Paul reports an agreement with them about the validity of the mission on which Paul and his partner, Barnabas, were engaged. The only additional requirement was that they make a collection of money for the "poor." These "poor" are probably the believers in Judea. Paul takes this very seriously. Later we find a number of references to his organising such a collection across his mission areas, so that he could finally bring it to Jerusalem. It was more than an obligation. It became a symbol of solidarity of Gentile

Christians with the Judean church and in some sense echoed Old Testament visions of Gentiles bringing gifts to Zion at the climax of history.

So far, Paul has explained the basis of his authority, and shown that while his authority is not derived from the apostles, his gospel, and so his authority, has been recognised by them. That should settle any criticism that Paul was acting on his own authority or was out of touch with the true church of the apostles, let alone that he was preaching an invalid gospel. The apostles who counted were on his side, not on the side of those who wanted to circumcise Gentiles. Luke, writing some 30 or so years later, also reports some of these events in Paul's life. At some points his sources appear confused about just how many times Paul visited Jerusalem. Luke has more visits than Paul mentions. Acts 15 also records a meeting in Jerusalem where it was decided not to impose circumcision on Gentiles. That sounds similar in very general terms to what Paul reports of his second visit (in Acts it is his third). It is however complicated because Acts appears to report problems about eating with Gentiles as part of that discussion, whereas Paul himself here in Galatians reports that as an issue which came up later. Fortunately we have firsthand evidence in Paul, but Luke's later accounts are also useful in giving further background information. Despite coming from so much later, it is interesting that Luke has also preserved some of the main features of the conflict.

Paul and Peter in Conflict

In Galatians 2:11-14 Paul continues his account of his stance, but this time it is more controversial. Paul reports an occasion when Peter (Cephas) came to Antioch. While in Antioch Peter and other Jewish leaders, like Paul and Barnabas, shared in common meals with Gentile believers. All belonged to Christ. All belonged together. Then some Christians came from James in Jerusalem. From that point Peter stopped eating with the Gentiles. Paul explains his withdrawal on the basis of his fear of "the circumcision party." By this he probably means: the Christians still insisting that all Gentiles be circumcised. It is possible it means Jews in general, especially non Christian Jews suspicious of the Christian movement. Were Christians in Judea facing criticism that their new movement was undermining the Jewish people? Was it a political withdrawal? Or was it more than that? For some it would have been a matter of being faithful to God's word, as they saw it. That meant insisting on circumcision and for some it meant not mixing with Gentiles at the meal table.

Whatever the real reason, Paul was appalled that Peter and even Barnabas should sacrifice fellowship with Gentiles because of it. For Paul it meant a betrayal of the gospel itself, which declared that all people, Gentiles as well as Jews, were acceptable in God's sight. There must be no discrimination against Gentiles. The challenge now was to live as a human being, inclusively, not "to live as a Jew," where that excluded others.

Paul, Christ, and Scripture

There are serious conflicts about authority here. They include conflicts about the authority of scripture. Paul sees similar conflicts playing themselves out in Galatia. Some insisted on biblical authority to the letter. Paul insisted that Christ and Christ's inclusive grace is the ultimate authority and that this must mean setting aside those commands of scripture which conflict with it. Fellowship with God through Christ must be the chief value to be upheld and that included fellowship with each other. His opponents would have argued that all this is possible without setting aside any biblical commands. Paul saw it differently. In some ways, to put it anachronistically, it was a version of the debate over fundamentalism.

The rest of Galatians shows Paul arguing the validity of his stance. If the only way to salvation is by following the biblical law, then, for Paul, that raises serious questions about the need for Christ and his work. Christ is central for Paul. That is Paul's starting point. Paul sees total adherence to the biblical law and total adherence to Christ as incompatible. To include Gentiles must mean setting some parts of the law aside. Paul goes further: Christ's way is so totally new and adequate that there is no need for Gentiles to keep the biblical laws and, more radically, the same applies to Jews. Otherwise one gets oneself into the impossible situation in which Peter and Barnabas found themselves where they were acting contrary to Christ's way.

In claiming that Christ is the all-sufficient basis for our relating to God and that matters such as circumcision, observance of special days, and foods and the like can be set aside, Paul raised a host of new issues and generated widespread opposition which would dog him throughout his ministry. If Christ is the way, do we abandon scripture altogether? Paul does not go that way. Instead he argues that there are signs in scripture that God envisaged such a change would benefit more than Israel and that when it came, the biblical law would cease its role. The Law was something preliminary, useful for defining boundaries, even a kind of enslaving power to keep people under control and expose their need for change. Paul could not deny that God gave the Law, but he refused to allow it to remain central.

Against the argument that without the Law people simply go off the rails, Paul insisted that the Spirit created a new basis for moral life and reproduced in the believer the fruits of love. The result is that such a believer more than fulfills the valid demands of the Law, which we find in the commandments to love and not to steal, murder, commit adultery, and the like. In effect Paul still valued highly such commandments, while others which had been used to mark the Jewish people off as separate he saw as expendable.

Yet in all of this Paul saw the gospel he preached not as a breach with biblical faith or Jewish religion, but its legitimate fulfillment. Not everyone, including many Christians, saw it that way. It is to our great advantage that we have copies of letters which he wrote in which he argued the defence of his stance and in the process probed to great depth the meaning of human life before God.

3B. 1 Corinthians 11–14

By chapter 11 Paul is well into his letter to the Corinthians. The opening verse of chapter 11 really belongs more closely with chapter 10. There Paul has been dealing with one of the many issues which seem to have come up at Corinth and about which people like the friends or family of Chloe have reported (1:11) or the Corinthians have written themselves (7:1).

Self-Assurance

Unlike the Galatian churches where the problem seems to have been Christians wanting to impose biblical law on Gentiles, in Corinth we find signs of a self-assured Christianity where people have used the freedom they assert they have gained in Christ to do many things which are turning out to be destructive or at least dangerous.

It begins with the tendency of some to see themselves as especially wise and skilled in public speaking, an important value in those days. This seems also connected with a hero-worship of leaders, with groups identifying themselves as belonging to Apollos or Peter or Paul. This is divisive. It comes first on Paul's list of issues which he needs to confront. We belong to Christ, not to leading preachers. Paul is quite happy to resist the seduction of having his own loyalists. He does not see life's meaning to consist in winning power and affection because his life is in Christ and there is all the acceptance he needs and can want. He challenges those who think they are so wise and have "arrived" to think again. He pits against all such self-elevation and elevation of leaders the stark fact of the cross. Love poured out even to the point of death is the true wisdom and the true power for life.

Others have used their new sense of freedom to live in ways which seem to ignore moral values and the need to let faith affect the way we live. In one case that led to sexual immorality. In other cases, it led to Christians taking other Christians to court. They may claim wisdom and cleverness, but they can't even work through conflicts creatively with love. That kind of Christianity is not working.

Paul also has to take on prostitution. In no way should the Corinthians be meeting their sexual needs through prostitution, acceptable as it was in society of the time. Paul does not favour casual sexual encounters of this kind because he sees sexual intercourse as forming a personal bond and belonging therefore in a deep and lasting relationship. He is unhappy with those who, perhaps inspired by his own single lifestyle, idealise singleness and avoid marriage. Paul fears that to suppress one's sexuality could lead to inappropriate sexual behaviour such as visiting prostitutes. So in 1 Corinthians 7 we have the fascinating situation that Paul, who prefers singleness, mounts a case for marriage and insists, following the best models of the time, that it is something which should be mutually fulfilling for both man and woman.

Paul also has to deal with problems about attitudes towards food. He had abandoned the very cautious stance of some Jews of avoiding eating meat altogether lest they be contaminated by it. That could be because it came from unclean animals. It was more likely to be because the slaughtering was accompanied by religious rituals and often took place in pagan temples. Paul is happy to affirm that the believer is free from such worries and can eat such meat, but he is not happy that some go so far as frequenting the temple restaurants. People who do that are being naïve, argues Paul, about the subtle influences in such contexts.

Against the self-assuredness of the Corinthians, Paul recalls the story of the generation of Israel's peoples who escaped from Egypt. That act of salvation did not guarantee that they would reach the promised land. It was a common warning, made famous in Psalm 95. Today if you hear his voice, do not harden your hearts, like the wilderness generation, because they failed to reach the land. Paul is wanting to say: becoming a Christian and being baptised is no more guarantee one cannot fail, than the Exodus was that those leaving Egypt would enter the promised land. To make the connection he playfully connects Christian baptism with the crossing of the Reed Sea.

Gender

Chapter 11 begins with another of Paul's concerns. Women are abandoning their normal way of dressing in worship. They are effectively setting aside the social indicators that they are women. It is as though they are denying their difference from men and their gender. It may seem a trivial matter, but Paul saw danger. He did not think that Christ wanted women to become like men. They should remain as women and value themselves. Paul had a traditional view based on his understanding of Genesis. He saw men as reflecting God's glory and women coming next in a kind of hierarchy. But at the same time his faith in Christ pulled him in an opposite direction. Women were just as important as men. Somewhat playfully he sets men up only to bring them back to earth when he says: "For as the woman came from the man [as in the Genesis story, 2:19-23], so also men come through women [as in birth]." Paul is unhappy with any notion that God devalues us in our being ourselves, as women or as men.

Communion

The chapter goes on to another problem in the church gatherings. The more well-off believers were apparently coming together to share a meal and the poor would turn up late in time for sharing Holy Communion, but get very little to eat. Paul points out to the Corinthians that this reflects lack of understanding of what the Eucharist is about. They are not discerning the meaning of sharing Christ's body when they behave like this. For surely as all share the one bread they also need to demonstrate that they belong together. And surely the whole thing is a vision of justice and sharing. In our previous chapter we explored the background of this vision. How can they go on celebrating communion when they are denying communion and fellowship at the level of practical living, where it especially matters? Their celebration is being turned on its head to become a celebration of selfishness.

Gifts

Problems of worship continue in chapter 12. Paul will have taught the Corinthians about the Spirit. It was a way of talking of God's presence. It became a way of saying that Christ was present. Sometimes Paul even speaks of the Spirit of Christ. From early times Christians saw among themselves the signs of God's presence in new ways. The promise to which people looked forward had arrived. They really were enjoying the gift of the Spirit, even though they were still very aware that this was only the beginning. Paul therefore speaks of the Spirit as a kind of advance instalment of how it will be when God's kingdom finally comes in full.

As the church lived with a sense of God's Spirit in their midst they identified particular gifts and abilities which emerged as a result. They called these "gifts of the Spirit." Many had to do with leadership. Some were very practical. Some were ways of expressing worship. But Paul is worried about the trends in Corinth. He even suggests there is a danger they could get carried away with their religious experiences and then be no different from other religions in which they were once carried away. They could even end up doing things that were tantamount to cursing Jesus rather than blessing him.

So Paul tries to bring the Corinthians down to earth. He reminds them that the various gifts all come from the one Spirit. The emphasis is on oneness. If you find the gifts are creating division, then something has gone seriously wrong. People are different. Gifts are different. Not everyone has every gift. This is good common sense. It also reflects the need we have to support each other. We are together the body of Christ, not a lot of individuals pulling in different directions. So unity is the theme again, as it has been through much of the letter. This time Paul reminds them of their baptism. It is one baptism, one Spirit, one Christ. In the previous chapter he had reminded them of participating in one loaf, one communion.

He also uses the familiar image of the human body. We need every part. All parts need to work together harmoniously. Otherwise we are in danger. It is not Paul's intention to disqualify any of the gifts. He lists them all, including the ones he sees as less important like speaking in tongues, a form in which some people worshipped with words that went beyond ordinary speech and made sounds, which to some sounded like other languages. That sounded a bit magical and Paul was especially worried that such gifts could set people off onto an adventure in self-indulgence which would miss the point of faith altogether. So he interrupts himself to make one of the most famous statements about religion ever written.

Love

1 Corinthians 13 relates directly to the concerns Paul had with what is going on at Corinth. It does so in a way which crystallises some central truths and has endeared this passage to generations of people inside and outside of the church ever since. In one sense, therefore, it speaks for itself. In another, we cannot really feel its texture unless we read it in context.

Paul begins this passage where he left off in the previous chapter: speaking in tongues. He will return to this phenomenon in the following chapter. It seems to have been a distraction. It means nothing, says Paul, without love. The same is true of some of the other things which the Corinthians prized: prophecy, knowledge, wisdom, ability to work miracles. None of this matters if the most important component is missing: love. Elsewhere Paul puts love at the head of the list of the fruits of the Spirit. When the Spirit of Christ comes into our lives he fills us with love, so that we in turn can express that love to those around us. That is what it means to live out the gospel, to walk in the Spirit.

Paul spells out some of what this love means. It is generous and outgoing. It is not hateful or divisive. It has no need to engage in self-promotion. We can see the themes of Paul's letter recurring. It does not try to win power and form factions for self-importance. It does not disregard the poor and their needs. It does not treat people as things or exploit others sexually or in other ways. It does not deny the value of being woman or being man. It does not pride itself in being superior. Paul's thinking reflects his claim about the cross: that act of powerless love is the true wisdom, the true power. Paul is not, of course, talking about a submissive, non-confronting love, that says yes to everything. Quite the contrary, neither Christ nor he himself in this letter models that kind of love. Rather this love is engaged, sometimes passionately, sometimes with argument, sometimes gently, but always respecting and honouring others as people of worth and within the faith community seeing others as forming a unity with oneself which must be upheld.

Paul continues to bring people down to earth by reminding them that even with this love, it does not mean that he or anyone else ceases to be a human being with human limitations. He does not know everything. There is more to come. He has not arrived. But at the centre is his faith and his hope and, for him, most important of all: love.

Speaking in Tongues and Prophecy

In chapter 14 he returns to the question of speaking in tongues. He himself also speaks in tongues. He does not want to reject it. But he does want people to put it in perspective, because it has been getting out of hand in a way that has been disruptive in the gatherings. It has made outsiders who come in think the believers are off their heads. In all this Paul assumes, like the people of his time, that things like speaking in tongues were abilities which people developed and were under their control. They were not necessarily proofs of God's involvement at all. In fact it is quite clear that Paul believes that people can misuse their gifts — even sin with them. They may have their origins in the work of the Spirit; we might say in response to the Spirit. But in themselves they are almost neutral in quality and like many things, capable of being used helpfully or harmfully.

Notice that here, too, Paul is concerned that people love and respect each other. Love and respect need to govern what they do with and to each other when they gather. The common good remains paramount. Faith is not about me seeking spiritual fulfillment. It is about us celebrating love in ways that we build one another up.

There is a segment in 14:34-36 which many see as out of place and some manuscripts lack. It insists that women do not speak in church gatherings — contrary to what Paul had written in chapter 11. The passage may well have been added from a later period when people (primarily, men) had changed their minds about the place of women and wanted them to be more subordinate.

3C. Romans 1–3

Paul commences his letter to the Romans with the usual greeting. As in other letters his additions are all significant. He describes himself as "servant" or "slave" of Christ Jesus. That is both a statement of his humility and of his authority. He is not about promoting himself, as some others seem to be, but Christ. Paul confidently asserts his apostleship, linking it with the claim that his role is not only given by God but planned by God. In the way that prophets of Old Testament times claimed a special place in God's actions, so Paul claims a special place in the bringing of the good news. Again, it is not Paul's good news, but God's good news and Paul is about to extrapolate — all this before he has even mentioned the address-ees, the Romans!

Good News

Having set himself in perspective (1:1), he turns to the "good news" (1:2) to make sure it, too, receives the right profile. It is not something which Paul dreamt up or which is the invention of a new sect, but something deeply rooted in the scriptures. That mattered very much, especially because some were suggesting that Paul's preaching amounted to a betrayal of Israel and its scripture. The next two times in Romans that Paul focusses on the good news we find the same emphasis: it is according to the scripture (1:17); it fulfills the witness of the law and the prophets (3:21).

In 1:3-4 he gives substance to the good news: it is about Jesus. In a very condensed statement Paul strings together some key elements. They are each important for the gospel about Christ. They read as though they have been repeated as central statements of faith for some time. They may even have been known already to the Romans. At least the Romans would have known their substance. Thus Paul is starting on common ground with the Romans. He is asserting the faith they hold together.

The key elements are concerned with Jesus as Son of David and Son of

God. Their starting point is the ancient Jewish hope that God would raise up a descendant of David to be a new king over Israel. Some espoused this hope in a military form and looked to the Son of David to defeat Israel's enemies and liberate the land from evil influences. Christians asserted that Jesus fulfilled the hopes for such a Messiah, but not on the military model. 1:3 begins by telling us that Jesus is descended from David and so qualified to be the Messiah, also called God's Son, like the kings of Israel of old. 1:4 then tells us that God installed or appointed him as Messiah, Son of God, at his resurrection. Since his resurrection Jesus sits enthroned at God's right hand as Messiah, Christ, and Son of God.

As we saw in the previous chapter, this was one of the earliest ways in which Christians interpreted the meaning of Jesus' death and resurrection. It uses the language and ideas that belonged to Israel's ancient coronations and so to Israel's hopes for a king Messiah. This is probably why Paul assumes the Romans will also share these views, especially because their churches seem to have been founded very early. As the early Christians made such claims they would have been aware that it was never going to be adequate and that in some ways it was dangerous, because it was so easily misunderstood. It had, after all, been misunderstood when Jesus was crucified and he was lumped together with freedom fighters and accused of wanting to be such a King of the Jews. It was also rather unsatisfactory when you moved beyond the world of the Jews and spoke with people who had no such expectations for a Messiah and did not come from that background of thought.

To speak of Jesus as Son of God in a non-Jewish world had to mean something different. Already within the Jewish world people used "Son of God" in other senses. Some spoke of God's wisdom or Word as being like God's child. Very early some declared that God sent Jesus in the same way that God sent the prophets and equipped them with the Spirit. It was not far from that to declare that God sent Jesus as God sent the divine Word or Wisdom. Even here in Roman 1:3-4 we find two different ways of speaking of Jesus as "Son of God." He becomes the enthroned Messiah, the Christ, and in that sense Son of God at his resurrection (1:4). But 1:3 suggests he is already "Son of God" as he begins his earthly life and other passages go much further, suggesting God sent his Son into the world, so that he was Son of God even before he was born on earth (8:3).

The main emphasis Paul is bringing here is that the good news has its foundation in the event of Jesus' death and resurrection. Later he will argue that this is also the foundation of hope that God can do what seems impossible to us. Paul is not thinking about magic and miracles of a sensational kind. Rather he means that God can change the lives of people, who seem hopeless and godless. They can be set back into a right relationship with God. This applies to everyone without exception. That is the good news. No one is too bad or too hopeless. God's love and goodness (righteousness) reaches out to all. Paul is going to explain all this in a series of arguments. It is really the same message which Jesus demonstrated by his words and actions: no one, not even the most depraved sinner, is beyond God's love.

Paul and the Romans

In 1:5 Paul has still not got to the point of mentioning the Romans. He is still saying things about himself and the gospel he represents. His call to be an apostle was an illustration of the grace and goodness of God. Elsewhere he expands this even further. Here he notes that his call to be an apostle was part of this goodness of God reaching out to unworthy people such as himself.

At the same time this statement helps Paul make the transition to the next element of the greetings: the addressees. Paul's call is to be an apostle to the Gentiles (1:5). The Romans, too, lived among Gentiles and many of their number would have been Gentiles. So 1:6 reminds them of this. This is a sensitive issue as we shall see. Yes, some of them are Gentiles and they live in Gentile Rome. Yes, Paul is an apostle with a special role in relation to Gentiles — as we saw when considering Galatians. But Paul did not found the church at Rome. So he can't assume the authority of a founder. On what basis, then, is he approaching them? Would anyone have worried about this? Very probably they would have. News would have spread about Paul's disagreements with Peter and others. We can see from what Paul goes on to say that Paul assumes the Romans were well aware of the problems. In fact part of the reason for writing Romans was that Paul needed to explain himself and "get on side" with the Romans.

So finally in 1:7 Paul comes directly to the Romans and gives his usual greeting. He then continues with the usual assurances of thanksgiving (1:8) and mentions his desire to visit (1:9-15). But this is all much more than formula. Paul is so serious he uses language employed in swearing oaths: "God is my witness" (1:9). People used to lie; Paul is saying: he is not lying, when he mentions regularly praying for them. Did some think he was just wanting to take advantage of the Romans for his own purposes? These genuine prayers also included a desire to visit them (1:10). He wants to strengthen them (1:11). Careful, Paul! They are not your flock! Such caution then prompts him to put it another way in 1:12. He doesn't imply that the benefit would be one way. He really means mutual strengthening. Without that some might have found his approach rather presumptuous and arrogant. Perhaps they still did, but Paul was trying to be sensitive.

Paul's passion is not about to subside in over-sensitivity, however. In 1:13 he re-asserts his purpose: to bear fruit among them ("among them" is easier for them to take). 1:14-15 links his passion to his call. It is to bear witness to the gospel to all Gentiles, the Greeks (representing the dominant culture of the region and including those at Rome) and the barbarians (representing foreign cultures, often seen as inferior). "Wise" and "foolish" is not an exact match with Greek and barbarians, but it is clear that for Paul God's goodness crosses all the barriers of discrimination. Everyone matters and is of value. Even though he is not the founder of the Roman churches and even though there have been numerous reports which might make his visit difficult for some, Paul runs with his passion, with his call. That includes bearing witness to the good news also in Rome.

The same confidence builds to a crescendo in 1:16, where Paul declares that he is fully confident in the gospel he preaches. He is not ashamed of it — as some thought he should have been. So 1:16-17 comes back to the substance of the gospel. In 1:3-4 he had put it in very traditional terms. Here he asserts it in terms which will play an important role in the rest of the letter.

Back to the Good News

In 1:16 he declares what the good news achieves. It brings to bear the power of God in people's lives in a way which saves or liberates them. It does this not just for some, but for all who believe it, who respond to its offer. Paul is being sensitive when he writes: "to the Jew, first, and also to the Greek." Paul is recognising that the good news came first to Israel — against those who seem to be arguing that he doesn't any longer care about his own people. "Greek," here, stands for all other people, because Greek language and culture was the dominant culture of the day.

In 1:17 he turns to the actual substance of the good news in very brief terms. The traditional term "righteousness" means God's goodness and includes the notion of God's generosity and will to set right again things that have gone wrong. In the gospel we hear about God's goodness. Paul is not meaning that in a general sense (God is always good). Rather he is referring to Jesus. In Jesus we see God's goodness demonstrated. It is a goodness that seeks to liberate people. Later, when Paul spells that out further, we see that it has to do with liberation from powers that alienate people from God, from themselves and others. That shows in actions, traditionally called "sins," but it comes from being tied up in a destructive way of being, which Paul calls "sin."

"Sin" is the opposite of goodness. So the good news is about helping people change from being caught up in sin to being engaged in goodness and showing that change in goodness and generosity in their lives. The rest of 1:17 emphasises that this possibility is there for the taking. Faith means taking the offer which God's goodness presents. That is the way to life, life that is free and good. Paul even has room for a quotation from scripture, because for him this has been the real intention of scripture all along. It is not something recently invented which leaves the scripture behind.

What Has Gone Wrong

As we noted in the introduction to this chapter, Paul next performs a manoeuvre designed to stop Jews making special claims. In 1:18 he speaks of God's anger. It is directed against people who refuse to recognise what they see of God and especially when they then make gods of animals and birds and other creatures that contradict God's true nature. So Paul begins like many Jewish preachers of his day and we can imagine Christian Jews in Rome hearing the letter read to them nodding in agreement, almost cheering Paul on.

When Paul then asserts that getting God's nature wrong leads to getting one's own nature wrong, they would also hail his argument. Paul's chosen example, homosexual behaviour, would have won their approval, because both he and they would have understood homosexual actions as deliberately perverting what is natural. Paul would not have thought, as many have come to believe today, that for some people their homosexual orientation is not the result of deliberate perversion, but something natural to them.

Paul then expands the theme to all acts of sin. The common thread is alienation: from God, from oneself, from others. Alienation is the state of sin and the result is sins: acts of sin. Later in Romans 7 he expands the theme of alienation, using popular psychology of his day (and ours) to show that people easily become hopelessly confused. They want to do what they know is good, but end up doing the opposite — and not for want of trying. In fact, the harder they struggle, the worse the situation becomes. Such people are living not only in sin, according to Paul, but in death. They need to be brought back to life. There needs to be a resurrection. They need the power of the gospel to set them free.

By the end of Romans 1 people hearing the letter in Rome would probably be very much in agreement with Paul, possibly even admiring the powerful way in which he wrote. They would then find chapter 2 something of a shock. Shocking your listeners was one of the techniques which ancient writers used. Paul uses shock here to pull the rug out from underneath those who would be feeling very good about Paul's attack on sin in the world in general in chapter 1. For now Paul begins to shift his attention to Jews in particular. It is not yet apparent in 2:1; but it becomes clear in 2:17.

Sin is just as rampant among people who believe in God as among people who don't. Paul suggests that it is even more serious for people who know the commandments and then ignore them. You can't hide behind being a Jew (or being a Christian, for that matter), as if that makes you immune from facing up to things. Paul appeals to common sense and common wisdom in stating that everyone has to face up to God and God's response will be based on what we are and what we have done, not on things like whether we are Jews or not. Echoing his sensitivity in 1:16, where he wrote "to Jews, first, and also to Greeks," he repeats it provocatively in 2:10. Jews, first, at the judgement! Only goodness counts. Against his fellow Jews he declares that even the things that mark them out as Israel, like circumcision, are no guarantee of real goodness.

By now the listeners at Rome are likely to have felt rather uncomfortable. That will have been Paul's intention. If everyone is brought down to the same level, whether Jew or Greek, what then are we to make of Israel being God's chosen people? What advantage is there in being a Jew? Paul won't let the boat capsize. In 3:1-8 he reassures us that being a Jew does have advantages, but mentions only one: the scriptures. Of course, they are only an advantage if you use them. Paul is not suggesting that God has abandoned Israel. He will spend three chapters later arguing that God still has a special place for Israel — but not at the expense of others. He is certainly not implying that we may as well all become like sinning pagans if God is going to forgive us anyway. Already people had said such things about Paul's version of the good news (3:8).

Paul has created a whirlpool. He has undermined people's assumptions. It is going to take quite an effort to put something secure in their place. There will be loose ends. Paul presses on. In 3:9-20 he sweeps towards one of his main points. It is that no one is exempt from needing God's goodness. No one has special privileges which will let them get away with sin. All have sinned.

Back to the Good News Again

Having established that everyone needs the power of the good news of which he spoke in 1:16, Paul returns to the substance of that good news. The words of 1:17 come back. Now God's goodness has been shown (3:21). Paul is careful to remind them that the scriptures witnessed to it in the law and the prophets, as he did in 1:2. The new element is "the Law." As part of the scriptures the Law witnessed to the goodness of God which was to come in Christ. But that goodness has now come independent of the Law. That means God's goodness has come independent of the systems which the Law introduced and which became the basis for Jewish life and faith, from the temple to circumcision and much else.

This claim would worry many Christian Jews because controversy had surrounded Paul about his attitude towards "the Law" in this sense. Jews should surely not give up their religion, represented by "the Law." The issue was far from simple. In any case Paul argues that they should now base their lives on the good news, not on the Law, and rather see the Law as something which pointed forward to the good news.

In 3:22 Paul expands the phrase, "God's goodness." As we noted in discussing 1:17, he sees it not as something timeless (God is always good), but as a special action which God undertook, an action of goodness and generosity in sending Jesus. In 3:22 as in 1:16-17, the emphasis is on taking up the offer in the good news by believing and acting on it and on the fact that this is possible for everyone — no discrimination. 3:23 reinforces this openness by returning to the conclusions drawn from 1:18–3:20. Everyone needs God's goodness and generosity. There are no exemptions. In 3:23 Paul reminds the listeners: everyone has sinned. He also says: they have missed out on the glory they could have had. This is another way of saying that people have not become what God made them to be. Paul thinks about this as something glorious, sharing God's glory, being like God. That has been lost; they have fallen short of God's glory. They need to be brought back to what they were made to be. That is the whole point of the good news. It offers people the way back, the way to freedom and restored humanity.

Images of the Good News

In 3:24-25 we have another occasion in which Paul uses very condensed statements which probably reflect established traditions of his day. They are packed full of meaning. In fact 3:21-26 is all a single, long, and complex sentence in Greek. Many parts are unclear and people still argue about their possible meaning. Here we will only note some of the main points and how they fit with what Paul is saying as a whole.

In 3:24 Paul says we are "justified." The Greek word means here something like: we are brought back in a right relation with God. Then he uses a word which means "freely, as a gift." He is underlining the generosity of God's goodness. He reinforces this with the words, "by his grace," which means: based in his love.

The next word speaks of "liberation" or "redemption." It belongs to the images of the slave market. Slaves were bought and sold. They could also be bought free when someone paid a ransom or price for them. The Psalms speak of God ransoming or redeeming Israel from Egypt. It was a common image for liberation, setting people free; so it fitted well what God was doing in Christ. People didn't make all the details match, as though they looked at all the details and matched them. That would lead to an over-literal understanding of the word and result in absurd questions such as: who paid a ransom? Jesus or God? Who was it paid to: God or the devil? People simply used the image to mean: liberation.

In 3:25 there is also a bookshelf of special terms. Paul changes the image again, this time thinking of the temple and annual Day of Atonement. God made Jesus the basis for Atonement. Paul uses a word which could mean simply that: "the basis of atonement." But it could also mean the lid of the ark of the covenant where in the ancient ritual of the Day of Atonement the high priest sprinkled the blood. He is using the language of sacrifice, but as with the language of redemption and slavery, it is not wise to press the details too closely. Paul is simply finding another way of saying: God set us right with himself.

Redemption (liberation) and atonement are different ways of explaining this. 3:25 uses yet another way: forgiveness or passing over of sins, but even that is not altogether clear. What remains clear — because Paul states it twice in 3:25 and 3:26 — is that all of this was to demonstrate God's goodness (righteousness). God is good and shows this by setting people back into a right relationship with God. So these complicated sentences are illustrating what Paul had written in 1:16 and repeated in slightly different words in 3:21: God has shown his goodness (righteousness) to us and that is good news, because goodness in God's terms means generosity and love and wanting to bring people back into a good and right relationship with himself.

Implications of the Good News

In the final verses of chapter 3 Paul pauses to state the implications of what he has been saying. Does anyone have the right to claim a privileged status before God ("Where is boasting?" 3:27)? It is excluded because the basis for a relationship with God rests not on privilege or possessing God's Law and observing its rituals, but simply on saying yes to God's offer in faith. So Jews, even very observant ones, are not in a right relationship with God based on their observances, but because God offers such a relationship freely to all. In 3:29 Paul underlines that this means that God is as much God of Gentiles as God of the Jews. In 3:30-31 he returns to a very sensitive issue: if you put everyone on the same level, doesn't that make the Law — God's gift to Israel — obsolete? Isn't Paul undermining God's Law? Paul rejects this accusation. Even though he is happy to set much of it aside (like circumcision), he argues that the good news upholds all that matters in the Law.

Later in Romans 8 he will show that the new life which begins for people when they accept God's generosity demonstrated in Christ leads to a lifestyle marked by love. When people live this lifestyle they more than fulfill what the Law sees as important. Paul argues that people's behaviour changes as they themselves change in their attitude and focus. New relationships do wonders for people. A new or renewed relationship with God works exactly like this. The fruits are there for all to see, even if it is a process which takes time — a lifetime.

So Paul is heading off criticism of the way he proclaims the good news. It sounds like he is saying that before Christ everything was hopeless and the faith of the Old Testament was useless. This is especially so, the more he works hard to undermine any special privilege. Everyone is damned until Christ came along. When, however, you look closer, you see that that is too literal a reading of Paul. In Romans 4 he hails Abraham as the model of true faith and a right relationship based on it. So at least Abraham is an exception. So too are those people of whom Paul speaks in 2:12-16 whom God will affirm in the judgement day, whether they are Jews or not, because they lived according to God's will.

But Paul leaves us in no doubt: the basis of life with God is acknowledging that God approaches us with love and generosity, nowhere more dramatically and powerfully portrayed than in the life and death of Jesus. To accept that offer of a relationship with God means letting that love transform us: letting ourselves be forgiven, moving from anxiety and fear to trust and hope. It also means becoming part of the movement of God's life and generosity, sharing God's passions and goals, letting the Spirit of Christ fill us. It never means receiving some kind of guarantee about going to heaven with no ongoing, transforming relationship. It is being baptised into Christ and thus into a community of people in whose lives the Spirit of Christ is welcomed and active. Such faith certainly does not abolish the Law. It sustains it (3:31). In the rest of Romans Paul explains in just what sense this is true and in what sense it is not. Paul agrees neither with those who simply want all the Law's demands to continue to be met nor with those who want to abandon it altogether. Some people would find it very difficult to see any other alternative — and still do. Paul hopes the Romans will see the difference and understand his carefully worked out stance.

3D. Colossians 3:18–4:1 and Ephesians 5:21–6:9

Both Colossians and Ephesians address concerns about households and reflect both the values of their world and the impact of the Christian gospel.

Colossians 3:18–4:1	Ephesians 5:21–6:9
	21Be subject to one another out of reverence for Christ.
18Wives, be subject to your husbands, as is fitting in the Lord. 19Husbands, love your wives and never treat them harshly.	22Wives, be subject to your husbands as you are to the Lord. 23For the husband is the head of the wife just as Christ is the head of the church, the body of which he is the Savior. 24Just as the church is subject to Christ, so also wives ought to be, in everything, to their husbands. 25Husbands, love your wives, just as Christ loved the church and gave himself up for her, 26in order to make her holy by cleansing her with the washing of water by the word, 27so as to present the church to himself in splendor, without a spot or wrinkle or anything of the kind — yes, so that she may be holy and without blemish. 28In the same way, husbands should love their wives as they do their own bodies. He who loves his wife loves himself. 29For no one ever hates his own body, but he nourishes and tenderly cares for it, just as Christ does for the church, 30because we are members of his body. 31"For this reason a man will leave his father and mother and be joined to his wife, and the two will become one flesh." 32This is a great mystery, and I am applying it to Christ and the church. 33Each of you, however, should love his wife as himself, and a wife should respect her husband.
20Children, obey your parents in everything, for this is your acceptable duty in the Lord. 21Fathers, do not provoke your children, or they may lose heart.	6:1Children, obey your parents in the Lord, for this is right. 2 "Honor your father and mother" — this is the first commandment with a promise: 3 "so that it may be well with you and you may live long on the earth." 4And, fathers, do not provoke your children to anger, but bring them up in the discipline and instruction of the Lord.

22Slaves, obey your earthly masters in everything, not only while being watched and in order to please them, but wholeheartedly, fearing the Lord. 23Whatever your task, put yourselves into it, as done for the Lord and not for your masters, 24since you know that from the Lord you will receive the inheritance as your reward; you serve the Lord Christ. 25For the wrongdoer will be paid back for whatever wrong has been done, and there is no partiality. 4:1Masters, treat your slaves justly and fairly, for you know that you also have a Master in heaven.	5Slaves, obey your earthly masters with fear and trembling, in singleness of heart, as you obey Christ; 6not only while being watched, and in order to please them, but as slaves of Christ, doing the will of God from the heart. 7Render service with enthusiasm, as to the Lord and not to men and women, 8knowing that whatever good we do, we will receive the same again from the Lord, whether we are slaves or free. 9And, masters, do the same to them. Stop threatening them, for you know that both of you have the same Master in heaven, and with him there is no partiality. NRSV

These two passages are very similar. Both deal with matters relating to the household: (1) husbands and wives; (2) children and fathers; (3) slaves and masters. The passage in Ephesians is much longer than Colossians, especially in dealing with marriage. As with the rest of Colossians and Ephesians careful study shows many similarities. The most common and convincing explanation of these similarities is that Ephesians was written after Colossians. It uses ideas and phrases from Colossians, sometimes with slightly different meanings.

As explained in the introduction to this chapter, some see both Colossians and Ephesians as coming from the period after Paul's death when his faithful followers sought to keep alive his authority and wisdom. They wrote in his name, not to deceive, but to put themselves under Paul's authority and represent that authority to the people of their day. While Colossians seems to be dealing with some specific situations, Ephesians reads much more like something written for broad circulation. Alternatively, some see both letters, or at least Colossians, coming directly from Paul and account for the different emphases and lines of thought in these letters from what we find in the undisputed letters of Paul by a change in his circumstances.

The Context in Colossians

Colossians 3:18–4:1 must first be seen in the context of the letter itself. Colossians 3:12-17 focuses on unity and worship. Just before that the author has emphasised the basis of that unity. People have made the change, leaving the old life behind and beginning the new life. Echoing the imagery of baptism the author declares that they have been raised with Christ. They are a new creation where "there is no longer Greek and Jew, circumcised and uncircumcised, barbarian, Scythian, slave and free; but Christ is all and in all!" (3:11). This is very interesting because he is soon to speak of slaves and masters. 3:12-15 emphasises mutual love, including humility, gentleness, compassion, patience, and forgiveness.

3:16 briefly mentions worship. It is about hearing God's word, encouraging each other, and giving thanks to God. Worship belongs as part of the new lifestyle which demonstrates love and compassion. 3:17 looks out across the whole of life and declares that it all belongs within the new lifestyle — the Christ-way of life. So when 3:18 speaks directly to wives and then to husbands we need to see this in the light of what the author has just said about love.

The Context in Ephesians

When we look at Ephesians, we find that it has much more about the new life. There, too, we find a focus on unity, but the emphasis is on unity among those exercising various gifts of leadership (4:1-16). Most of what follows takes the form of warnings about what Christians should avoid (4:17-32). 5:1-2 affirms the need to walk in love, but by 5:3 the author has returned to warnings again, clearly concerned about dangers to the Christian life. By 5:19-20, just before our passage, he turns to the theme of worship, just as Colossians does in 3:16. The transition is slightly more abrupt. That is probably why Ephesians adds the words: "Be subject to one another in the fear of Christ" (5:21). Colossians had already covered that mutuality very adequately.

Household in the World of Colossians and Ephesians

Colossians is very brief in its instructions to wives: they are to be subject to their husbands, as is fitting in the Lord. Ephesians begins in almost the same way, but strengthens the statement by adding "as to the Lord."

Colossians does not mean: only when it is fitting, but rather: do this because it is fitting.

Before we explore these instructions in more detail, it is important to look at them as a whole and understand their background. We cannot understand them unless we understand what it meant to be a wife, or a husband, or a slave in those days. Reading scripture and taking it seriously means listening to it as far as possible within its own world. It is just as important to do this in reading scripture as it is in any relationship. It is a most unpleasant experience when people don't listen to you but only hear what they want to hear and then get it all wrong because they don't understand your world.

In the world of Colossians and Ephesians households consisted of a family where the husband was normally the head of the household and responsible especially for affairs beyond the home and the wife was responsible for domestic matters. Reasonably well-to-do families also had slaves. These might be individuals or they could be families. The slaves had been inherited or purchased and they did not have freedom. They were the possessions of their owners. Children were the responsibility of the father who might make slaves responsible for their education.

Clearly both Colossians and Ephesians assume that among those who will be listening to the letters are members of households, including slaves. Stable family life was where each member of the household knew his or her position of importance and did not try to change that. People were obviously not equal. Freedom was limited or not there at all, in the case of slaves. A peaceful household had to be based on such inequality. In addition the unequal power frequently led to violation of the rights of the weaker members of the household, especially slaves.

Both Colossians and Ephesians uphold the common values of the day: the maintenance of good (but unequal) household relationships. There is no indication that they sought to change the system. Slavery remained. Women remained subordinate. Men ruled. But they brought to that framework their Christian faith. What people commonly saw as good and what Christian faith taught as good were by no means identical. The result is some tension. We can see it as we look at each set of instructions.

Wives and Husbands

Already in the instruction to wives in Colossians we find the words "in the Lord." It was quite common in the world of the day to declare something to be "fitting." It means something like: this is how everyone knows things should be. Adding "in the Lord" to this brings in another factor: the values Jesus taught. Colossians does not say what the implications might be, unless we look back to the verses which come just before our passage. There we see that the Lord puts love and compassion at the centre. The values of Jesus are echoing all around us as we hear 3:18. So 3:18 would certainly not support abuse or injustice. There is a tension in the statement: eventually it will declare such submission inappropriate, but that is not the position of 3:18.

In Ephesians we are faced with a fascinating contradiction — at least on the surface. It begins by asserting that we should submit to one another (5:21). It adds that we should do that "in the fear of Christ," which probably means: as we take Christ and his message seriously and honour it. It has the potential to undermine all the hierarchies which follow: will masters be willing to submit to slaves? If everyone submits to everyone else then we have an impossible situation where no one submits to anyone. 5:21 is not, however, talking nonsense and means something like: take into account the needs of all others and respect them. Love them! That is revolutionary, but for the author of Ephesians it does not yet go so far as to call into question the household system of his day.

Ephesians supports the household system by appealing to Christian tradition. As Christ is the head of the church, so a husband is head of his wife. No reason is given why it could not read "as Christ is the head of the church, so woman is the head of man." The author simply assumes this applies to husbands, not to wives, probably because he reflects the common values of his day. It is a given for him, not to be questioned. Perhaps he thought of "head" as meaning "source" (like "headwater" of a river). Perhaps he was thinking of Genesis 2 according to which God created woman by taking a rib from man. Referring to Christ as "saviour of the body" (5:23) may suggest that the author thinks of the male as protector and therefore as head. The effect is to reinforce the traditional values of the day: women are to obey their husbands in everything. The Christian values now serve to support the traditional ones, a position which would remain influential for centuries to come and keep women in a secondary position in society and the church.

Colossians urges husbands to love their wives and not to abuse them. This reflected a common value of the times and it certainly fitted a Christian stance, except that ultimately the stance of Jesus would undermine the subordination and inequality. Here in 3:19 the unequal power is assumed. That is why there needs to be the warning about abuse of that additional power.

Ephesians has massively expanded the instruction to husbands. Once again it uses the Christian gospel to reinforce the instruction. Playfully the author speaks of Christ's love for the church as like the love of a husband for a bride. The ritual of washing of the bride on the wedding night fits the imagery well. Sexual intercourse similarly becomes a way of talking of unity between Christ and the church. The point of this elaboration is to emphasise love for one's wife. This is very radical and goes far beyond just warning against abuse. But it stops short of seeing one's wife as an equal. In fact it reinforces the inequality by putting the husband in parallel with Christ and the wife in parallel to the church. Ephesians is not at the point where it could say to women, love your husbands as Christ loved the church, because it does not assume such equality. But even to make Christ the model for the loving sows revolutionary seeds capable of making traditional marriage a place of love but also of ultimately subverting its inequality.

Children and Fathers

Colossians 3:20 urges that children are obedient. This assumes they will be present when the letter is read. Obviously children are assumed to have a place in the gathering. This already values children highly. "In the Lord" keeps the gospel values in view. 3:21 has a matching instruction to fathers. Mothers do not feature because it was not their responsibility. Parenting was not shared as in most cultures of our day. In its own way, Colossians shows some awareness of the fragility of children and their vulnerability to abuse at the hands of parents.

Ephesians reinforces the instruction to children by referring to the ten commandments. Perhaps the reference to the promise attached to the commandment is nothing more than reinforcement that it is important. It may, however, reflect the idea that such stability augurs well for the future. The instruction to the fathers also has child abuse in mind. The standard upbringing included corporal punishment and this seems to make an appearance here. In time, gospel values would change people's approach to bringing up children, but instruction accompanied by threat of punishment remained a norm for centuries.

Slavery

Slavery is part of the social order, according to both Colossians and Ephesians, so the issue is: how to be a good Christian slave and good Christian master. Colossians urges complete and genuine obedience. It also urges slaves to see themselves as accountable ultimately to Christ and promises them an inheritance. This is slightly subversive: slaves do not usually expect an inheritance. By bringing Christ into the picture as the true (and only) master, Colossians is indirectly sowing seeds which will subvert slavery itself. This is clearly the case in the instruction to the masters. They are firmly reminded of their place and cautioned against abuse.

Ephesians makes similar points in addressing the slaves. God does not treat slaves and masters differently. Similarly masters are left in no doubt that they are not free to do as they like, but will be held accountable.

This did not become in either Colossians or Ephesians a rejection of slavery. That would take time. Slaves were frequently exposed to sexual abuse. Both passages pass over this problem in silence and we are left wondering what slaves might have to endure, but surely not from masters who has espoused the new faith. Slavery and the good news are irreconcilable, but at this stage the good news reached only so far. At least it was seeking to influence the way people operated within these household systems. Resistance to structural change would remain strong.

Engaging Colossians and Ephesians Today

These two passages have been important in shaping family life within the Christian tradition. They need to be read in their contexts. When we do so, we can see why the authors wrote in the way they did. They were reflecting the most respected values of their day, which saw stable households as important for society. It was a compromise which stood in tension with the direction of the good news. We can sense that tension in the statements of the passage. We now recognise the abuse of slavery and of making women subordinate to men. We now approach the bringing up of children differently, usually more informed by the values of the gospel.

These passage also illustrate the importance of rightly discerning what remains valuable and relevant for us today in biblical material and what needs to be set aside, though respected as belonging to a different mindset and culture. Part of that process will be when we engage such scriptures critically in the light of our current knowledge and wisdom. Part of it will be when we set such passages beside others in scripture which call for more radical and just ways of men and women living together.

CHAPTER FOUR

The Gospels: Putting the Story Together

A Scribe for the Kingdom of Heaven

Exciting things are happening in your congregation. If you can imagine yourself as a scribe in the community where the Gospel according to Matthew was being written you will know what I mean. As a scribe you are one of the few people who know how to read and write. That made you very important. All over your world at that time scribes were essential for local communities. They had a very busy time helping people understand official documents, reading bills and letters, and writing letters for people. In your Jewish surrounds you were also often called upon to look up passages in the Law and explain them to local people. Sometimes even the priests needed you to help them understand points of Law.

And here you are in a community of Christians about half a century after Jesus. As one of the people who could read, you sometimes read aloud the stories of Jesus when you all meet together for worship, just as you did before things became too contentious in the synagogue gatherings. A few times you read the Gospel according Mark right through from beginning to end. And people listened and listened — to every word. It was, after all, also a major source of entertainment in an age when there was no radio or television. People used to gather together to hear a book read out loud.

You stood up before them all with the scroll. The words were all hand-written in black ink in columns. So as you read, you rolled the scroll from right to left. It was a big effort which required much skill, because there were no breaks between the words. You just had to know. You would know the right way to read, GODISNOWHERE!

Why is it exciting in your congregation and especially for you? Because one of the other scribes has decided to put it all together into one new gospel. For years you have had the Gospel according to Mark, and a book of sayings of Jesus, and beside this an increasing number of stories which have been circulating about Jesus. Now it's all going to brought together into one big gospel. What a task!

We call the writer of this new gospel, Matthew, because some time in the second century when the Church wanted to assign an author to each gospel, it concluded that this one must have been written by Matthew. We have no idea whether this conclusion was correct and in some ways it doesn't matter. Perhaps he was a founding figure among the communities where the gospel came to be written. But we are calling the writer, Matthew, anyway. He obviously had no interest in drawing attention to himself as the author because he never mentions it. The real author, from a faith point of view, was Jesus. It is, after all, the gospel of Jesus Christ (*according to* Matthew).

Mark (also a late attribution) states from the start: "The Beginning of the Gospel of Jesus Christ." People must have come to love Mark's gospel in your community. Matthew chose to base his new gospel on Mark's gospel, revising it and supplementing it as he went. It was a huge task when Mark wrote, about 15 years earlier. He apparently had no full-length gospel to use as his base. Instead he seems to have gathered together groups of sayings and stories which people were using in his community at the time. For instance, it is easy to see how people linked parables which had the theme of seeds together. We now find them together in Mark 4. In the previous two chapters Mark seems to have worked in a series of stories about Jesus being in conflict with his fellow Jews over interpreting the Law. The story of Jesus' last days in Jerusalem had been a special focus for a long time. Mark was able to draw that into his gospel.

There was much besides which he wove into his composition. It is a remarkable writing — much more than a collection of stories and sayings. Even deciding which order to put things was a task in itself. Should you gather material together because of similar themes, like all the miracles together? Or should you spread them around? Most of the stories had been doing the rounds for so long that no one had an overview of when they originally happened — except of course for events like Jesus' baptism and death and resurrection. Mark did some wonderful things in his arrangements. He seems to have deliberately set side by side an account of the disciples being very blind to what Jesus was showing them and an account of Jesus healing a blind person. He also tells the story of Jesus' feeding 5000 and then 4000 in a way that celebrates the good news of the gospel coming to both Israel (represented by the 5000) and the wider world (4000).

Mark was writing for churches full of Gentiles who had turned to the faith, so his gospel celebrates that fact. It is a wonderful climax when finally a Gentile centurion acknowledges Jesus as the Son of God at the cross, after everyone else, including Jesus' disciples, either rejected him or misunderstood him. Outsiders, including the women, get it; the others don't. People in Mark's congregations would hear echoes of political propaganda in parts of Mark. Roman emperors claimed to be Son of God and to bring good news to the world. By contrast Mark proclaims the good news of Jesus Christ and his image of the Son of God is a broken figure on a cross. His Jesus challenges traditional notions of greatness with the assertion that the truly great person is one who cares for others and is lowly. Jesus was exactly that.

So people had preached from Mark, taught from Mark, used Mark in small groups, argued from Mark. It was a gospel to treasure, although in some respects it did not quite match the needs of Matthew's communities who had a much stronger Jewish background. Parts of Mark grated with some, especially where he interprets a saying of Jesus to mean that biblical food laws should be abandoned because they never made any sense. How can food or things external to a person make them unclean! Mark's community had reached this conclusion only after years of grappling with the question which once set Paul and Peter at loggerheads. For them, as for Paul, the logic of the gospel demanded that they abandon all such practices, including circumcision, because they create barriers between people, especially between Jews and Gentiles.

Matthew's communities, to which you belong, found that all a bit too radical. You have been brought up to honour God's Law and see no need to drop parts of it. In fact, the matter is very contentious and belongs to the deep sense of grief many of you are feeling. Not so long ago it looked like your group might win over the other Jews and that the main line of interpreting the Law in the synagogue would be that of Jesus. That hope did not prevail and you found yourselves attacked as betraying Israel and setting aside God's Law. People rejected the claim that Jesus was God's Messiah. Stories are beginning to circulate which are designed to denigrate your faith, such as that Jesus was illegitimate and that the disciples stole Jesus' body and hid it and then made up the idea of his resurrection. Families split apart; friends were divided. There is a lot of pain and anger on both sides.

Both sides are also still trying to come to terms with the disaster of 70 CE when the Romans destroyed the holy temple of God in Jerusalem. Your group has been arguing that that never would have happened if the people had listened to Jesus. Some of you, like Matthew, declare quite openly that it was God's judgement on Israel for rejecting the Messiah. Imagine when these accusations are flying about in a family!

These are very tense times. Parts of the gospel of Mark are sometimes an embarrassment in these discussions. A revision is called for, quite apart from the need to bring all the other material together. As a fellow scribe you must have conversations with Matthew about this great undertaking. The days ahead will be exciting as you see the project develop. There on Matthew's table is the Gospel according to Mark. On the other side is the book of sayings, which we know he must have had — Luke had it, too — but which has not survived on its own. We know it only from what Matthew and Luke have in common and call it "Q." And there in the middle is the freshly dried scroll. As you look closely you still see the strips of the papyrus plant which have been stuck together and Matthew had markings as guidelines for his writing. There must be notes and plans scribbled on older pieces. It would be too much to keep all that in one's head and the final product which we have today reveals careful detailed effort in design, especially in the first half of the work.

It is going to be very important to counter the accusation that Jesus was trying to undermine the Law. That needed to be said right up front. But first something had to be said to counter the innuendo about Jesus' mother and then something about Jesus and John the Baptist and Jesus' baptism. Then the time would be ripe to address the issue of the Law.

At the moment Matthew is carefully copying a genealogy into the first columns. He has a smile on his face because he knows he is doing something slightly subversive. Instead of a list of males, he is including women, not with every man, but only four and all of them were in some sense outsiders, either because they were Gentiles or because they were subject to sexual innuendo like Mary. Others will notice the neat pattern of three lots of fourteen generations or six lots of seven; now for the climax, the seventh seven! People who played with numbers could hardly fail to see the point.

Matthew will work on these early columns further while you return to work. He knows his Bible so well that his story of Joseph and Mary and Herod and the magi is full of echoes of Israel's story, of its Joseph, of Moses going down to Egypt, of Balaam's star and Balak, the wicked king. People were used to this way of storytelling. It was the ancient equivalent of flashbacks in movies, when images of the past dance with images of the present to create new levels of meaning. Out of it we see Jesus as a new Moses. We also shudder at Herod's threat to kill the king of the Jews because we know how the story will end. It will also end with the promise that Jesus will always remain with his people, just as it begins by calling him Emmanuel, "God with us."

We divide biblical writings into chapters and verses, following the pattern developed by the Archbishop of Canterbury, Stephen Langton (chapters), in the 13th century and the publisher, Robert Estienne (verses), in the 16th. For Matthew it was simply columns; column after column, perhaps eventually with some markers to show where selected readings might begin and end. He had already written a number of columns and rolled some way into the scroll before he turned his attention to Mark. We now see the result in Matthew 3. Some lines are absolutely identical, copied with not a single change. In others a word here or there is replaced, perhaps by a more familiar word, or a sentence is rearranged.

It was careful, detailed work and takes the same careful detailed attention to detect. Sometimes Matthew makes additions which stand out. In 3:2 he summarises John's message with exactly the same words used to summarise the message of Jesus in 4:17 and the disciples in 10:7. This is because he apparently wanted to align Jesus and John more closely. It fits the emphasis he wants to put on God's Law or will. This helps counter those who claim Jesus abandoned God's Law. It also helps keeps those Christians on their toes who think having the label "Christian" and calling Jesus "Lord" is all there is to it.

Soon the process becomes quite complicated because the book of sayings ("Q") also contains material about John and about the temptations of Jesus. Matthew weaves the two together into one. The result is to emphasise Jesus' role as the one who will judge the world. John's famous words confronting his compatriots with their failure to live up to their claims comes in almost identical wording in both Matthew and Luke. Mostly, however, Matthew treats Q as he does Mark, with minor rearrangements and just occasional revision. He can supplement Mark's very short account of the temptation with Q's longer one. It is all coming together well. The temptation story shows Jesus doing what Israel in the wilderness failed to do: he is totally obedient to God's will.

Your next visit to Matthew's project finds him already well on into the opening stages of Jesus' ministry. Looking over his shoulder you can see why Matthew seems so satisfied. He has been able to rearrange Mark's gospel in such a way that the opening section about Jesus' ministry has two clear parts: Jesus' teaching (chapters 5–7) and Jesus' deeds (chapters 8–9). For the teaching he uses the collection of sayings from Q found in Luke 6. It has already been widely used in your community and expanded. It fits ideally here. Matthew borrows the detail about Jesus going up a mountain from Mark's scene where Jesus appoints twelve disciples. You cannot help but think of Moses. Jesus is like Moses, though even greater. His words begin with promises of blessing, shaped especially to encourage believers to take their faith seriously and show it by their attitudes and deeds.

Then comes a very clear statement about the scriptures in which Jesus states that he did not come to abolish or abandon them. To the contrary, he came to make sure they were fulfilled and followed to the letter. Matthew drew from Q the saying that not even a stroke of the Law is to pass away. He surrounds it with warnings against those who think or teach otherwise. He then expounds what this standard of righteousness or goodness implies. Not just murder, but murderous attitudes and hateful behaviour is wrong; not just adultery, but adulterous attitudes to other men's wives. Divorce is not to be tolerated. Oaths are no longer acceptable. There must be no more revenge and no hate, only love, even for one's enemies.

That should make its mark, for those who doubt Jesus' faithfulness to the Law. At the same time it also shows that Jesus did not apply the Law in a wooden fashion where everything was considered of equal importance and authority. People mattered most, not rites and rituals. Later Matthew will again draw on Q when he quotes Jesus as saying: "Woe to you, scribes and Pharisees, hypocrites! For you tithe mint, dill, and cumin, and have neglected the weightier matters of the law: justice and mercy and faith. It is these you ought to have done, without neglecting the others" (23:23).

As you watch, Matthew has worked out a neat way of talking about devotional practices (giving money; praying; and fasting) where they all follow the same pattern of words. Then in the middle he has placed the Lord's Prayer. Next come statements about trust and anxiety, about hypocrisy and being judgemental, and finally Matthew concludes with sharply worded warnings to believers. He even takes one of John's warnings to his compatriots as trees that bear no fruit and transfers it to Jesus' warning to the disciples.

In the rest Matthew takes what once belonged to confrontation between Jesus and his contemporaries and turns it into something which clearly addresses Christians of his day. This is a favourite strategy of Matthew. It has the effect of helping people hear the risen Jesus speaking to them in the present. Matthew's passion throughout is to re-present the stories and sayings of Jesus in a way that they are right on target for the hearers of his day — obviously an effective preacher.

This time it's your turn to smile. You had noticed that Matthew left out Mark's opening episode of Jesus' ministry where he conducts an exorcism. Perhaps Matthew had spoken of his hesitation about exorcisms, which also becomes apparent elsewhere. But he has not ignored the important statement about Jesus teaching with authority but not as the scribes. Instead he brings it at the end of Jesus' teaching in what we call the Sermon on the Mount, but in a slightly altered way. That's why you smile. Instead of "not as the scribes," he writes, "not as *their* scribes." By implication you are now in the picture! Jesus is the true scribe, and you know that you and Matthew are also scribes of the kingdom.

Matthew will continue his strategy into the next stage, where he draws together stories illustrating Jesus' deeds. For this he mostly has to rely on Mark, but there is at least the story of the centurion and his servant which is found in Q and the account of would-be disciples who failed to rise to the challenge. He weaves all this together, generally following Mark's order, but bringing forward some stories which come later in Mark (like the stilling of the storm, the healing of Jairus' daughter and the woman, and the Gadarene demoniacs) and leaving Mark's stories about controversy about Jesus' deeds on the sabbath till much later after he has presented Jesus as the one who offers the light yoke. See Appendix B for detail.

By the time of your next visit the strategy is complete. In case you hadn't noticed Matthew draws to your attention the fact that he has ended the block in 9:35 with almost exactly the same words as he began it in 4:23, which speak of Jesus' teaching and deeds. This is neat. It was also a great help to people listening to the gospel being read aloud. They could tell that the block had ended by the echo. It was in fact a favourite device for people writing at this time. It achieves what we can more easily achieve by formatting. People of Matthew's time only hear; they do not see the text.

Over the next weeks Matthew will continue his project, revising Mark, adding Q and other materials which had come his way, and putting it all into a meaningful pattern which became a vehicle for God's word to address the people of his day and also help them answer their critics. There are many highlights. Into Mark's scene of Peter's confession Matthew inserts Peter's call to be the foundation rock of the new community. Peter tries to walk on water and fails. The message is clear. The congregation receives instruction about dealing with matters of discipline, but it comes in a context which stresses the care of the shepherd and the importance of forgiveness.

Q's material in which Jesus confronts hypocrisy and malpractice among teachers becomes a full-blown confrontation of the Pharisees, a scarcely veiled allusion to the leading party of yours and Matthew's day. It leads right on without interruption (Matthew leaves out the widow and her small coin) to the prediction of the temple's destruction as God's judgement on their sin. Yet Matthew expands the climax of Jesus' teaching which he found in Mark 13 by three parables, clearly shaped to confront believers, who had lost their oil, buried the wealth (talents) of the gospel, and would face judgement because they failed the all-important test of love for those in need.

Matthew's account of Jesus' last days follows Mark very closely. The additions are designed to underline God's involvement and response to the events. Earthquakes heighten the effect. Visions, as in the Joseph story, wink to the hearer that what occurs is a travesty. Matthew reinforces the acclamation of Jesus as Son of God and by contrast accentuates the responsibility of the people for what happened. He writes as a Jew confronting fellow Jews. You understand this well and feel it because it reflects the tensions of your day. You would be shocked to hear how it was turned later into something anti-Jewish and was made to inspire hate and genocide. That was not its meaning in your context.

Matthew must have been exhausted at the end and he must have nearly run out of space in a normal-sized scroll. He ends as he began: with openness to the world. The coming of the magi prefigured the results of Jesus' command to tell all peoples the good news. Your community now includes some Gentiles and more are sure to follow. You find yourselves in transition, no longer considered to belong in your synagogue and finding more openness in the direction of those communities which gave you Mark but which still seem strange.

Things would be quite different in another part of your world. You could have been in Luke's community. Then, with your talents, people would call you a secretary rather than a scribe. Luke is also a name given by later generations, but which we will assume. Though not a Jew Luke is also well steeped in scripture. He, too, is fond of Mark and has Q at his disposal, and also some wonderful stories you have never heard of like the parables of the Prodigal Son and the Good Samaritan.

Luke also seems bothered by the Jewish synagogue, but for different reasons. It has become embarrassing that their numbers are on the increase and that they are questioning why Luke's Christians, who are mostly not Jews, are using their scriptures. Perhaps they have become an irrelevant sect, a dead end. This is certainly not Luke's view. Also using Mark as his base Luke sets out to give a fresh account which will help to set such things to right and demonstrate everything is in order.

Like Matthew, he, too, spends two chapters (much longer than Matthew's) telling of Jesus' birth. Both John and Jesus are heroes, with Jesus always the greater. Luke follows Mark's lead of using the language of political propaganda. It was not Augustus the emperor or his successors who brought peace on earth, but Jesus. He alone is the true Son of God. Luke's use of political allusions extends to the songs which come from the lips of faithful Jews who surround Jesus and John. Mary, Zechariah, Simeon, Anna, espouse the hopes of liberation. Luke dares to claim that Jesus is the fulfillment of these hopes. He shares the view that ultimately all nations will join Israel and Christ will come again to rule from Jerusalem in a kingdom of peace.

So, far from abandoning Jewish heritage, Luke and his largely Gentile churches are in the mainstream. It is the synagogue which has lost its way. Luke focuses on continuity, both by citing scripture and imitating its style, and by emphasising that the key people around Jesus and Jesus himself were devout Jews, fully observant of the Law. He shares this approach to the Law with Matthew and both draw their inspiration from the sayings in Q.

Luke's way of dealing with Mark's more radical approach to the Law is to leave out such passages. He drops a great slab of Mark's text, reaching from Mark 6:45 to 8:26. For Luke Christian Jews are fully observant and so are Gentiles. They do what the Law requires of Gentiles. Luke makes that clear in his second volume where he sees it as a resolution of the council of the church meeting in Jerusalem. There is, however, an exception: circumcision is no longer required and Jews may eat together with Gentiles. Apart from that the Law remains intact. Luke even pictures Paul as fully Torah-observant, an image which stands in tension with Paul's own views expressed in his writings.

It is not clear to what degree Jews of Luke's time would have found his argument convincing. They would probably have scoffed at Luke's claim to be Torah-observant. But Luke is not trying to dialogue with them. He is trying to emphasise continuity between Israel and Jesus and between Jesus and his church. That is why he writes a second volume setting out how the continuity was sustained since Jesus. He pictures the first Christians as meeting in the temple. They are the true Jews. He plays with numbers to make the same point. Not only are there twelve apostles (Judas is replaced to make up the numbers), but there are 120 as the core in the upper room at Pentecost. Pentecost is the festival of harvest and also the celebration of the giving of the Law, God's Word, at Sinai. It was accompanied, as legend of the time had it, by tongues of fire, with only Israel hearing God's Word and resolving to do it. Such allusions and symbols underline Luke's view that here is true Israel, not some sect setting off on a tangent.

Luke also took great care about how he commenced his account of Jesus' ministry. Where you saw Matthew produce the block of material from 4:23–9:35 to depict Jesus' teaching and deeds, Luke has opted for an alternative strategy. He picks up the account which he found in Mark 6 where Jesus fronts up to his home synagogue and makes that his opening scene. In it he shows Jesus identifying his Spirit-given task in the scripture itself. He then depicts a positive response followed by a wrangle over miracles, where the locals felt they had missed out. The scene develops into a confrontation with Jesus defending his actions by citing Elijah and Elisha and their outreach to Gentiles. The locals then explode in fury and Jesus barely escapes. The story functions as a model for what will come in both the gospel and in Acts. Initial positive response in both gives way to hate. Jesus is crucified. Unbelieving Jews hound Christians.

Luke's method of using his sources differs from Matthew. For long periods you would see Luke with only Mark in his hands. Then for long periods you would see only Q in his hands. In fact from 9:52 to 18:14 he does not use Mark at all. If you could spend time with Luke, you would also detect the methods he uses and the emphases he seeks to bring. In some ways we can find his own summaries of what he has done in speeches in Acts. This is especially so when Peter addresses the Gentiles. There he states simply that God anointed Jesus with the Spirit and that he went about doing good and healing all who were oppressed by the devil because God was with him, but they put him to death.

Given the conflicts which Luke and his community faced, we can also understand why he also gives much emphasis to the role of the Jewish leaders in having Jesus killed. Unlike Matthew, however, Luke frequently depicts Jesus as more sad than angry about Jerusalem and holding out to her people the hope that one day the trampling by the Gentiles would come to an end. Luke does not indicate a timeline for this. The disciples ask Jesus about it and he refuses to answer, telling them instead to go out and witness by the power of the Spirit to what has happened — just as Luke himself was doing by writing his two volumes.

Luke's sense of continuity not only counters the fears that his communities may have lost the true path. It also gives major emphasis to the church and its continuity with the earliest days and with Jesus, himself. Continuity through leadership was important. Peter was a key figure. Paul, whose life is made to match Peter's at many points, is a hero. Faith for Luke has a strong element of belonging to a community with roots deep in the past. The marks of the life of faith are the kind of compassion shown by the Good Samaritan and denied by the rich man to Lazarus. Salvation, a favourite word in Luke, like peace, means healing and wholeness as well as forgiveness. Hope includes individual hope beyond death, but also includes a universal dimension with strongly Jewish elements and centred on Jerusalem. The focus is not on Jesus' death as a means of atonement for sins, but on the bravery of Jesus and inevitability that faithfulness will face danger and death.

Luke's version of Q contains a version of the promises of Jesus which appears to be much earlier than Matthew's which reflect considerable expansion and elaboration for new settings. In Luke's we are probably still able to detect what must have been Jesus' own emphasis, which promised good news to the poor and the hungry. In Luke we hear Jesus' emphasis on the hope of the kingdom as an agenda for change and renewal in the present from the opening scene of his ministry. The stories become models to challenge Luke's hearers to see social justice and appropriate use of wealth as integral to being a follower of Jesus. You would find Luke's ways of writing very different, but the underlying message far from strange.

A selection of passages to which this section alludes: scribes in Matthew's community: 13:52; Mark on "blindness": 8:14-21 with 8:22-26; 10:35-45 with 10:46-52; Mark on the feasts for Jews and Gentiles: 6:33-44; 8:1-11; 8:14-21; the centurion: Mark 15:39; Mark on food laws: 7:1-23; Peter and Paul in conflict: Galatians 2:11-14; anti-Christian stories: Matthew 28:11-15; split families: Matthew 10:34-39; destruction of the temple as judgement: Matthew 22:1-14; 23–24; Balaam and Balak: Numbers 22–24; upholding the Law: Matthew 5:17-20; expounding the Law: Matthew 5:21-48; alms, prayer, and fasting: Matthew 6:1-18; not as *their* scribes: Matthew 7:28; the centurion's servant: 8:5-13; Luke 7:1-10; additions about Peter: Matthew 14:22-33 compared with Mark 6:46-52; Matthew 16:16-23 compared with Mark 8:27-31; Peter's authority and the congregation's authority, Matthew 16:18 and 18:18; hypocrisy and judgement: Matthew 23–25; Matthew adds to the passion story: visions, 27:19; the people's self-curse, 27:25; earthquakes, 27:51-52; 28:2; Luke and the Law: 16:16-18; Acts 10–11; 15; Luke on Paul and the Law: Acts 21:17-26; Luke on Christian beginnings and Pentecost: Acts 1–2; Luke's opening scene of Jesus' ministry: 4:16-30; Luke on Jerusalem's destruction: 19:41-44; 21:20-24; 23:29-30; Parables of the Good Samaritan and the Rich Man: 10:25-37; 16:19-31.

4A. Mark 6:30–8:26

When Matthew or Luke rewrites parts of Mark, we have the advantage of comparing the result with what we find in Mark and noticing the similarities and differences. Often it gives us clues about Matthew's or Luke's emphases and even their context. This is not the case with Mark, where all we have is Mark. We do not have Mark's sources. We just know he had them. All the same when we look carefully at Mark we discover that this is much more than stringing together remembered stories and much more than an historical report of what went on in the life of Jesus some 3 or 4 decades back. The passage we consider in this section makes this very clear.

Overview of the Passage

The passage contains a number of episodes. 6:30-44 is the feeding of the 5000; 6:45-52 is the walking on the water. 6:53-56 reports Jesus' healings in Gennesaret. Then 7:1-23 is a story based in controversy about washing hands before eating. 7:24-30 moves to Gentile territory and reports Jesus' encounter with a Syrophoenician woman, whose daughter Jesus heals. 7:31-37 reports Jesus' healing of a deaf and mute man. 8:1-9 brings us the feeding of the 4000, sounding very similar to the feeding of the 5000, but this time in Gentile territory. 8:10-13 tells us of Jesus' return to Jewish territory and dispute with Pharisees wanting a sign of authentication from Jesus. 8:14 reports a conversation between Jesus and the disciples which begins by noting that they had forgotten to bring bread with them and ends with Jesus asking them whether they understood the two feeding miracles, focussing on the number of baskets left over after feeding the 5000 and the 4000. Finally 8:22-26 reports the healing of a blind man in Bethsaida.

Special Features

Though the passage reads like a sequence of events which unfold one after another and there is nothing more to it, on closer inspection we see some more interesting features. Food or bread keeps being the focus of attention. Already just before our passage there is the disastrous feast of Herod Antipas which leads to John the Baptist's death. Then food is clearly the focus in the feeding of the 5000. Even in the walking on the water Jesus refers back to the bread. The controversy in 7:1-23 is initially about the disciples eating leaves without first washing their hands and the response of Jesus broadens the issue to all food. Bread features again in the following episode where Jesus provocatively declares that it is wrong to take the children's bread and give it to dogs and the woman replies that dogs can at least eat the crumbs under the table. Bread is again the centre of attention in the feeding of the 4000 and features in Jesus' discussion with his disciples after they discover they have forgotten the bread. Jesus then develops the theme of bread further, warning against the leaven (bread) of the Pharisees and asking whether the disciples noted how many baskets of bread were left over after feeding the 5000 and the 4000.

Another feature of the passage is that Jesus keeps moving around, in particular from Jewish territory to Gentile territory and back, with the result that there is a major feeding miracle in each area. People steeped in scriptural knowledge would also hear echoes of biblical stories: the manna in the wilderness and the crossing of the sea. What are we to make of these features?

Clues from a Conversation

It is useful to begin near the end of our passage where Jesus talks with the disciples because here he refers back to what has gone before and expects the disciples to understand a deeper meaning. 8:14 tells us that the disciples had forgotten to bring bread, except for one loaf (which would have been too small to be enough for them). What are they to do? Mark is almost leaving it over to our imagination. Assuming we are hearing the story read as a whole, just a minute or so earlier we heard that a similar situation confronted the disciples when they found themselves with Jesus in a hungry crowd of 4000 people. They had no idea what to do, even though a short time ago back in Jewish territory they had seen Jesus miraculously multiply the loaves and fish and feed everyone with 12 baskets of left-overs. Given all that experience Mark is showing that the disciples are particularly dull and slow to catch on. Mark leaves us to imagine that it would not have occurred to them that Jesus might do something with the one loaf.

Instead of following that theme further Mark tells us that Jesus warned the disciples against the leaven of the Pharisees and Herod. Leaven was how you made bread, so the reference is to the bread of the Pharisees and Herod. If you had been listening to Mark being read, about three minutes ago you heard about Herod's food, his birthday party. As a result of it John the Baptist met his death. The story is like a dark cloud on the horizon. Jesus, too, would meet his death at the hand of ruling authorities. People of Mark's day and those before them faced similar dangers. The warning made a lot of sense.

What about the leaven of the Pharisees? Food was a common image for teaching. The invitation to learn God's Law was like an invitation to a feast. God's word is food and drink. But not all food is good for you. In Mark Jesus is warning against the teaching of the Pharisees. Again, if you have just been listening to Mark 7, you know exactly what is meant. It is the teaching being propagated by those who opposed Jesus, especially in that episode. It included teaching about purity which demanded that people perform ritual washings before eating. It also included laws about clean and unclean food and many other distinctions between clean and unclean, most of them rooted in biblical law. In the time of Paul there had been disputes about whether Christian Jews should eat at the same table as Gentiles. By Mark's time a decade or so later these problems had been resolved, at least in his community, but they were still important enough for Mark to celebrate the solution.

The solution was to set such rules aside, including the biblical ones, because they had created a barrier between Jews and Gentiles. Ephesians, written about this time, speaks of a dividing wall of hostility which consisted in part of the biblical commandments about such things. The barriers are to be broken down.

Breaking Down Barriers

This is the main theme of 7:1-23. It begins on a particular matter, ritual washing of hands before eating, but ends with the blanket assertion that Jesus declared all foods clean and that distinctions between clean and unclean were invalid. We now recognise that there was an increasing concern with ritual washing at the time of Jesus' ministry. It is reflected in the large numbers of stone jars in use in Jewish areas (stone jars were not susceptible to impurity) and the number of immersion pools. It is very likely that Jesus' initial response to such concerns is reflected in Mark 7:15. The point is made with a subtle sense of humour, typical of Jesus. Probably it was not a frontal attack on purity but meant something like: it is not so much what enters a person that makes them unclean but what comes out of them. In a similar way the prophets had declared that God desired mercy not sacrifice (e.g., Hos 6:6), but meaning God preferred mercy to sacrifice.

Once Christianity spread into the Gentile world, the issues of separation and impurity became more acute. Most agreed that the biblical requirement of Genesis 17 that all Gentiles joining the people of God be circumcised should be waived. Paul and others went a good deal further and argued that a relationship with God depended on responding in faith to God's generous goodness and that this was something open to everyone. It did not require particular rites either before or afterwards. The requirements of the Law, beyond those ethical ones with which everyone agreed, had no place. They should be set aside, especially the ones which caused separateness and, as some saw it, discrimination. So people like Mark took up Jesus' saying in Mark 7:15 and interpreted it much more radically, because they believed that this was required in the new situation. Had it all been clear from the start and had Jesus meant it this way, the major disputes over the Law in early Christianity would not have arisen in the way they did.

So Mark is passing on stories and sayings of Jesus in a particular way, as he and others were interpreting and re-interpreting them for their own day. This then makes sense of what Mark has been doing in our passage. He shows Jesus warning against the leaven of the Pharisees. That leaven is the teaching which creates barriers between Jew and Gentile. It is to be set aside. In Mark's view Jesus declared or showed all food to be clean.

Seeing More

Returning to 8:14-21 we find that Jesus confronts the disciples for lacking understanding. They have eyes, but do not see; they have ears, but do not hear. This is a quotation from Jeremiah 5:21 and a common image for people failing to understand. What are the disciples meant to understand? Part of the answer is: Jesus can do something with even a single loaf. But the main point is far beyond that: they fail to understand the symbolic meaning of what he has done. They should recognise the dangers of the Herods of this world. They should also recognise the dangers of the teaching represented by the Pharisees, for instance, in chapter 7, which creates barriers, including when it is biblical teaching.

Jesus then continues with questions designed to elicit true understanding, but with little prospect of success. How many baskets after the feeding of the 5000? 12. And after the 4000? 7. Now do they understand? According to 8:21, apparently not! What should they be understanding? The numbers have some meaning here. Most of Mark's listeners would have recognised the connection. Back in Mark 5 they heard the story of a 12 year old girl in Israel and a woman who suffered a haemorrhage for 12 years. Just before that Mark told the story of Jesus in Gentile territory healing a deranged man among the tombs. That panel of events celebrated the coming of the good news both to Gentiles and to Israel. Our passage reflects a similar twofold panel. Jesus feeds 5000 in Israel and he feeds 4000 in Gentile territory. What about the 12? It was a standard number associated with Israel who saw themselves as consisting of 12 tribes. What about the 7? This, the so-called perfect or universal number, doubtless reflects the wider world of the Gentiles. Now do the disciples understand? Do we?

Mark celebrates the inclusion of both Israel and the Gentiles in God's offer of the good news in Jesus. What about the leaven of the Pharisees? It symbolises the barriers that would prevent the good news being as freely accessible to Gentiles as to Jews. We can now see that Mark has put these stories together not only for their own sake and because they reflect early tradition but also because together they celebrate a major theme about the food of the gospel which is freely available to all.

Looking more closely at the feeding of the 5000 we see that it also has echoes of Israel. Some have suggested even the figure 5000 may be symbolic, recalling the 5 books of the Law (the first 5 books of the Old Testament). The 5 loaves may do the same. Certainly the description of the people as sheep without a shepherd (6:34) echoes a common Old Testament description of Israel. Setting the people down in groups of 50s and 100s would recall Israel's army formation in the wilderness. However, none of these elements feature in the feeding of the 4000, which otherwise follows the pattern of the first story very closely.

Crossing Boundaries

Other features of the passage confirm this design. Immediately after the controversy in 7:1-23 when Jesus declares the barriers invalid, we find the story of Jesus' meeting with a Gentile woman (7:24-30). That story is rather daring. It celebrates the crossing of a boundary. It probably functioned like that well before it came to be written up in Mark's gospel. It is somewhat daring because it pictures Jesus changing his own stance. He begins negatively, reflecting the prejudice which many of his contemporaries probably would have shared. Gentiles are dogs. Israel are God's children. No food for Gentiles! But then the woman challenges this stance and Jesus changes his stance, responding to the challenge. Jesus crosses the boundary.

Did Jesus really start with a prejudiced stance like that or was this a fiction of a storyteller wanting to highlight the contrast? Does it reflect Jesus' conservative background? In any case the most notable thing about Jesus was that he kept crossing boundaries and people who had suffered discrimination kept retelling these good news stories. It suits Mark's purpose well to tell the story directly after the episode in which he shows Jesus declaring the old barriers invalid.

Seeing and Not Seeing

Mark's listeners keep hearing that the disciples miss the point. It is unlikely that Mark has something against them or their successors, although some have suggested this. It is more likely that Mark is showing up the disciples as a way of challenging his own listeners not to miss the point. Mark sometimes makes this emphasis dramatically. Just after 8:14-21, where Jesus suggests the disciples have eyes but do not see, Mark tells the story of the healing of the blind man at Bethsaida. The contrast is powerful. Mark does something similar in the way he uses the healing of the blind man, Bartimaeus in 10:46-52. The disciples have just been embroiled in a number of episodes in which they worry about power and status whereas Jesus has been trying to get through to them that the real greatness lies in service and compassion, finally ending on the note of declaring that as Son of Man he did not come to be served but to serve. The disciples fail to understand and will go on to see the cross not as a sign of greatness and compassion but of failure and defeat. In stark contrast Mark immediately goes on to tell of Bartimaeus' healing. The disciples are blind. Bartimaeus sees! What did Mark's listeners do? What do we do?

Signs and Symbols

On the other side of the conversation of Jesus with his disciples we find the Pharisees asking for a sign. This seems slightly mad. Jesus has just produced two very clear signs through the miraculous feedings. Anyone of the time with a basic knowledge of the scriptures would have recognised these signs as demonstrations that Jesus is repeating the signs of the great story of Israel. The Pharisees fail to see this. Mark is almost making a joke of their closedness. This will have reflected his experience and the experience of his community in dispute with some of the Pharisees of their time. We should not assume that all Pharisees were like this. But for Mark, these ones were, and his storytelling puts these episodes side by side to make a powerful impact.

Mark does more than tell stories. He shapes them, puts them in order, and links them in ways that point to deep meaning. Our passage celebrates that the good news is for all. It also warns against using the Bible in ways that discriminate or that undermine the good news, even to the extent of requiring that some parts be set aside. Mark invites his listeners (and us) to become involved, especially by the way he portrays the disciples. They began as the first heroes of faith in the early chapters. They end by running away, first the men — in contrast to the women — then even the women fall silent through fear. Mark is interested in much more than telling stories about the past. He wants to re-present Jesus in ways that people will grasp the good news for themselves. That is why he called his account a "gospel" (the word means literally: "good news").

4B. Matthew 15:1-20

In 15:1-20 Matthew rewrites Mark 7:1-23. In fact most of the surrounding chapters in Matthew are a rewriting of Mark. In Mark we looked in particular at Mark 6:30–8:26. Matthew takes over nearly all of this material. It is easiest to see this if we look at the table below:

Matthew	Mark
14:1-2 Herod wonders about Jesus	6:14-16 Herod wonders about Jesus
14:3-12 Death of John the Baptist	6:17-29 Death of John the Baptist
	6:30-31 Disciples return from mission
14:13-21 Feeding of the 5000	6:32-44 Feeding of the 5000
14:22-33 Jesus and Peter walk on water	6:45-52 Jesus walks on water
14:34-36 Healings at Gennesaret	6:53-56 Healings at Gennesaret
15:1-20 Dispute over purification	7:1-23 Dispute over purification
15:21-28 The Canaanite woman	7:24-30 The Syrophoenician woman
	7:31-37 Healing of the deaf mute man
15:29-39 Healing and feeding of the 4000	8:1-10 Feeding of the 4000
16:1-4 Demand for a sign	8:11-13 Demand for a sign
16:5-12 Conversation with disciples	8:14-21 Conversation with disciples
	8:22-26 Healing of the blind man

The Beginning

Much is the same, but there are some variations. There are also variations within each story. One useful exercise is to examine each passage in full comparing similarities and differences and noticing any particular tendencies. The technical term for analysing such similarities and differences is "Redaction Criticism (or Analysis)." Matthew also stands on its own. People were not hearing both accounts one after another. They were just hearing Matthew. We have an advantage in having Mark as well, so that we can make such comparisons.

Matthew begins like Mark with an account of the execution of John the Baptist, although he has reduced the detail considerably, taking only 10 verses to tell what Mark had said in 13. Then we notice that Matthew leaves out Mark's story of the disciples returning from mission. In Mark Jesus sent them out in 6:7-13, just a few verses previously, just after he had reported how the local people of Nazareth rejected Jesus (6:1-6). Putting the sending of the disciples between Jesus' rejection in his hometown synagogue and the execution of John helps us sense that the disciples, too, might face danger. Matthew, however, has made some rearrangements. He reports the sending out of the disciples back in 10:1-16, where he combines it with Mark's earlier material about the naming of the disciples and with material he found in Q. That was all too far back to refer now to the return of the disciples from mission.

Instead Matthew makes his own transition to the story of the feeding of the 5000. He says that John's disciples came and told Jesus about John's death (14:12). This is slightly awkward because the execution took place some time back, even though the story is being recalled here. Nevertheless it has the effect in the story that we see Jesus taking the disciples aside not to rest from their mission, as in Mark but in response to John's death. So death hovers behind Matthew's story of the feeding of the 5000 and some who heard Matthew's gospel would probably have thought about Jesus' own death and the way he broke bread with his disciples on his last evening with them.

The Feedings

The feeding of the 5000 in Matthew is similar to what we find in Mark except that Matthew removes the reference to the people as like sheep without a shepherd, the Old Testament image of Israel. It may be simply that he chose to use the image earlier (9:36). He also lessens the emphasis we found in Mark on symbols of Israel. Slight changes put the focus not on symbolism but on the sheer magnitude of the event.

We find a similar emphasis in the account of the feeding of the 4000. In fact Matthew has made the two events match closely. As the feeding of the 5000 begins with Jesus healing people (something Matthew has added in), so the feeding of the 4000 begins with Jesus healing people. To make this possible Matthew has merged together Mark's two stories: the healing of the deaf, mute man and the feeding of the 4000. In doing so he has taken away the specific reference to the man and turned it into a story of Jesus healing people generally.

More significantly, Matthew has changed the locations. No longer is the feeding of the 4000 happening in Gentile territory. Both times Israel is being fed. The second time it is on a mountain. For people steeped in the Old Testament the connection of healings and feedings on a mountain would remind them of the prophetic hope that one day God would gather Israel to Mount Zion, where there would be healing and a great feast. Matthew is making a strong point about Jesus. He fulfills the promise of the prophets. The story now re-enacts that vision. As people heard the story they could make the connections and commit themselves to the great vision of justice and peace. Those who thought of the eucharist would know that this vision is at its heart.

If we skip over to the conversation which Jesus has with his disciples about the feedings, we find that the focus there, too, is on the magnitude of the miracles. It is not on the symbolism of the 12 and the 7, but just on the wonder of what Jesus had brought. And only at the end do we find the warning about the leaven, the false teaching. Gone is the reference to Herod. Only the Pharisees remain and to them Matthew adds, as he often does, the other leading group: the Sadducees. The disciples still struggle to understand, but finally they do understand, unlike in Mark.

The Disciples Lack Faith Not Understanding

It is a constant feature of Matthew's gospel that he modifies Mark's picture of the disciples. He may well have been aware that Mark was using them as a ploy to challenge his listeners. Matthew seems concerned to show them greater respect. Their problem is only rarely that they do not understand. Their problem, according to Matthew, is lack of faith, whereas in Mark they keep missing the point. The message in Matthew for the disciples is that they should really believe that Jesus is the one who brings the promise of new life.

It fits Matthew's view of the disciples that he leaves out the story which follows in Mark, the healing of the blind man at Bethsaida (Mark 8:22-26). Mark was using it cleverly to contrast with the disciples' blindness. But in Matthew they are not blind; they see very well; they need to act on that in trust. Matthew therefore leaves out the story.

Matthew is concerned with leadership and responsibility in the church. In the story of the walking on the water Matthew appears to be his creative best. He supplements the story he has from Mark with the detail that Jesus invited Peter to walk. He did and then failed. But he could. There is no suggestion that Matthew is using an independent story, although this is possible. It is more likely some poetic or creative licence on his part is being used to powerful effect. It points forward to 16:16-19, where Jesus will commit his cause to Peter, calling him the rock and declaring he will have powers over the deep forces of evil (symbolised earlier in the story by the sea). Later Jesus gives the same authority to the congregation at prayer (18:18-20), especially in tackling difficult issues of discipline (18:15-17), but always in the context of love and compassion (18:12-14 and 21-35!).

Changing Focus from the Gentiles

So far we have said nothing of Mark's major theme: that Gentiles are now as welcome as Jews to receive the bread. Mark has worked that in very skilfully with effective use of symbolism. Again, Matthew was probably aware that this was Mark's doing. He chooses to do things differently. He, too, will show that Jesus welcomes Gentiles. In his last action in the gospel the risen Jesus tells the disciples to go and teach all peoples. That is part of their authority to act of Jesus' behalf. But Matthew chooses not to use the two feedings to symbolise Israel and the Gentiles.

So he puts the emphasis elsewhere in the feeding of the 5000, not on the symbols of Israel. He no longer suggests the people at the feeding of the 4000 are Gentiles. He removes the focus on the numbers 12 and 7 in Jesus' conversation with the disciples. He still keeps the provocative story about the woman, now labelled a Canaanite — like Israel's enemies of old. He adds much more into that story, especially to show that Jesus' mission was only to the lost sheep of the house of Israel; a mission to Gentiles would come later. Israel should be ashamed that here a Canaanite (like the centurion earlier in 8:5-13) recognises who Jesus is, whereas Jews did not. He reinforces this by having her address Jesus as "Son of David."

Modifying Mark's Radical Approach to Scripture

By changing the focus of this section of his gospel Matthew can also avoid a problem. The problem is Mark 7:1-23, where Mark suggests that Jesus set aside purity laws as making no sense. How can external things make a person unclean! Mark saw this as the implication of Jesus' teaching and so gave it as Jesus' teaching. It justified abandoning what he and others saw as barriers between Jews and Gentiles. Such teachings espoused by Pharisees and others (including Christians who took a more literal approach to scriptures) were the leaven to be avoided. The passage is central to Mark's theme of celebrating the inclusion of Gentiles without discrimination.

Matthew belonged to those circles of early Christianity who were not willing to go that far. Earlier Matthew had reported that Jesus refused to let any part of the scriptures be set aside: not a single stroke (5:17-19)! Matthew could not possibly take over Mark 7:1-23 without some modification. By comparing the two stories we can see his main changes.

Matthew 15:1-20	Mark 7:1-23
1Then Pharisees and scribes came to Jesus from Jerusalem and said, 2"Why do your disciples break the tradition of the elders? For they do not wash their hands before they eat." 3He answered them, "And why do you break the commandment of God for the sake of your tradition? 4For God said, 'Honor your father and your mother,' and, 'Whoever speaks evil of father or mother must surely die.' 5But you say that whoever tells father or mother, 'Whatever support you might have had from me is given to God,' then that person need not honor the father. 6So, for the sake of your tradition, you make void the word of God. 7You hypocrites! Isaiah prophesied rightly about you when he said: 8'This people honors me with their lips, but their hearts are far from me; 9in vain do they worship me, teaching human precepts as doctrines.'" 10Then he called the crowd to him and said to them, "Listen and understand: 11it is not what goes into the mouth that defiles a person, but it is what comes out of the mouth that defiles." 12Then the disciples approached and said to him, "Do you know that the Pharisees took	1Now when the Pharisees and some of the scribes who had come from Jerusalem gathered around him, 2they noticed that some of his disciples were eating with defiled hands, that is, without washing them. 3(For the Pharisees, and all the Jews, do not eat unless they thoroughly wash their hands, thus observing the tradition of the elders; 4and they do not eat anything from the market unless they wash it; and there are also many other traditions that they observe, the washing of cups, pots, and bronze kettles.) 5So the Pharisees and the scribes asked him, "Why do your disciples not live according to the tradition of the elders, but eat with defiled hands?" 6He said to them, "Isaiah prophesied rightly about you hypocrites, as it is written, 'This people honors me with their lips, but their hearts are far from me; 7in vain do they worship me, teaching human precepts as doctrines.' 8You abandon the commandment of God and hold to human tradition." 9Then he said to them, "You have a fine way of rejecting the commandment of God in order to keep your tradition! 10For Moses said, 'Honor your father and your mother'; and, 'Whoever speaks evil of father or mother must surely die.' 11But you say that if anyone tells father or mother, 'Whatever support you might have had from me is Corban' (that is, an offering to God) – 12then you no longer permit doing anything for a father or mother, 13thus making void the word of God through your tradition that you have handed on. And you do many things like this."

offense when they heard what you said?" 13He answered, "Every plant that my heavenly Father has not planted will be uprooted. 14Let them alone; they are blind guides of the blind. And if one blind person guides another, both will fall into a pit." 16Then he said, "Are you also still without understanding? 17Do you not see that whatever goes into the mouth enters the stomach, and goes out into the sewer? 18But what comes out of the mouth proceeds from the heart, and this is what defiles. 19For out of the heart come evil intentions, murder, adultery, fornication, theft, false witness, slander. 20These are what defile a person, but to eat with unwashed hands does not defile."	14Then he called the crowd again and said to them, "Listen to me, all of you, and understand: 15there is nothing outside a person that by going in can defile, but the things that come out are what defile." 16 17When he had left the crowd and entered the house, his disciples asked him about the parable. 18He said to them, "Then do you also fail to understand? Do you not see that whatever goes into a person from outside cannot defile, 19since it enters, not the heart but the stomach, and goes out into the sewer?" (Thus he declared all foods clean.) 20And he said, "It is what comes out of a person that defiles. 21For it is from within, from the human heart, that evil intentions come: fornication, theft, murder, 22adultery, avarice, wickedness, deceit, licentiousness, envy, slander, pride, folly. 23All these evil things come from within, and they defile a person."
	NRSV

Our focus is not every detail, but the main, important changes. The conclusion of the dispute in Matthew shows us where he saw it going. It was about washing hands as an act of purification. That is how the dispute arose and that is the point of the episode. It is not about setting parts of scripture aside. So Matthew cuts out Mark's important comment in 7:19. Matthew has no argument with the focus on internal rather than external, but rejects the idea that one has to choose between the two. In this sense Matthew reflects the view of the prophets and the psalmists who also emphasised that God wanted love and faithfulness more than sacrifices and rituals, but he wanted these as well.

With a few changes Matthew has brought the story into consistency with his own approach to scripture. He could not use this episode to justify breaking down barriers between Jews and Gentiles and so abandons that emphasis, rewriting this section of Mark to make a different, but also very challenging, point. Matthew obviously highly regards Mark's gospel, especially its emphasis on who Jesus was, but there was also room for disagreement and it shows. Even so, the heart of the gospel remains firmly fixed on compassion and inclusion, and Matthew has given us a reworking of Mark's stories which highlights the great vision of the prophets which underlies our celebration of the eucharist and in which, as 15:21-18 and 28:16-

20 show, all people have a place. That vision symbolises the goal of God's goodness and sets the agenda for our lives now and the future.

4C. Matthew 18–19

In these chapters we have another opportunity to see the way Matthew has put together his gospel. The table below sets out its main sections on the left side and the right side where there is parallel material. Material from Mark which Matthew is rewriting is in ordinary font. Other material is in italic font.

Matthew	Mark and Q
18:1-5 Who is the greatest?	Mark 9:33-37 Who is the greatest
	Mark 9:38-41 The other exorcist
18:6-9 Warning against abuse	Mark 9:42-50 Warning against abuse
18:10 Angels and little ones	
18:11-14 One sheep strays	*Luke 15:3-7 One lost sheep*
18:15-20 Dealing with discipline	
18:21-22 Forgiving 77 times	*Luke 17:4 Forgiving 7 times*
18:23-35 Parable of unforgiving servant	
19:1-2 Journey to Jerusalem	Mark 10:1 Journey to Jerusalem
19:3-9 Marriage and divorce	Mark 10:2-12 Marriage and divorce
19:10-12 Celibacy	
19:13-15 Jesus and the children	Mark 10:13-16 Jesus and the children
19:16-22 The rich young man	Mark 10:17-22 The rich man
19:23-30 Dangers of wealth	Mark 10:23-31 Dangers of wealth

Before Matthew 18–19

Matthew follows Mark closely even before Matthew 18–19. We have seen how he does so in Matthew 14:1–16:12. The rest of chapter 16 also follows Mark, but with significant additions about Peter's special role. In Mark, Peter is the first to acknowledge Jesus as the Messiah. This happens at Caesarea Philippi (8:27-30). But in Matthew the disciples have already hailed Jesus as Son of God when he walked on water (14:33). So Matthew changes the focus in 16:13-20 from who Jesus is (as in Mark 8:27-30) to who Peter is and what he and the church must do.

The rest of chapter 16 follows Mark closely as does chapter 17, except that Matthew adds a short episode about the temple tax in 17:24-27. We have seen earlier how Mark puts a lot of emphasis on leadership and Christian community from chapter 8 onwards. On three occasions Jesus tells the disciples he is going to face suffering and death, and on each occasion they are preoccupied with their own models of greatness where success means escaping from suffering and having authority and status over others. We reach the second of these in Matthew 18:1-5. The third must wait until Matthew 20:20-28 because Matthew has so much more to add.

Matthew 18 and Abuse

The major addition which Matthew makes is in chapter 18. Leaving out Mark's short section about another exorcist — which Matthew probably saw as not having a lot to say to his situation — Matthew continues with Mark 9:42-50, the warnings against abuse. He had used the saying about plucking out eyes and cutting off hands already back in 5:29-30, when speaking of sexual abuse. That theme is still in the background here. Matthew also includes a similar warning he found in Q to strengthen the point (found also in Luke 17:1). It was necessary to make absolutely clear to people that any form of abuse or exploitation should have no place in the community. The focus is initially on children, but it applies equally to people of all ages. Some even think that Matthew's "little ones" refers to all believers and not just to children. Matthew also adds a saying which only he preserves, which speaks of angels of little ones in God's presence, a way of saying they are very special to God (18:10).

Matthew and People Who Go Astray

At this point the attention shifts to people who go astray and how to deal with them. Matthew draws on the parable of the ninety-nine sheep which he and Luke know from the sayings source we call "Q." Luke keeps it in what was probably its original setting: conflicts over Jesus reaching out to the lost. There Jesus uses the parable to argue: surely a shepherd would go out to find a missing sheep. Why can't you think of God like that? That is what I am doing — we can hear Jesus saying.

Matthew is using the parable in a new way. He has slightly rewritten it so that it speaks not about a sheep being lost, but about a sheep going astray. In his church context it is referring especially to members of the church who go astray, either because they have been led astray by abuse or because they themselves have been the abusers.

He then moves straight on to the situation where it is necessary to confront someone about wrongdoing. The teaching in 18:15-20 is found only in Matthew. It is similar to advice we find in some Jewish groups of the time. It is also a striking 1st-century example of handling conflict which still speaks its wisdom today. You go directly to the person and talk about it. You don't shame people in front of others. This also means you don't gossip about the person to others. If speaking one-to-one does not work, take some others with you. In the last resort it may be necessary to deal with the matter in the congregation as a whole.

These are basic guidelines which have formed the backbone of more developed systems which now exist in the church for dealing with wrongdoing and which are necessarily more complex and refined. It is important to note that Matthew pictures the congregation needing to do such things and says it does so with the support of Jesus. In fact the words about discipline and defining what is right and wrong (18:18) are the same as those spoken to Peter in 16:19. The promise of support is enhanced in 18:19-20. Jesus is right there with the congregation when it deals with such matters in the spirit of prayer. Jews made a similar claim about God's special presence (the *shekinah*) being present wherever two or three gathered to interpret God's Law. Here we have a Christian version of that faith.

Taken on their own, the instructions in 18:15-20 can lead to abuse of power and to claims of infallibility. History teaches us to be wary of such claims. Matthew also makes sure we do not hear these words on their own. We recall that immediately before them he tells the parable about caring for the straying sheep. That same caring comes through strongly in the words that follow the section on discipline. Immediately Matthew brings in the saying about forgiveness which he and Luke knew from Q. Not just 7 times, but 77 times people are to be forgiven!

Matthew then reinforces this emphasis by adding a parable, which he alone knew: the Parable of the Unforgiving Servant (18:23-35). There is no room then for an unforgiving congregation or church. Compassion and forgiveness are the context in which we deal with matters of discipline. This does not mean that we sweep wrongdoing under the carpet. Matthew is certainly not suggesting that. It must be faced. It is only when we face up to what we know needs forgiveness that we can know what forgiveness is about and benefit from it.

It must always be our aim both to help people face up to their truth and to help them find their feet again. Facing up to their truth has to be a change in attitude and has to include a response which will right any wrongs committed where that is possible. Often it is not possible and it is dangerous to see this as paying off a debt in a sense that earns our forgiveness. Forgiveness is a gift of grace and requires courage to give and to receive. Response to facing up to ourselves will see us wanting to do what we can to restore what we have damaged and do even more, but this is to be seen as an expression of restored respect and regard for the other or others, not a mechanism to rid ourselves of responsibility.

Matthew 19: Marriage, Divorce, Celibacy, and Children

In Matthew 19, Matthew brings us back to Mark 10 and three familiar episodes follow. The first is about marriage and divorce, which we have touched on elsewhere. Matthew makes some modifications. As in 5:32 he allows for the requirement that divorce must follow where adultery has taken place — a widespread view at the time, which most would no longer share. But Matthew puts this saying which he has trimmed and revised from Mark 10:11-12 (omitting 12 altogether) into the conversation with the Pharisees (19:9).

He keeps the private conversation which Jesus has with his disciples after the controversy which originally included the sayings in Mark 10:11-12 and instead gives it new content. It is now about being a eunuch for the kingdom of God (Matt 19:10-12). This is a very dramatic way of asserting that some people will see it as their gift to remain unmarried. Matthew may well be preserving Jesus' personal response to those who claimed he should have been married like most other men of his time. In the conversation Jesus is especially careful not to insinuate that everyone else should do the same. Paul finds he must be equally careful when he reports this as his stance in 1 Corinthians 7:1-7.

As in Mark 10:13-16 Matthew follows the marriage theme with a section about children. Both gospel writers would have been aware of the need to give instructions to congregations about matters of marriage and family, and these anecdotes served the purpose well. Matthew's main change is to take out Mark 10:15 and use it earlier in 18:3 where he speaks of becoming like children.

Matthew's Rich Young Man

19:16-22 is famous as the story of "The Rich Young Ruler." This title is a mixture of the three different versions of the story. Only in Matthew is he young. Only in Luke is he a ruler. In Mark he is a rich man looking back on his youth. We looked at Mark's story in the first chapter. It is very interesting to see how Matthew retells the story. Luke leaves it much as it is, apart from adding that he was a ruler (most of the rich belonged to the ruling class). Matthew's changes are much more interesting, and show us more of Matthew's pastoral concern, not just to retell stories of Jesus, but to do so in a way that made an impact and spoke to the people who would be listening to his gospel.

The versions of Matthew and Mark are set out in the table below.

Matthew 19:16-22	Mark 10:17-22
16Then someone came to him and said,	17As he was setting out on a journey, a man ran up and knelt before him, and asked him,
"Teacher, what good deed must I do to have eternal life?"	"Good Teacher, what must I do to inherit eternal life?"
17And he said to him, "Why do you ask me about what is good? There is only one who is good. If you wish to enter into life, keep the commandments."	18Jesus said to him, "Why do you call me good? No one is good but God alone.
18He said to him, "Which ones?" And Jesus said,	19You know the commandments:
"You shall not murder;	
You shall not commit adultery;	'Do not murder;
You shall not steal;	Do not commit adultery;
You shall not bear false witness;	Do not steal;
	Do not bear false witness;
	Do not defraud;
19Honor your father and mother;	Honor your father and mother.'"
also, You shall love your neighbor as yourself."	

20The young man said to him, "I have kept all these; what do I still lack?" 21Jesus said to him, "If you wish to be perfect, go, sell your possessions, and give the money to the poor, and you will have treasure in heaven; then come, follow me." 22When the young man heard this word, he went away grieving, for he had many possessions.	20He said to him, "Teacher, I have kept all these since my youth." 21Jesus, looking at him, loved him and said, "You lack one thing; go, sell what you own, and give the money to the poor, and you will have treasure in heaven; then come, follow me." 22When he heard this, he was shocked and went away grieving, for he had many possessions.
	NRSV *modified by W. Loader to make it more literal*

Reworking the Initial Exchange

Matthew trims the beginning of unnecessary detail, as he usually does, and brings us straight to the question, but notice he has modified the question. In Mark the man says, "Good Teacher," to which Jesus responds by asking him why he calls him "Good." Matthew drops "Good" and that means he must change Jesus' reply. Probably he sensed that some might hear Jesus' reply as inferring that Jesus was not good. To avoid this he re-jigs the conversation. He changes the man's original statement, so that he asks what good deed he must do. That sets up Jesus' reply. Jesus questions why he asks about what is good.

In making such modifications Matthew would not have considered he was falsifying history because he knew like everyone else that stories were passed on orally and in approximate fashion. Without perfect recall and written records people telling stories necessarily had to improvise the likely conversations around a special saying or the point that that was being made. As long as the point was being made clear there was little concern about variations in the surrounding conversations. We see this time and again. Mark will have done the same as the stories came to him and people before him did this, too, especially when the stories were not written down. Then once they had been written down people like Matthew could check the original, but even then there is considerable freedom in rewriting the material. Most of the changes from then on are about improving style, removing misunderstandings, or enhancing the main point. We see how Matthew has been at work in this way in this passage.

Matthew still keeps the focus on God. There is only one God. In both versions the man asks about eternal life. Matthew reinforces this by adding it again to the conversation. Jesus says: "If you wish to enter into life, keep the commandments." There is another short interchange added by Matthew, but then the answer comes as in Mark: the commandments. As in Mark we should note that part of the answer has already been given when Jesus points to God. Jews recited daily the acclamation that there is one God, as do followers of Islam. It puts God in first place. Then the commandments follow on this basis. It is almost like this covers the first half of the ten commandments, at least those directly related to God.

The Commandments

As in Mark, so in Matthew, Jesus cites some of the ten commandments. Matthew has revised Mark slightly. Instead of the form "Do not kill" etc., he brings the commandments as they appear in the scripture: "you shall not kill" etc. He also drops, "Do not defraud" from Mark's version, because it is not one of the commandments. But then he adds a commandment which is not one of the ten, but which is an appropriate summary of all the commandments relating to people: "You shall love your neighbour as yourself." It would be silly to suggest that Matthew thought Jesus' answer in Mark was wrong or inadequate. Rather he wants to make the same point and simply shapes some of the minor details to improve the overall effect. The message is essentially the same, but Matthew's is an improved version.

Youth and Maturity in Faith

The next statements are interesting. Matthew leaves out of the man's answer the words, "from my youth," but he introduces into his story the idea that the man is a youth. It is like he has swapped the words around, but it changes the image of the man. In the next verse we see the probable reason. Matthew makes an addition. He tells the man what he must do, if he wants to be mature or grown up. Mostly our English translations use the word "perfect" for the Greek word *teleios,* here because that is one of its meanings. But it is also the common word for "mature" or "grown up." Matthew has playfully changed the conversation so that Jesus now tells the young man how to grow up in his faith. That is why he changed the previous verse around to make him young.

Matthew leaves out the note about Jesus' affection for the man, as he often does with such detail, but he keeps intact the main focus of the story. As in Mark Jesus challenges the (young) man about the poor. That exposed what was missing in his approach to the commandments. He could keep rules and tick boxes but when challenged about an aspect which underlies the commandments, he gives up. He hadn't done anything wrong, but he hadn't grasped what was right either. He could not contemplate the level of compassion for the poor which in his case would lead to selling all and giving his wealth away and following Jesus. Following Jesus meant following Jesus' way of understanding the commandments. They are not boxes to be ticked but guides to the compassionate life. The man missed that point. That was lacking.

Jesus did not go around asking everyone to sell their possessions and give them to the poor. He did so with some, but with others he asked that the commitment to the poor and to compassion be worked out in other ways. Matthew would have been aware of this. There are not two standards: for the perfect and for ordinary people. Matthew is speaking about faith maturity for all. Handling wealth is as challenging now as it was then, probably much more so. Matthew follows the rest of Mark's discussion of wealth closely, including the seemingly impossible situation people realise they are in when they look at themselves and that only by God's grace can they live with themselves.

Into the middle of this conversation Matthew slipped a saying which he and Luke knew from Q, in which Jesus promises the disciples that they will share with Jesus in future leadership (19:28). But Matthew goes on to deal with the problems which leadership pose. In 20:1-16 he tells a parable about labourers who all received the same wage, though some were hired very late in the day. In Matthew's gospel it now seems directed at people claiming they should be first. Matthew surrounds the parable on either side with the saying with which Mark ended his section: "many who are first will be last and last will be first" (19:30; 20:16; Mark 10:31), as we saw in chapter one. From there he returns, fittingly, to Mark's account of the ambition of James and John (20:20-28).

4D. Luke 10:25–42

This section of Luke contains two stories: Jesus' encounter with a scripture teacher specialising in the law (10:25-37) which includes the Parable of the Good Samaritan, and Jesus with Mary and Martha (10:38-42). The encounter with the scripture teacher is very similar to what we find in Mark 12:28-31 and Matthew 22:35-40, where both describe him as a scribe.

The Question

The encounter in Matthew and Mark takes place while Jesus is in Jerusalem. Matthew closely follows Mark at this point. So does Luke except that he leaves out the encounter. Almost certainly this is because he chose to use it earlier as an introduction to the Parable of the Good Samaritan. Alternatively he knew another version of the story and chose not to include it twice.

One of the small differences between Luke's story and that of Matthew and Mark is that the opening question is different. They have the man ask which is the greatest commandment. Instead, Luke's "scripture teacher" asks, "Teacher, what must I do to inherit eternal life?" (10:25). This is the same question which the rich ruler asks Jesus in Luke 18:18, based on the story in Mark 10:17-22. It looks very much like Luke made this change deliberately. It means that the focus on what follows falls less on what is greatest and more on what is necessary.

The Answer

Jesus' answer in 10:27 includes part of the daily affirmation of faith made by Jews, called the *shema*. The Hebrew word *shema* is its first word, and means "Hear!" It continues: "Hear, O Israel, the Lord your God is one." Loving God with all one's heart (means: mind) and soul and strength and understanding comes from Deuteronomy 6:4. Jesus' answer adds Leviticus 19:18, "You shall love your neighbour as yourself."

In the encounter with the rich man (ruler in Luke) Jesus quotes some of the ten commandments. He quotes a summary of the commandments, its two main principles. The orientation is the same. A living relationship

137

towards God and towards other human beings is the evidence that someone has eternal life or shares the life of God. It is also the way to that life,
when people turn away from other gods and goals (traditionally called re-
pentance and conversion) and turn to receive God's offer of a new life. Jesus makes this clear and embodies this in his own life. In this sense to respond to Jesus is also to respond to God. Luke is getting us to the heart of
Christian faith.

Luke then suggests the man wanted to justify himself, perhaps in the
sense that he wanted to feel good about himself as having already taken the
right path. So he checks with Jesus: "Who is my neighbour?" That sounds
like a straightforward question, but at another level it is a little strange. It
assumes some people do not qualify to be my neighbour. Jesus' answer also
turns out to be a little strange, although at first it looks very straightforward.

Good Samaritan?

The Parable of the Good Samaritan is perhaps the most famous of all Jesus' parables. It is a story which stands on its own and speaks to every generation. When we look at it closely both in the context of Jesus' world and
in the context of Luke's story, we find it has some very sharp edges.

Samaritans were Jews living mainly in the area of Samaria to the north
of Judea and were commonly believed to be descended from people of Israel who had lived there over the centuries. Many Judeans looked on them
as not true Israelites, accusing them of having married with local non-
Israelite peoples, especially after the Assyrians conquered their territory in
the early 8th century BCE.

The Samaritans lived in tension with their southern neighbours. This
tension was so great that they set up a temple of their own in which to worship God on Mount Nablus. There are still Samaritans living in Nablus today. They have their own ancient version of the Pentateuch (the first five
books of the Old Testament) which has only a few minor differences in it,
mainly about the location of the temple.

We see some of this reflected in Jesus' encounter with the Samaritan
woman in John 4. There we read about the rival temples (4:19-21) but also
that Jews and Samaritans did not get on (4:9). 4:9 may mean: they did not
mix at all or it may mean they never used the same instruments and con-

tainers. Certainly for many Jews the Samaritans were an inferior race with an inferior religious culture.

The Priest and Levite

So Jesus is being very provocative when he makes a Samaritan the hero of his story, the one who really shows what it means to share God's life. Jesus is also being provocative when he pictures personnel from the Jerusalem temple acting in ways that were uncaring. The story assumes that they were worried about keeping the biblical commandments about purity, especially in avoiding touching corpses, which made a person ritually unclean. It was not a sin to do so, but it should be avoided as much as possible. When someone dies in your own household then you have no choice. Family obligations, also enshrined in scripture, overrule the purity rules.

Both the priest and the Levite (also from a priestly group but with more mundane temple duties) put their purity concerns first. Jesus' story, which appeals to common human concern for others, challenges their priorities and in doing so challenges the priorities being set by many in his day, including those who thought he should keep away from disreputable people because they could render him unclean.

The Perspective of Jesus

Jesus rejects giving so much attention to such matters. He did not support the growing tendency to bring such purity concerns into everyday life in a way that disrupted human caring and created barriers between people. To God people mattered most, not meticulous observances designed to protect the holy from the unholy. On another occasion Jesus said: "The sabbath was made for people, not people for the sabbath" (Mark 2:27). Jesus was not rejecting the sabbath, but putting it in perspective. It is also unlikely that Jesus was rejecting the purity laws of his day, but setting them in perspective. In Jesus' hands concern for human need overrode such provisions, not just in the immediate family, but with everyone. Everyone was a neighbour. Love should show no limits.

The Samaritan responded to the desperate man with practical love that went as far as not only rescuing him but helping him recover. The "outsider" got it right. The "insiders," as they saw themselves, were so pre-occupied with their religion and with what they thought worried God that they failed to follow the direction of God's compassion. They become a symbol of people in every generation who are obsessed with not doing wrong and who rarely do any good and who think this is pleasing to God.

Subverting the Question

The story is powerful and speaks for itself. But then there is something strange. The teacher of scripture had asked, "Who is my neighbour?" (10:29). According to Luke Jesus turns to him now with the question: "Which of these three showed himself a neighbour to the man who fell victim to the brigands?" (10:36). Jesus changes the question around. The man's question assumes some people are not our neighbours (such as Samaritans!). Jesus rejects such discrimination. So he turns the question on its head. The very man whom the teacher would disqualify as neighbour was the hero of the story. Everyone is a neighbour and everyone is called to care. Failure to be neighbour is not about who is worthy but about who is loving and who is not. We are all called to be neighbours, to be loving people.

Mary and Martha

Luke ends with a short, but also famous episode, in which Jesus spends time with Mary and Martha (10:38-42). There is more than one way to understand this story. Many find it hard to understand. Martha is the practical one doing all the work and then Jesus tells her off. Is that fair? Isn't Martha more like the Samaritan in the previous story and Mary more like the priest and Levite? What is going on?

One interpretation argues that we should not see Jesus' words to Martha as an attack on practical work. The words are more focussed than that. They address her busy-ness and her worrying. They suggest that Martha is preoccupied and captive to these concerns and therefore missing out on something. Many see this as addressing the unjust structures which define the role of women as staying with housework and not straying into what they see as the realm of men, which include the more valuable things such as learning and teaching.

Seen in this light Jesus is subverting a standard prejudice about women and women's position. They should not be left to the chores. They have as much right as men to engage in reflection and study. Mary models this stance, by behaving in a way normally assigned to men. Mary stands for the woman who is free and that freedom, Jesus declares, must not be taken away from her (10:42).

Short anecdotes like this make their point and then leave us to go on our way. They hardly answer all the questions. They provoke us. That is how they work. We then have to work out the implications. The anecdote is not saying household work is not important. It is challenging preoccupation with it. And in the light of what we learn from the heart of the gospel we also affirm: women are not to be discriminated against. They are not to be excluded.

For men, too, there are important insights: they have as much a role in doing behind the scenes work as women. In the Christian community men and women are to be affirmed in their distinctiveness and in their common humanity. All receive God's gifts to share. All must be free to do so. There is no room for prejudice and discrimination. Such values are now being affirmed more often in society than ever before but we are still a long way from removing prejudice and abuse against women. There are still tendencies in some circles to question women's obvious leadership strengths and to carry on as though the only worthy images of God are all male and reflect what have been male preoccupations: might and power.

Another interpretation looks far less sympathetically at Luke's story and sees Mary at the feet of Jesus as a symbol promoting women's subordination to men and to the church. That would then be in stark contrast to other emphases which flow from the heart of the gospel. There is no doubt that the story has been made to bear both good news and bad news for women.

Love is a key theme in Luke. Loving is the sign of eternal life, God's life. This is a common theme among all the writers of the New Testament. For Mark it was what was missing with the rich man who kept the commandments. For Matthew it will be what matters most on the day of judgement. Not those who say, "Lord, Lord," but those who love will be the true sheep. They will be people who loved because there was need, not because they saw Jesus or God in others. They are then surprised to hear: when you did it to them, it was like you did it to me (Matt 25:31-46). Paul has to make a similar point when writing to the Corinthians who seem to be carried away with their own religious experiences. The result is his famous love chapter in 1 Corinthians 13.

From these sample passages illustrating key themes in Mark, Matthew, and Luke, we move to the gospel of John and the remaining writings of the New Testament. There, too, we will encounter similar themes, but also some special emphases.

CHAPTER FIVE

John and Beyond: Faith and the Future

"God Is Love"

Imagining oneself with the mind and experience of someone of great age living in the late 1st century is a challenge. You could find yourself ignored, pushed to the side, spoken to as if you were a child, or, perhaps, loved and respected for your wisdom and experience. You actually find yourself in a very caring community. When people around you say, "God is love," they mean it. There are a number of you who have been part of this community for years. Your memories reach right back to the fledgling communities which first formed in your region when the disciples came.

Those memories have become more and more important to you as the years have passed, though not everyone sees it that way. One of your colleagues has just written about those connections. When it was read in your house church your heart warmed. We know it as 1 John. Yes, he was one of those like yourself who remember the coming of the word of life. It was music to your ears. The melody of love comes over and over again, including those wonderful words, "God is love." These are the values you have stood for. The younger people need to hear this. How sad when this is missing.

Your joy is tinged with such sadness, because recently a large number have left your house churches and gone off to set up their own. They don't think you are spiritual enough. They claim the Spirit is on their side. They make claims about Jesus which seem out of touch with what you remem-

143

ber. You remember Jesus as a really human person in whom you met God, not as a kind of heavenly being without real flesh and blood. He was baptised just as you were. He died just as you will one day — perhaps not so very far away. They think we dishonour him by remembering he was human just like us, but we think they have misunderstood. Why couldn't he have been really human as well as really being God for us? The ideas seem wrong and the breaking up of the community hurts. They have taken copies of the gospel which they say justifies their claims, but you still have copies and treasure them because it remains the basis for your faith and the inspiration of your community.

In your old age you can see the important things. Details don't matter much and you are finding it increasingly hard to remember them, especially recent events. Increasingly you hold onto those wonderful acclamations of faith which have become favourites in your faith communities: "God is love"; "God is light"; Jesus is the light of the world. He is the bread of life. He is the resurrection and the life. He gives the water of life. He is the true bread, the true vine, and you belong to the branches. When you think of Jesus, you see it simply and profoundly. Jesus and God are one. When you reach out to Jesus, he touches your hand, and his hand touches God the Father and you sense that deep oneness which gives life and hope to the world.

Your community has its own gospel. You love the way it begins. Jesus is the Word who was with God from the beginning and really is God. It's hard for you to think of God and not think of Jesus. They belong together as one. You remember how the Jews used to speak about the Law as God's word, a light for our feet and a lamp for our path. God's word and wisdom was like God's most intimate companion from the beginning and helped create the universe. God's word was water for the thirsty, bread for the hungry. All this is true of Jesus now. He is the only word and truth and life. The old Law which God gave pointed forward to him.

All the old rituals which the Jewish people observed — and many still do — were there like reflections of what was to come in Jesus. Now that you have the grace and truth of Jesus, the ways of the past, including the Law, belong to the past. The true bread is not the manna in the wilderness or the Law, but the life which Jesus gives and the life you celebrate when you eat the bread and drink the wine together. The true vine is not old Israel, but Jesus himself and all connected to him.

These are deeply comforting thoughts. They connect you to Jesus and God and ultimately to the whole creation. They give you that deep sense of belonging within the community of faith and love. And you know that this will be with you forever. It is a sharing in eternal life, now and beyond the grave. Jesus came that you might have life and have it in all its fullness. Some people found this life by meeting him in flesh and blood. Others found this life after he was dead and gone and yet mysteriously alive and present and people witnessed to their faith. There was no difference. It was the same Jesus, offering the same generous love to all without discrimination.

But now there is pain. Most of your life there has been pain. Pain and joy have gone together. You know about discrimination. In your youth you were a Samaritan girl growing up in a village through which sometimes the Galileans passed on their way south to the temple. You remember how they refused to greet you, walking by on the other side. It was as though you were like the lepers who had to be kept away from everyone else. Your mother explained the conflict. You were also Abraham's people. You were also Israel. But they didn't recognise you. There was nothing you could do.

Not all Galileans and other Jews behaved this way towards your people. You will never forget the day when one of the most unlikely women in your community came running back from the well in the middle of the day saying she had met the Messiah. A Jew had sat down with her at the well and had even asked for a drink from her water. Whatever happened next, she couldn't get over it. Her life was changed. He had set aside all those barriers and instead of giving him her water, she came away feeling that he had brought real water to her thirsty soul. It lifted her up and made her well. No discrimination against her because of her race or because she was a woman or because she had had so many marriages.

It started something. And that was when you joined the movement. You have often wondered what was really said. The few words in the gospel story were surely not the whole story, but they capture the spirit of the encounter. They also fill in some of the gaps so people know what the tensions were, especially over rival claims about where the temple should be, at Jerusalem or on Mount Gerizim in Samaria. The story was told over and over again before it finally came to be written down. Its present version is rich in symbolism and thrills your heart each time you heard it read. You especially like the almost humorous way it plays with the image of water as the woman takes it literally and thinks Jesus is offering a permanent water supply which will save her the drudgery of having to go to the well each day. People in your community know how to retell these stories very creatively so that they come alive for each new generation.

So that was joy bursting into a situation where you often felt the pain of being treated as a second-class human being because you were a Samaritan and a woman. The joy has remained with you, even through the turbulent times when your community was in great strife. It seemed to begin with questioning that there was room for you and your community within the broadly diverse groups which made up Judaism of the time. People of different persuasions attended synagogue gatherings. That was normal. But over a long period of time the tensions became unbearable, with accusation and counter-accusation. They left their mark on the way people told and retold the story of Jesus. Your gospel reflects these conflicts.

When people hear the story in John 9 of the blind man who was healed but then expelled from the synagogue, they reflect on the split which occurred in their own time. In fact, the story seems deliberately shaped to echo these events. The arguments in the gospel between Jesus and his compatriots about what he was claiming about himself also reflect arguments of your teachers with synagogue authorities.

They accused you of giving up belief in one God by making Jesus a god. Every time your people said Jesus and God were one, they thought you were claiming Jesus was God and God was not God. Every time your teachers had to explain that this was not the case. Rather Jesus was truly the Word of God expressing God's being, but always in obedience to God the Father, never acting independently and certainly never a separate god. Part of the problem arose when your community made the link between Jesus and God's Word or Wisdom and said they were identical. It was already a matter of controversy in Judaism, because sometimes it sounded like the Word or Wisdom was like a senior angel beside God or even a second god.

Your people insisted on the fact that Jesus was not a second god. They also insisted on the fact that Jesus was a real human being, not a god or an angel in human disguise. The non-believing Jews never questioned this, but in recent times some of your people have and that led to the split referred to earlier. So the pain continues. It has been really quite confusing. Some have left the church because they feel you claim too much for Jesus. Some have left the church because they feel you don't claim enough.

That is why it has been so important for you to keep in touch with your memories and especially the memories of the community. For a while it was enough to keep telling the well-known stories. Each time they were retold, they would be adjusted to reflect the current needs. The story of the feeding of the five thousand now fills a chapter of 71 verses in your gospel, whereas at first it was a brief account of a miracle.

Faith could hardly be satisfied in just repeating the miracle story. There was so much more. Already in Mark's community we see that people wanted to speak about more than the pieces of bread. They saw Jesus as offering the food of salvation to both Jews and Gentiles. In your gospel this has gone much further. Now we find a conversation in which Jesus contrasts the manna and the wilderness and the Law with the true bread which he offered. He even claims, directly, "I am the bread of life."

And then we find a connection to Holy Communion in the symbolism of eating his flesh and drinking his blood, a shocking notion if taken literally, but deeply meaningful as a way of speaking of sharing his life. It is not as though Mark knew all this and chose to leave it out. It is rather a matter of how stories developed as they were told and retold. There was more to tell than just what happened. There was the ongoing story of who Jesus really was and the life he brought. In your community that theme now finds its way into nearly every story and the Jesus who speaks is really the risen living Jesus who brings faith to life.

Some of your people needed to learn that lesson early. People of your world love the sensational, much as people do today. For some the main thing about Jesus was the sensational miracles he performed. Why follow Jesus? Because of the miracles he performed. This was a worry. There's much more to faith than that. Where is "the Word" in that? So your gospel makes it very clear at a number of points that Jesus was not happy with such an approach.

At the end of chapter 2 it reports that many "believed in his name" because of the miracles, but Jesus did not believe in them. It continues to refer to Nicodemus who claimed Jesus must be from God because of the miracles. Jesus is very confronting in his reply, telling Nicodemus he must be born from above if he really going to see what matters and stop using earthly values. Jesus also rejected the response of people to the feeding of the 5000, when they were so impressed they wanted to crown him king. Such faith misses the point.

It is not that believing in miracles was a problem — not for most people of your times, who found it easier than we do today. The problem was that people did not go to see the greater reality to which the miracles pointed and which they sometimes symbolised: Jesus brings the offer of a life in relationship to God which feeds people in a much deeper sense, draws them into community, and sends them into the world to spread God's love.

So people kept retelling the stories in ways that brought out these connections. The result is a gospel which is in many ways quite different from the others. In it, Jesus speaks at greater length and uses a different kind of language, the language used in your community, rich in symbolism. Those gospels only mention a confrontation about Jesus as Messiah once, right at the end where Jesus stands before the high priest. In your gospel it happens virtually from the beginning. The same is true about Jesus as Son of God. In your gospel it is a constant theme.

You have some of the same stories, like the feeding of the 5000, the expulsion from the temple, and events at the end of Jesus' life, but mostly the stories are different. Your gospel reports that Jesus went to Jerusalem four times during his ministry, which it assumes lasted about three years. The other gospels assume only one visit and a ministry of less than a year. They say that Jesus died on a Friday which was also the Day of the Passover. Yours says that Jesus died on a Friday, but the day before Passover Day, which was a Saturday. Such differences are inevitable in a world in which communication was much more difficult than in ours and in communities which were energetically telling and retelling stories.

In your gospel your Jesus knows the pain which faces the community. It had been a tradition for centuries, reaching right back to Old Testament times, to try to put together what a great leader would have wanted to say to future generations. This is the basis for the book of Deuteronomy. In Mark we find it in chapter 13, which Matthew has followed in chapter 24, but added an extra chapter. Luke has drawn some traditions together to present Jesus' final words to the disciples at the Last Meal. In your gospel Jesus' final words at the meal have extended to nearly five chapters. They are famous words of comfort which generations have cherished ever since: "Let not your heart be troubled! Believe in God! And believe in me!"

Just as the disciples will be left behind, so we are all left behind, at least in the sense that we no longer have Jesus. But then there is the promise. The Spirit will come and in that sense Jesus will come to be with his community. The theme in chapter 14 is comfort. The theme in the following chapters and in the end of chapter 13 where the speech begins is the need for love and unity in the face of danger. Your gospel has been shaped to address your situation. Jesus' main concern in his prayer is for unity. And you know that despite that there has been disunity. Your pain will be felt by others across the centuries. Your gospel has a wonderful way of being real for every generation.

The climax of your gospel, like the others, is Jesus' arrest, trial, and death. Jesus speaks of it during his ministry more often than in the other gospels and does so in distinctive ways, rich with double meaning. So he tells us that as Son of Man he will be lifted up. At one level this alludes to his crucifixion. But to the eyes of faith there is more: the same word also means exaltation. Through his death he will be lifted up to God! Similarly he speaks of the glorification of the Son of Man. To the ears of unbelief this is a crazy way to speak of crucifixion. To the ears of faith it celebrates that through this event Jesus returns to the glory of the Father whence he came. Similarly, again, he seems to be abandoning his disciples, separated from them for all time, but his going away means he will return to enable them through the Spirit to go far beyond the limits of his ministry.

The world sees in the cross a disaster, a failure. In one sense it represents the victory of sin over goodness, hate over love. Yet, paradoxically, it also reveals the victory of love over hate and of goodness over sin. It is exposure; it is judgement. It is a revelation both ways at once. Revelation and finishing the work of making the Father known is the primary focus, rather than sacrifice for sins, as in Paul. It is the turning point. Resurrection celebrates what faith sees, but where unfaith is blind. This is the return of the Son to the Father, his exaltation and glorification. This marks the new beginning of the faith community as the Spirit of Jesus fills the community and enables it to bear fruit. That is the joy which we share with you.

We call your gospel, The Gospel according to John, for similar reasons that we name the other gospels. It never mentions its author. None of them did. In the next century some people were sure it came from the community of the apostle John, hence its name. But John was not an uncommon name even then. Some also spoke of an elder called John. If there is a clue for us, it is in the reference to "the disciple whom Jesus loved," who seems to have been an important person in your community, who recently died but who had contact with Jesus perhaps mainly near the end of his life. Perhaps he was the inspiration for many of the stories. Inevitably people later equated him with "John," but this is little more than a guess. If only you could tell us more! But, then, you might remind us again that the real author of the good news is Jesus and we might do better to respect what these authors have done. They do not make themselves important. They are there to turn our attention to Jesus and ultimately to God.

There is a writing which bears the name, John. John of Patmos wrote the Book of Revelation. Its language and style show that this is not the author of the gospel, nor of 1 John and the related 2 and 3 John. There is little indication you would have ever heard of this work, although some of its images would be familiar. For instance, it too speaks of Jesus as a lamb who overcomes evil.

Revelation is an unusual work consisting mostly of a series of visions introduced by revealed letters to seven churches. The often bizarre imagery belongs to a style of writing called "apocalyptic" (revelatory or unveiling), used to reveal to people what has been happening in the world of their time, usually in contexts of political oppression. In the case of Revelation the setting is Asia Minor, modern-day Turkey, and the crisis is that local Roman authorities are enforcing emperor worship and persecuting those who refuse. The visions are thinly-veiled allusions to this imperial abuse. They hold out hope that one day soon Rome would be overthrown and God's empire established with Christ as king and paradise as a place of healing and living by God's light. Its visions of hope also have a timeless quality because they point beyond John's time. Its visions of oppression also find echoes in later centuries, wherever people experience the political monsters, so much so that every now and again people have imagined Revelation was written just for them rather than for a 1st-century setting where it belongs. Its story has made it a vehicle of inspiration and also for some confusion both for its complex symbols and for those parts where it reflects an unforgiving stance.

In your time the faith has spread widely. Through your gospel you know of other Christian communities different from your own, like those associated with Peter. Your "beloved disciple" always seems ahead of him. Is that how you feel generally about your church, perhaps? We know of letters which people wrote in his name. The second, 2 Peter, is very late and is closely connected with a very short one called Jude. Some think 1 Peter may be Peter's own, but, a bit like Ephesians and Colossians and the later works attributed to Paul, 1 and 2 Timothy and Titus, it is just as likely to come from someone working in the long shadow Peter's influence cast. Somewhere in your time, late in the first Christian century, the well-crafted sermon, "To the Hebrews," began its circulation.

From your own community we know 2 and 3 John, and from them we see that your anxieties must have continued. Not all groups got along well and not all leaders behaved as they should. It must have been very hard not surrender to these idolatries. Your colleague's closing warning is still relevant in our day.

A selection of passages to which this section alludes: God is love: 1 John 4:7, 16; God is light: 1 John 1:5; Jesus the light of the world: John 8:12; 9:5; the bread of life: 6:35, 51; true bread: 6:32; true vine: 15:1; resurrection and the life: 11:25; the Law and Wisdom as life: Proverbs 8:22-31; Sirach 24; life in fullness: John 10:10; the old and the new gift: 1:17; the Samaritan woman: John 4:4-42; Jesus and God: 5:16-24; 10:22-39; 14:8-11; communion: 6:51-58; miracle-centered faith: 2:23–3:5; 4:48; 6:1-15; different dating of Jesus' death in relation to the Passover: 18:28; 19:31, 42; compare Mark 14:12-16; Luke 22:7-13; Jesus' prayer for unity: 17; exaltation double meaning: 3:13-14; 12:32-33; glorification: 12:23; 13:31-32; 17:1-5; Jesus' return to send the Spirit: 14:12-17; the cross as victory and vindication: 12:31; 16:8-11; the "beloved disciple": 13:23-24; 19:25-27; 20:1-10; 21:1-8; 21:20-25; 18:15-18.

5A. John 1–3 in Overview

"In the beginning was the Word." What a fantastic beginning to John's gospel! "In the beginning God created the heavens and the earth" is how Genesis begins. John's gospel disputes nothing of that but begins with the focus on communication. God in communication! That is therefore how John's gospel sees Jesus.

Word

Israel's traditions had spoken of God's word or wisdom being ever present with God, like an intimate companion. Sometimes it almost sounds like Wisdom is God's child (Prov 8:22-31). At times people simply said: the Law is God's Word and Wisdom. But then they would say that this divine Word was part of God's being from the beginning.

These are very complicated, but beautiful, ways of saying that God is not aloof but engaged. They are images. God is not silent, but like a conversation of goodness. Jews could think of Wisdom or the Word as God's companion. Christians would later develop the doctrine of the Trinity which also has its roots in the playful image of communication: the Father, the Son, the Spirit — yet they are one.

John's gospel begins differently from the other gospels. Mark takes us straight to John the Baptist. Matthew leads us into a list of Jesus' messianic pedigree. Luke begins with the romance of angels and visitations to Mary and Elizabeth. John takes us to the heart of his theology. He will tell the story of Jesus, stringing together anecdotes and sayings, as others did before him, but always against the background of seeing Jesus as God's communication to humankind.

He colours every scene with these insights. Every conversation reflects it in some way. John's is the most thoroughgoing and creative of all the portraits of Jesus. If we think of a spectrum with photographs at one end and abstract art at the other, John's is closer to the abstract end. Whatever words appear on the screen, behind them is a clear pattern of thought. Jesus is the Son sent by the Father from the heavenly world to offer a new relationship with himself and so with God. Few will respond to the invitation. He will return to the Father having faithfully carried out his work, even through suffering and death. Then he will appear to his own to send them with the aid of the Spirit on the same mission to bring life and light to the world.

As Jews spoke of scripture, especially the Law of Moses, as light and life for the world, John declares that Jesus is light and life. What Israel claimed for scripture he claimed for Christ. Images of the Law now become images of Jesus: not only word, light, and life, but also the water of life, the bread of life, the true vine. The result is a change of focus. People who had looked to the Law for life should now look to Jesus. The scriptures themselves are not that life; they point to it by their witness, just as John the Baptist did at the beginning of Jesus' ministry according to John's gospel. Only Jesus is the bread, the true bread.

These claims are central to John's gospel. They upset people who still wanted to put scripture at the centre and call it God's word and light and life and so sought to continue the traditions of Israel's worship. They uplifted others who could now see Israel's scripture and its patterns of worship as prefiguring the one to come, who has not come. Most of them were also Jews, but they had come to see and value their religion in a new way.

In John 1:1-18 we see some of the emphases already. John the Baptist also needs to be seen in proper perspective. Like the scriptures and the Law he is not the light; but he is an important witness to it (1:6-8, 15-16). The

Law is God's gift (1:17). Now the ultimate has come and we see the glory of God in human flesh (1:14). He has made the Father known (1:18).

It is very likely that John — or perhaps already someone before him — has taken what was a hymn of praise to God's word and wisdom and applied it to Christ. The hymn may well have spoken of wisdom coming to Israel in the prophets. Now in John's version the word comes in Jesus. Certainly in the rest of the gospel we find a similar taking over and transforming of what people had said about the Law.

The Lamb of God

Having set the scene with these wonderful words, John brings us his version of the encounter between Jesus and John the Baptist. It contains many echoes of what we find in the other gospels, especially in Mark. John, or perhaps people in his community before him, has reworked these stories. The major emphasis is on putting John in the right perspective, to the extent that we may wonder if there were people at the time of the gospel who were beginning to revere John the Baptist more highly than Jesus. 1:20 makes the point with triple underlining: John is not the Messiah!

In 1:29 John then points to the true Messiah. People could describe the Messiah as a ram or a lamb. This happens here. Here is the lamb of God who removes the world's sins. Removing evil from the world and setting up a kingdom of goodness and peace was one of the Messiah's tasks. But the image of lamb and of sins might also make listeners to John's gospel think of lambs used in daily sacrifice or the lamb eaten on Passover evening.

It often happens in John's gospel that we find what seems a simple and straightforward statement, which on reflection turns out to be jewel that seems to sparkle in a number of directions at once. The writer deliberately sets up such moments in the text. It is likely to be happening here. John invites us to imagine the links and make the connections.

Differences between John and the First Three Gospels

One peculiarity of John's gospel is the date of Jesus' death. Jesus dies, according to John, when the Passover lambs were being slaughtered on the day before the Passover. The Passover Day began at sunset with the Passover meal, which included eating lamb. According to John's account the Passover that year fell on a sabbath, a Saturday (strictly speaking, Friday sunset to Saturday sunset). This is different from the first three gospels, which report that Jesus' last meal was the Passover meal and that Jesus was executed on the Day of Passover, which was not a Saturday but a Friday.

Did John deliberately change the date to picture Jesus as slaughtered like a Passover lamb? Or did Mark (whom the others simply follow) want to portray Jesus' final meal as a Passover meal for similar symbolic reasons? We may never know who was right, historically, although the lack of evidence elsewhere of the actual meal itself being a Passover meal slightly favours John.

Similarly the first three gospels and John differ over the length of Jesus' ministry. Did it simply run from Jesus' baptism for less than a year, climaxing in Jesus' single visit to Jerusalem at Passover weekend at which he was killed, as Mark suggests? Or is John the one who is correct in suggesting a number of visits to Jerusalem and a ministry lasting about three years? Evidence again slightly favours John because all of the gospels assume Jesus must have had more to do with Jerusalem than just the week suggested by Mark and the others.

John's gospel, then, is an interesting mixture of an overriding theology which unites everything under the theme of Jesus as the Word of God and at the same time contains some stories and sayings which have a strong historical claim. More than this, the stories and sayings in John frequently reflect the language and ideas which belong to its overriding theology in a way that Jesus almost speaks a different language from the Jesus of the other gospels. Here, however, the others probably reflect the language of Jesus more closely and consistently. They combine different sources which all reflect this language and even beneath the elaborations of John's account we can find clear traces of the way Jesus spoke elsewhere. Occasionally, where all four gospels carry the same story we can compare the differences and similarities.

In moving through John 1 in overview, we encounter some more differences between John and the others. John 1 tells the story of the call of the disciples in a very different way from what we find in Mark 1:16-20. Similarly there are differences about when John the Baptist's ministry ends and when Jesus' ministry begins. In Mark Jesus' ministry commences after the arrest of John the Baptist. In John both operated side by side for a while. Again John's gospel is probably more correct.

Moving On to Greater Things

After John's opening in 1:1-18 the rest of John 1 focuses on Jesus as Israel's Messiah. In the rest of the gospel we see that Jesus' messiahship is just one way among many of pointing to the deeper truth announced in 1:1-18. Jesus is the Son sent from the Father to offer us life. At the end of John 1 there is a surprise.

In 1:50 Jesus responds to Nathanael's sense of wonder that Jesus miraculously knew of him by asserting that there are greater things to come. One might think of greater miracles, but that is not where John leads us. Instead he reports Jesus' claim that people would see "heaven opened and the angels of God ascending and descending on the Son of Man" (1:51). When John speaks of Jesus elsewhere as Son of Man and pictures him as glorified in heaven, he refers to what happens as the climax of Jesus' ministry. The world sees him lifted up on a cross. Faith knows that this is also his return to be glorified with God. People listening to the gospel would probably have had no difficulty making such connections because the idea was not new and most would not be hearing this gospel let alone the Christian message for the first time.

Such listeners might also smile to themselves at what immediately follows. "On the third day" is language we usually find used to describe Jesus' resurrection, which belongs closely with his exaltation to glory. Here is another example of different levels of meaning. In John. 2:1 it can simply mean "three days later." It is not always easy to know if it means only that. The likelihood that it means more than that depends on whether there are other factors which suggest more is going on. In this case we have the reference to the climax of Jesus' life in 1:51. We also have a meal with wine about to follow which can be seen as an allusion to the meals of the bread and wine that become the centre of Christian community after Easter. Sometimes we have to stand back and say: possibly. Partly it is about being familiar with where we know John does use this technique and then assessing whether there are enough indicators to suggest something else is going on.

Even so, whether "on the third day" has two levels of meaning or just one, there are certainly other aspects to the story which follows which have at least two levels of meaning. At a literal level there is a miracle in which Jesus produces wine for a wedding feast where supplies were running out. The result is a huge quantity of wine (around 550 litres, 120 gallons!) and more extraordinary that it is for people who had already drunk a good deal. There is no indication that John has any qualms about the alcohol or about the miracle, such as might concern us, both intellectually and morally. But there is already a wink, as it were, to the listeners simply in the vast quantity of wine, which suggests we should think a bit further.

Many of John's listeners would have been familiar with the great vision of Isaiah 25 about a feast in the last days in which wine would abound. Often people imagined that as a great wedding feast. They might also think of their own meals of bread and wine, which have their origin in that great vision and ultimately in Jesus' own use of meals to represent the good news. So the jewel is already sparkling in a number of directions.

The new wine Jesus brings is the relationship with God. The water in stone jars reflects the concerns with purification which were so popular in Jesus' day, stone jars not being susceptible to ritual contamination. Notice that John (unlike Mark) does not here (or anywhere for that matter!) disparage or ridicule such practices. Part of the subtle meaning in our story is that they can now be abandoned, since Jesus, the greater gift than the gift of the Law (1:17), has come.

The story glistens with more "extra meaning." When Jesus' mother tells the attendants to do whatever Jesus tells them, we can sense that applies at a much broader level. When the attendants wonder where the wine came from, we can almost hear John's listeners cry out: he comes from the Father. For those who already know John's story of the crucifixion, Jesus' words that his "hour has not yet come" point forward to that event, and his conversation with his mother recalls the conversation there in which Jesus commits his mother to the care of the beloved disciple.

The Temple Sign

The second story in John 2 takes us already to Jerusalem to a Passover. Again we have the problem of the difference between John and the other gospels. They suggest, probably correctly, that this was one of the events leading to Jesus' arrest and trial. It looks like John has deliberately chosen to relocate the story to a position very early in the gospel because it suits the theme he is developing. If the new wine replaces the old water for purification, the new temple replaces the old temple.

John's account of Jesus' action in the temple is similar to what we find in the others. The actual words spoken differ, as we have come to expect.

They also reflect some techniques which are typical of John. One of these is to use different levels of meaning to create a dramatic effect. People in the dialogue fail to understand the true meaning, but listeners to the gospel chuckle because they do understand. In 2:20, for instance, the Jews think Jesus is referring literally to the temple. John says in 2:21 that Jesus refers to his own body. The effect in any case is that the old temple is replaced by a new temple, the risen person of Jesus and, by implication, his community. This theme continues in 4:21-24, where Jesus tells the Samaritan woman that the temple is to be replaced with a new kind of worship.

More Than Miracles

2:23 then tells us that many people in Jerusalem "believed in his name seeing the miracles he was performing." 1:12 had spoken of people believing in his name and so becoming children of God. So 2:23 sounds like a report of success. In 2:11 John tells us that the event at Cana in Galilee showed his glory to his disciples, but that was probably about much more than just the miracle we have seen.

2:24 continues with the striking comment that Jesus, literally, did not believe (the same word as in 2:23) in them! Why? 2:24-25 explains: "because he knew all people and because he had no need for anyone to give him evidence about people; for he, himself, knew what was in people." From elsewhere in John we learn that faith based solely on miracles is inadequate. People are fascinated with wonders. John wants them to look more deeply. It is much more important to find that Jesus brings the new wine than to believe he made so much wine at a wedding feast. John does not attack belief in the latter, but the all-important thing is the relationship with Jesus and ultimately with God. John is attacking a kind of faith in Jesus which he sees as inadequate.

This is apparent as we move from John 2 to John 3. The word I have translated "people" in 2:24-25 is the Greek word, *anthropos* (meaning a human being). 2:25 ends with John saying that Jesus knew what was in an *anthropos* (a person). 3:1 follows immediately with the words: Now there was an *anthropos* (a person). This is Nicodemus. He is an example of the believers of whom John has spoken in 2:23. He, too, focuses on Jesus' miracles and declares that Jesus is a teacher come from God and that God must be with him.

Usually we read John 3 without remembering John 2 and so we miss these important links. People broke the New Testament writings into chapters and then verses centuries after they were written. Mostly the breaks follow breaks in meaning, but this is an example of an unfortunate break, because Nicodemus illustrates a certain kind of faith. Usually we think he illustrates someone who does not believe. He does believe according to John and there were people who believed in Jesus the way Nicodemus did then and even today.

When Jesus challenges Nicodemus to be born from above, he is saying to him that he needs to take a different approach if he really wants to see and only then will he be born to new life. This is another example of John's playfulness. In the statement, "Unless you are born from above," the Greek words translated, "from above," can also mean, "again." John exploits this double meaning to create the dialogue. Originally, if there was such a conversation, it would have been in Aramaic where the double meaning would not have worked. John's dialogue, like most dialogues in stories told about history, was freely created. We smile as Nicodemus fails to see. Nicodemus is hopelessly out of his depth when he talks about literally being born again.

Part of this is saying: you have to see beneath the surface. Belief in miracles is fine, but unless you see what they symbolise and who Jesus is you will miss their point. Later John creates wonderful dialogues around miracle stories. He shows Jesus rejecting those who want to crown him king because he fed 5000 people. Those people needed to understand he was the bread of life ("I am the bread of life"). In a similar way the healing of the blind man in John 9 is really about seeing Jesus as the light of the world ("I am the light of the world") and the raising of Lazarus is about seeing Jesus as the resurrection and the life ("I am the resurrection and the life").

Seeing Greater Things

As the dialogue with Nicodemus continues, we see a conversation at two levels. Nicodemus thinks concretely at the literal level, the "flesh"; Jesus talks at the spiritual level, "the Spirit." You have to live at both levels. Nicodemus lives only at one. So Nicodemus will also misunderstand the climax of Jesus' life. He will only see Jesus lifted up on a cross and executed.

Faith will see instead the Son of Man ascending to where he was before, just as 1:51 had indicated.

3:16 introduces the wonderful summary of Jesus' life. It was God's initiative in love to send his Son to offer life. The focus is not on the quantity of that life — everlasting, as if that is the main point, but on its quality: life from God which we have now and which will endure. 3:17 puts it negatively: God's aim was not condemnation but the offer of hope. 3:18 indicates that our response to that offer determines God's response. We condemn ourselves by not believing. 3:19-21 explains how some respond positively and some, negatively. It suggests that some people deliberately choose darkness and death.

By this point in John 3 we have in effect left Nicodemus behind. John has Jesus make declarations about himself which are for all to hear. This often happens in John's gospel. 3:22-30 returns to John the Baptist and underlines John's inferior position, but by 3:31 we are back to general statements about Jesus. It is even possible to read them as statements by John the Baptist. Alternatively they are statements by the gospel writer for his listeners. In some ways it does not matter. John's gospel is offering us a summary of who Jesus is and using the pattern of language which forms the background to every scene.

So Jesus is the Son from above. He speaks on that basis. God has sent him. It sounds like Jesus is the bearer of information about the heavenly world, like a heavenly messenger, but that is not the focus. Rather what the Son communicates is not bodies of information or sets of teaching but simply the offer of life to be found in believing he represents God, and joining oneself in faith to him and so to God. This is what Jesus is all about. It is what Nicodemus fails to recognise.

John has made the story of Jesus wonderfully simple. It is about the offer of life to be had by a response of joining oneself to Jesus and his community in faith. The pattern for his thinking about Jesus is more developed than in the other gospels. Mark begins with Jesus' baptism. Matthew and Luke begin with his miraculous creation through Mary. None go back further than that. John does. He takes us back to the beginning and asserts that from the beginning God is the communicator and there is a Jesus shape to God's communication from the very beginning.

The human Jesus, whose humanity John never calls into question, is at the same time the divine Word addressing us and offering life. Beyond Easter and equipped with the Spirit those who share this life now bear it to others as they retell Jesus' story, just as John is doing. They are a community and temple which celebrates God's presence as new life in the symbols of worship, above all, the meal of faith, and in telling the story.

5B. John 4:4-42

This is one story with many parts. Just before it is a reference to Jesus and John the Baptist (4:1-3). John the Baptist features in 3:22-30 and perhaps right through to the end of the chapter. 4:1-3 mentions that Jesus baptised, but then corrects it to say his disciples baptised. The other gospels never say that Jesus ever baptised, although it is a reasonable assumption when we find the disciples baptising after Easter. Perhaps by the time John was written there was conflicting information. Perhaps 4:2 is a correction which came into the gospel in the final edition. We may never know. 4:1 remains, however, the ground why Jesus decided not to stay in Judea.

John 4:4-42 in Overview

4:4 tells us that Jesus returned to Galilee via the shortest route. That meant travelling through the territory of the Samaritans. Many Galileans avoided doing so and took the longer route on the east of the River Jordan. So this takes us to the setting of the story.

Before we pass along its various stages it is good to identify its main parts. 4:4-6 tells about Jesus' arrival at a well. 4:7 introduces the Samaritan woman and a conversation follows. 4:7-10 reports Jesus' request for a drink, the woman's response, and then Jesus' statement about living water. Next in 4:11-16 they have a conversation about this living water. In 4:17-18 Jesus brings out the fact she is living with a man to whom she is not married. 4:19-26 begins with the woman's awe at Jesus' knowledge and she then asks him about the rival temples of the Samaritans and Jews. 4:27-30 switches to the disciples who had gone to get food and return to be shocked that Jesus was speaking with a woman. She leaves to report her encounter to people in town and the possibility that Jesus is the Messiah. In 4:31-38 the disciples ask Jesus to eat but he switches the conversation to speak symbolically of his food as his mission. Finally in 4:39-42 we hear of the woman's impact and of the people coming to faith. The Samaritan woman becomes a hero of mission, but the story takes many twists and turns before it gets there and each one is rich in storytelling and symbolism.

Crossing Boundaries

The opening scene is very straightforward at one level. Jesus is tired just like any other human being after a journey. He sits by a well at midday, but here some of the symbols start to appear. It happens to be near Jacob's well which he gave to Joseph. Jacob is the famous ancestor who will reappear in the conversation in 4:12. Joseph was the saviour of the world around Egypt because he stored the grain from seven rich years. By the end of the story (4:42) the Samaritans will acclaim Jesus "the saviour of the world"!

One would not expect many people to be drawing water at midday. It was an activity for the cooler hours. But a solitary woman comes, perhaps because she was on the outs with other women. The story is simple. Jesus asks for a drink as she draws water. That seems straightforward for us, but as the woman indicates by her response — and Jesus does not deny — this was not to be expected. Jews and Samaritans do not mix or, at least, they would not usually use the same drinking vessels. Jesus is crossing a boundary erected by common racist attitudes.

There is another factor — possibly two — which also play a role. While 4:8 mentions that the disciples were not present because they had gone to town to get food, when they return in 4:27 they highlight another problem. Jesus is having a conversation with a woman in public. Many would have seen such a conversation in such a setting as inappropriate. Later we learn that she is also living in what would be understood as an adulterous relationship. This may explain why she turns up at such an unsuitable time of day to draw water. So Jesus may in fact be crossing not one, but three boundaries. She was a Samaritan, a woman, and a sinner. The anecdote is then typical of so many which people told about Jesus. He refused to write people off and refused the common prejudices of his day.

Well Water and Living Water

This is only the beginning. We are not even told if Jesus got his drink, because the story is more interested in a different kind of water. Jesus tells the woman that if she knew who he was she could ask him for living water (4:10). Here is a fine example of playfulness based on double meaning, as we found in the story of Nicodemus. "Living water" can mean running water as opposed to still water and is normally to be preferred as being of better quality. So it sounds like Jesus has a better water supply.

The woman takes Jesus literally, but wonders where he gets the water from. At this point John's listeners would already be smiling, as they would on the many occasions when people ask where Jesus is from or where he gets things from. It would have happened when the waiter asked about the origin of the wine. The living water is the gift of sharing in God's life which Jesus offers. But the woman has not grasped that. The drama intensifies when she asks another question: is Jesus greater than Jacob? Again we can imagine John's listeners calling out, "yes!" Jacob watered his flocks and he and his family drank from the well; Jesus offers the water of life to the world.

In 4:13-14 the conversation continues with Jesus affirming what John's listeners know. He offers a permanent supply of living water, eternal life! The woman still does not understand. In 4:15 she asks for this water — so that she would not be thirsty and not have to come every day to the well to draw water!

This is drama, almost like it is written for the theatre. A number of scenes in John's gospel have this character. They are very good examples of creative use of dialogue. Just as we have seen in the way Matthew revises Mark, so someone or some people in the community of the gospel of John had developed a very skilful and effective way of writing dialogues which helped bring out the heart of their faith. The dialogues work as drama because of all the clever allusions to what the listeners already know. It is a way of celebrating and reinforcing their faith.

Marriages

Perhaps the setting also enhances the sense of drama. Stories of men and women meeting at wells were not uncommon. They were usually courtship stories and featured in romances, including Jacob meeting Rachel (Gen 29:1-12). It was entertainment. But here the focus is something more serious. Still, this association of ideas is in the background and may explain the following conversation.

The conversation continues in 4:17-18. Jesus changes tack and asks about the woman's husband. It is a ploy to expose that she is in fact living with a man to whom she is not married. This was not to be tolerated at the time and fell under the heading of adultery. John's hearers would have known that and would have been in no doubt that Jesus would also have seen this as sin. As mentioned earlier, it may explain why the woman seems to be a loner — perhaps treated as an outcast. The fact that she has already had five husbands need not necessarily count against her. She may have been widowed or divorced five times. The exposure of this information does not lead to Jesus telling her off or cutting off contact with her. It just reinforces the fact that he does the opposite: he treats her as a person of worth and takes her seriously.

Temples

The woman is wonderfully persistent. In the story she does not sense that Jesus rejects her because of her life situation. With enthusiasm she inches closer to faith by sensing that Jesus must have prophetic powers to know so much (4:19). Faith matters to her so she comes straight to the point about one of the bones of contention between Jews and Samaritans: the rival temple. The Samaritan temple had been destroyed in 128 BCE, but the mountain of Samaria remained the centre for their worship.

Jesus' answer points beyond the dispute to a time when worship will be something very different and tied to neither mountain. It will be worship in the community of faith by the Spirit. John had already made that point in 2:13-22 which declares the risen Jesus the new temple. Jesus is also very straightforward about the rights and wrongs of the present time. The Jews are right and the Samaritans have got it wrong. God's work of salvation is coming through the Jews — concretely, through Jesus.

Rather than be offended by this straight talk the woman is a stayer. She raises the even more important issue of the Messiah, seen in Samaritan tradition especially as a teacher (4:25). Jesus responds directly; it's me, talking to you (4:26). At this point the disciples return, worried by their prejudices about women and the woman goes back to town, leaving behind her water pot, perhaps in haste to get away from these unsympathetic men or perhaps as a symbol that her attention has turned to a different kind of water.

Mission

Her report is tantalising. She asks people to come and see a man who told her all that she ever did. Perhaps this hints at the likelihood that they all knew what she had been up to and disapproved, which would make her report all the more convincing. Then she adds, tentatively: "Could this perhaps be the Christ?" The Greek definitely expresses some hesitation, but she is inching closer still to full faith. It is enough to bring out the townsfolk.

We are ready to hear what happens when they come, but instead John comes back to the disciples. They have brought food and offer it to Jesus (4:31). Jesus shifts the focus to symbolic food, just as he had shifted the focus to symbolic drink earlier (4:32). Like the Samaritan woman the disciples do not realise the change in level of meaning (4:33). The audience of John's gospel probably sighs at this point. The teaching which follows in 4:34-38 explains what Jesus means and goes on to reflect on mission. This includes the different roles of those who do the ground work and those who later bring in the benefits of that work. The interlude is reflecting on mission and clearly sees in the story of the Samaritan woman a model of missionary activity.

Finally we are back with the Samaritans in 4:39. Many believed because of the woman's testimony — tentative as it was. Jesus stayed with them. This has a literal meaning. It also suggests the presence of Jesus always with those who respond to his word. That mission, prompted by the woman's initiative, leads to many more becoming believers, independently of her testimony. They acclaim Jesus "saviour of the world" (like Joseph in his world, but in a much more important sense).

"Saviour of the world" in this story is full of meaning. It includes: not just Messiah of the Jews. It is all embracing. Jesus crossed the boundaries of racial, sexist, and moral prejudice. The woman came to faith, step by step, to become a hero of mission, even though the last words we hear from her are still tentative. The story assumes she made the full journey along with the people of her town.

The story will have its historical roots. But it also has much more. It has been reworked in a way which is typical of John's gospel. The dialogue, especially, playfully opens vistas of meaning which reach far beyond the literal details of the story. The story becomes a symbol, like an icon. It shines with ongoing meaning and invites those who listen to drink from the water of life themselves and then to engage in sharing that life in the world.

5C. John 6, John 13–17, and 1 John

The feeding of the 5000 appears in all four of our gospels.

The Feedings in the Gospels

We have seen how Mark uses the story to celebrate the nourishment of the good news coming not only to Israel but also to Gentiles as part of his grand composition which reaches to chapter 8 and includes the feeding of the 4000.

We have also seen how Matthew uses it differently, taking the emphasis away from Gentiles which he found in Mark and putting it instead on Jesus fulfilling the Old Testament hopes of bringing healing and nourishment to Israel.

Luke's is the shortest treatment because he takes only the feeding of the 5000 from Mark and the walking on water which follows it. He then leaves out the next large section of Mark with which Matthew had some difficulty, probably because Luke, too, had difficulty with Mark's radical approach to scripture. So Luke has only the feeding of the 5000 and places it just before the disciples realise who Jesus is and Peter acclaims him the Christ, just as later their eyes would be opened when Jesus broke bread with them.

John, too, has only the feeding of the 5000, but like the others it is linked with the story of Jesus walking on the water. But he then has an extensive conversation between Jesus and his disciples in which Jesus interprets the event at a number of different levels. This stretches out to one very long chapter of 71 verses.

Perhaps John (I use the traditional name for the author) knew Mark's gospel and was revising and expanding it. Perhaps he did not know Mark, but, like Mark, received the stories of the feeding and the walking on water together. There are many points in John's gospel where we cannot be sure which of these is the better explanation. Some suggest he had read Mark aloud many times in the past and this helped feed his version of the gospel.

Even if the author of John's gospel was in some way dependent on Mark, he also knew stories which were unknown to the others. In addition he was in a community where people had thought very creatively about some of the common stories, including the feeding of the 5000. We saw that already Mark went far beyond the literal meaning. Whether independently or not, John follows this lead. Now we hear not only that the good news is nourishment, but that Jesus himself declares: "I am the bread of life." John's pivotal emphasis, unlike Mark's, is not on the inclusion of Gentiles but on the sheer fact that to enter a relationship with God through Jesus is to receive the bread of life.

John's Story

Before John brings us these teachings, he recounts the story. The story is very similar to what we find in Mark without the special emphases on Israel which Mark may well have added. Some elements connect the story to what has gone before. 6:2 tells us that many were following Jesus because of his miracles. If we remember 2:23-25 and the story of Nicodemus, we will know that such following is no guarantee of true faith. When these people want to acclaim Jesus king in 6:14-15, Jesus will have nothing of it and goes away.

There are no immediate connections with John 5, which recalls events happening in Jerusalem. In fact the transition from John 5 in Jerusalem to John 6 in Galilee is rather abrupt if not rather awkward, because John 7 has Jesus back in Jerusalem having a conversation about the miracle he had just performed. But that miracle is now back in John 5 and quite some time has passed in the interim, including the Passover Festival. This has led some scholars to suppose that originally John 5 and John 7 belonged together and John 6 was added later, but by the same author or someone sharing the same general approach. It looks like the final editor or author who produced the gospel did not worry about smoothing out such awkward transitions and was more concerned with the message being conveyed.

The message is clearly that there is more to Jesus than miracles. The miracles are really signs which point to deeper truth. Mostly the dialogue tells us what that truth is, but not always. It was not the case in the wedding miracle at Cana nor in the healing of the official's son. It is not the case in the walking on the water which follows the feeding of the 5000 here. The author assumes people will see the parallels with Yahweh walking on the water and recognise the claim being demonstrated here: God is meeting us in his Word.

When the crowd succeeds in catching up with Jesus on the other side of the lake, Jesus challenges them because they saw the miracle only as a magical source of food. They did not see it as a sign (6:26). Then begins a dialogue in which Jesus does most of the talking and in which we find the image of food operating in a rich variety of ways.

The Bread of Life

Jesus tells them they should be looking for food of a different kind (6:27), just as earlier when he turned the attention of the Samaritan woman from literal water to the living water. Jesus refers to himself as the Son of Man and declares that the Son of Man will give them such food. This finds its echo in 6:53, where Jesus again refers to himself as the Son of Man: "I tell you, unless you eat the flesh of the Son of Man and drink his blood, you have no life in you." In both instances John's listeners will have recognised the allusion to the eucharist, where believers feed on Christ in bread and wine, representing his flesh and blood. It is typical of John to use such shocking language — it sounds like cannibalism and like a magical meal. These are dramatic ways of speaking of receiving Christ into one's life.

Most of the dialogue shifts focus to the present and rather than speaking of Jesus as giving food, speaks of him as that food. We see this happening in 6:30-35, where the obvious allusion to the manna in the wilderness becomes the basis of a contrast. Jesus' partners in dialogue want a sign from Jesus to justify his claims (much as they do in Mark 8:11-13). As if the feeding of the 5000 and the walking on water was not enough! They even point to the miracle of the manna as a sign. One can almost hear John's knowing listeners sigh in exasperation.

This gives Jesus the opportunity to contrast what he is doing with the story of the manna in the wilderness. It was a famous story which some Jews interpreted symbolically to say that the manna Moses gave was the Law. Perhaps our author had said similar things if he was once a learned teacher in his Jewish community. Now, however, he denies such a meaning. There is only one true bread and manna and that is Jesus, not the Law. In a similar way in 5:39 he complained that the Jews were going to the Law and scriptures as if they were the life instead of seeing that they pointed to himself as the source of life.

In 6:35 Jesus declares himself to be the bread of life. Then, echoing the story of the Samaritan woman, he says this bread satisfies hunger and he also satisfies thirst. We are a long way from the miracle of feeding 5000 people. It has been transformed into a sign which says: Jesus is the bread of life.

The following dialogue confronts disbelief. Jesus explains why some reject and some accept his teaching. This part of the dialogue reflects a problem many Christian communities faced. Many of their fellow Jews did not join them in the Jesus movement. The dialogue reflects ways in which people of the time thought about these problems. Ideas were in flux, so we find apparently contradictory statements side by side. No one can come unless God draws them, but also anyone can come, whoever believes.

6:47-51 brings us back to the central assertions about Jesus as the bread of life. 6:52-58 focuses initially on the question: how? How do we feed on this life? The answer comes from within the Christian community: in Holy Communion, in the bread and wine. This is not something automatic, but must be understood in the light of the rest of the chapter. The focus is personal faith not the properties of literal bread and wine.

6:26-58 is like a dialogue sermon and reflects some of the patterns of preaching of the day. It is a rounded unity, concluding where it began and expounding the biblical story of the manna in the light of Christ. It deals both with the fact of opposition and rejection, and with the central message that life is to be found in relationship with God through the Son.

Grumblings

6:59-71 is a new scene. Here there is also dissent, but it is coming not from unbelieving Jews but from among Jesus' own followers. John puts this on stage probably because these had been issues in his own day. Some Christians felt the claims about Jesus had gone too far. They "grumble" just as the Jews had "grumbled" (6:41). The grumbling is doubtless an echo of the words of Psalm 95, which refers to the "grumbling of Israel in the wilderness."

How could John and his fellow believers claim that Jesus came down from heaven? Isn't Jesus a human being? Aren't they in danger of making Jesus a second god? It is true that John's gospel makes claims about Jesus which go far beyond what the others say. None of them say Jesus came down from heaven. Mark's gospel shows Jesus as very reticent to make claims about himself. The disciples do not hail him as Messiah till halfway through the gospel and then get it wrong. Even the heavenly voices at Jesus' baptism and transfiguration, which affirm Jesus' sonship, never speak of origins.

So the potential was there for conflict. Others, however, were heading in a similar direction to John's gospel. Already Paul, writing some decades earlier, made a link between Jesus and God's wisdom and knew others who had done so. Sayings in Q also reflect the connection between Wisdom, the Law, and Jesus' presentation of God's word. None of these questioned Jesus' humanity. Nor did they appear to have seen any problem relating Jesus to God. In fact the image of Wisdom helped them to think about it.

For John's gospel it has become essential to believe that Jesus is God's Son, sent from the Father to offer light and life and truth. He alone is the Word. All other witnesses, such as John the Baptist and the scriptures, witness to him. John's argument is that Jesus' descent from above and Jesus' ascent, returning to where he was before, belong together. Any other view remains captive to a lower level of seeing and believing, like that of Nicodemus. For John this lower level is the level of the flesh, which in John is not something evil, but something rather useless on its own.

It is interesting John's gospel brings its own version of Peter's confession. He gets it right in form and substance, unlike in Mark. It looks like John knows Mark or Mark's tradition, but is rewriting it to good effect. But even in the inner circle of the 12 there is failure: Judas. This tells a well-known story; it also warns people in leadership in John's day.

John's gospel is rich in symbolism. It keeps shifting the focus from the literal to deeper levels of meaning, much more than any of the other gospels. The feeding of the 5000 becomes the jumping off point for the assertion now made directly by Jesus in the dialogue: "I am the bread of life." Similarly the healing of the blind man in John leads to: "I am the light of the world," a claim already introduced in 8:12 at the feast of Tabernacles where lights played a key role. And the raising of Lazarus leads to a claim about a very different kind of resurrection: I am the resurrection and life.

John 17 in the Context of Farewell Stories

There is one other passage which we shall briefly look at to complete our sampling of John's gospel: John 17. It is Jesus' final prayer. It is formulated in language typical of John's gospel. It belongs within a large section which covers Jesus' last night with his disciples: John 13–17. It was common in the ancient world to give special attention to famous last words and wishes of great people. The person who compiled Deuteronomy portrayed them as Moses' final instructions. In a similar way Genesis 49 gives us the final blessings of Jacob. There are many subsequent examples of final instructions. People tried to reconstruct what most would have said as their parting words. The result is a wide range of writings, called "Testaments." We have testaments of Adam, Abraham, Isaac, Jacob, Moses, and many more. The book, *The Testament of the Twelve Patriarchs,* is a fine illustration of careful ethical teaching, put together as wise words for all descendants.

It was inevitable that people did the same for Jesus. Mark has Jesus' words about the future in Mark 13. Matthew repeats and revises this and adds a further chapter (Matthew 24–25). Luke brings together some of Jesus' teaching about leadership into the scene of Jesus' last meal (Luke 22:21-46).

In John's community the attempts have gone much further. As with the awkward transition in chapters 5–7 the final author did not worry about the bumps, so in John 13–17, he has not smoothed the edges where expansions have occurred. This is most striking in 14:31, which almost certainly was at one time the end of the discussion between Jesus and his disciples. Jesus says, "Get up, let's go off!" John 18 then follows very naturally and so they went. But now we have another three chapters before they go, John 15–17.

It looks like an earlier version stopped at the end of John 14, but then someone (perhaps the same author) added John 15–17. It is not possible to fathom all the reasons for this or to discuss the passages in detail, but some differences stand out. As elsewhere in John they probably reflected concerns at the time of writing. Once again the method was to create a dialogue of what Jesus would have said. This was not made up in someone's imagination, but based on a combination of information available and what seemed most likely to have been said, in the absence of recording devices and material written down at the time. History in the ancient world always involved imagination. When we compare the gospels, it is clear that very little if anything was written down and remembered of conversations on Jesus' last night beyond the words and actions at the Last Meal and the warning about Judas. Jesus must have said more and we value the various attempts to fill out the missing details.

The Focus of the Farewell Speech in John 14

Up until John 14:31, in other words, in the earlier version of Jesus' last speech in John, the focus is on comforting the disciples in the face of Jesus' departure. While not denying the grief caused by Jesus' suffering and death, the speech highlights the good news. Jesus' death means his return to the Father. From the Father he will send the Spirit. Through the Spirit he will come to the disciples and he and the Father will live in and among them. They can take heart.

The words speak at two levels. In the story the actual disciples are worried about the impending dangers. Jesus promises them a future. In a short time they will see him again. John 20 and 21 will tell stories of Jesus appearing to his disciples. But the emphasis is on his abiding presence. Written with a view to saying something to all disciples, the message is similar, although the promise they will see the resurrected one does not apply. The rest does and tells them what do after Jesus. They will do greater things than Jesus himself, at least in the sense that by the power of the Spirit they will spread his message to the world.

In this speech we can almost see how the speech has been made. It makes use of the promise we find in the words of Jesus in Mark 13 that the Spirit would accompany believers when they faced courts. The Spirit would help them like a counsellor or advocate in what they should say. The person composing this speech takes this idea and extrapolates from it. The Spirit will accompany the disciples and all disciples as their helper, in place of Jesus, who was also in his own way such a helper. The main thing the Spirit will do is help them recall Jesus and his words to them.

The Focus of the Farewell Speech in John 15–17

When we look at John 15–17, the expansion of the last words of Jesus, we notice that the theme of the Spirit as advocate spawns more reflection. We also find there is a change of focus. Now the concern is unity and love among the disciples. This inspires the image of the vine. Jesus, not Israel, is the true vine but unity with Jesus means unity with each other.

We do not know whether the later parts of John 6 come from the same time as these chapters — perhaps they do — but it is clear that the words of Jesus now address a danger. We see this clearly in Jesus' final prayer. It, too, seems built on the basis of some remembered traditions, especially the Lord's Prayer. It reports Jesus' reflections before God on having completed the journey and task given him. He asks to return to the glory he once shared with the Father. The prayer is summarising the main point of the story of Jesus. He came to make the Father known.

But then halfway through the prayer the attention turns to the chief concern: disunity. When it says that this applies not only to the first disciples but all who follow John's listeners know that this is written for them. These are wonderful words. John's gospel starts the story with God's love in sending Jesus. Love remains the focus because salvation is about responding a call to enter that relationship of love. It is impossible to imagine this as something just about each private individual and God. It is also about love among believers. Unity among believers is not an optional extra, but belongs to the heart of faith.

The theme of mutual love comes much earlier in these chapters, especially in the scene where Jesus washes his disciples' feet and in the famous words: "I give you a new commandment, that you love another as I have loved you. By this shall all people know that you are my disciples if you have love for one another" (13:34-35). Possibly these words belong to the final revision when chapters 15–17 were added. It is in any case thoroughly consistent with the approach of John's gospel where salvation is not a thing, a place, a gift, but primarily a relationship characterised by mutual love.

Unity and Disunity in 1 John

If, as seems likely, John's gospel in its final stages reflects concerns about unity, do we have any further indications of disunity? Our evidence comes in part from 1 John. Strikingly similar in language, it is also strikingly different in the way it uses some of the language and in where it puts the emphasis. The writer implies he is a senior (elder) in the community who has been around from its early days and feels the need to call it back to its values. Probably he is a leading member among the communities where John's gospel was written and so shares its inspiration though in his own way.

In his letter there is a strong emphasis on love, but also strong warnings against failing to love and failing to recognise one's sin. This double focus on warning and comfort addressed a situation doubtless very well known to those who listened to it in the gatherings. The circumstances only begin to emerge for us from 2:18 onwards, where we hear that there has been a split in the community. Some people have left.

The warnings in 4:1-6 suggest that these people have not returned to paganism but have separated because of their claims to the Spirit. Their Spirit-inspired teaching seems to downplay the humanity of Jesus. 5:5-8 suggest they leave out Jesus' death in some way, either denying he really died or denying he died like any other human being. John 19:34-35 may reflect the same concerns when it goes to such lengths to argue that real blood and water came from Jesus' body, i.e. he was a real human being.

Quite possibly those who left interpreted John's gospel to suit their emphases. Perhaps it inspired them. As we have seen, it was controversial. The writer of 1 John who also stands under John's gospel rejects their claims about Jesus and sees their split as evidence of failure to love. He also suggests they were uncaring people anyway. 1 John is full of wonderful statements about love tinged with anger and sadness.

At times anger seems dominant to the extent that the author appears to give up on those who left and encourages people to cease praying for them because they have committed the unpardonable sin. That sin was to give up what the author says is the true faith. When we bring such statements into dialogue with the more rested heart of the gospel, we find that compassion cannot be held back by them.

The writer of 1 John is human. The love of which he spoke even exceeded his expectations and it does ours. There is even room for a Peter who denied Jesus. That is resurrection. John 21 celebrates this reversal of grace in another wonderful dialogue where instead of denying Jesus three times, Peter says yes three times to the question: "Do you love me?"

We find a similar tension in the final book to which we turn, the Book of Revelation.

5D. The Book of Revelation

This, the last book of the Bible, has been the happy hunting ground for all kinds of theories about the end of the world. There are good reasons for this. It speaks about the future. It does so in a veiled way, using symbols and images. It confronts us so often with a puzzle where we have to work out what each image refers to and then try to fit it all together.

Signs and Symbols

Fortunately most of the symbols and images can be deciphered. They are mainly not appearing for the first time. We know of them from other writings which came before John. We also know enough of the political and social problems of the Roman Empire and of Asia Minor (modern-day Turkey) where John and his communities lived. Most of the time we know who is meant.

This makes it essential when reading the Book of Revelation that we use commentaries by scholars who know these writings well and who know the world of that time well. That will help keep us from going off on speculative tangents and making up bizarre theories.

If we read it in its context with a knowledge of its use of symbols and a knowledge of the 1st century, we can see that it is mainly talking to Christian communities under serious threat from Roman authorities and from Jewish opposition. The woman sitting on seven hills, for instance, is an obvious reference to Rome. Babylon was the ancient enemy of Israel, so it is not surprising that Revelation refers to Rome under the name of Babylon and looks forward to its fall.

One of the major problems was the spread of emperor worship, which was particularly strong in Asia Minor. In a day when mortals could sometimes be hailed as gods it was a clever move for rulers to claim a special relation with the divine. In the east (including Israel) it was usual to speak of rulers in this way. Israel's king, for instance, was God's adopted son according to Psalm 2:7. Pharaohs were hailed as gods. Alexander the Great believed himself to be a son of God in this way.

While some treated the trend with scepticism — the emperor Vespasian, for instance, is alleged to have said on his death bed: I fear I am becoming a god! — others took it seriously and promoted it. They erected temples and set up images of themselves as idols to be worshipped. By agreement Jews were exempt from such worship. But once it became clear that Christians were not the same as Jews they faced the requirement to honour the emperor as a god. The more tension between Jews and Christians the more Christians were exposed. Martyrdoms followed. The situation was particularly acute in Asia Minor.

Crisis Literature: The Book of Daniel

People had faced such situations before. The Book of Daniel reflects a similar situation when the Greek king of Syria, Antiochus IV Epiphanes, decided to suppress Jewish religion in 167 BCE. He set up an altar to Zeus in the Jerusalem temple, required the priests to sacrifice pigs, as well as stripping the temple of its wealth to meet his own needs. The attempt at suppression lasted three and a half years.

In this context someone gathered stories about Daniel from earlier times and put together what we now have as the Book of Daniel, the first half in Hebrew, the second half in Aramaic (the only extensive passages of Aramaic in the Bible). Using the story of Daniel as a setting the author reported visions and dreams, perhaps inspired by accounts of dreams already in the stories. Now in the desperate situation of persecution Daniel presents some visions which go right down to the time of 167-164 BCE.

Sometimes the images are very strange. Fortunately the author sometimes explains the vision. This is so in Daniel 8. It speaks of a ram with two horns, one shorter than the other. The second horn grew after the first. The ram came from the east and charged west, north, and south and nothing could resist it. Then a goat came from the west. It "came across the face of the earth without touching the ground." It had a large horn between its eyes. It charged at the ram which was standing beside the river and broke both its horns and trampled on it. At the height of its power, however, the goat's horn broke and in its place four horns grew.

In one of them a little horn "grew exceedingly great toward the south, toward the east, and toward the beautiful land. It grew as high as the host of heaven. It threw down to the earth some of the host and some of the stars, and trampled on them. Even against the prince of the host it acted arrogantly; it took the regular burnt offering away from him and overthrew the place of his sanctuary" (8:9-11).

In the vision Daniel then hears the question how long this state of affairs was to last. The answer: 2300 mornings and evenings. This is just under three and a half years. Daniel has other estimates, all of them approximately this length of time.

In 8:15-17 Daniel asks for an explanation. The angel Gabriel declares that the vision is about the end of time — it certainly was as far as the author of Daniel was concerned! Then we receive the answer to the puzzle.

As for the ram that you saw with the two horns, these are the kings of Media and Persia. The male goat is the king of Greece, and the great horn between its eyes is the first king. As for the horn that was broken, in place of which four others arose, four kingdoms shall arise from his nation, but not with his power (8:20-22).

We know this history well. Of the Medes and the Persians, the latter came to be the leading power. Their last great leader was Darius. The king of Greece is Alexander the Great who defeated Darius and swept across the east as far as India, but then died in his prime at 33 in 324 BCE. His generals struggled over claims to the great empire and finally it was divided into four under four generals. In Israel's immediate vicinity Ptolemy took Egypt and Seleucus, Syria. Next we come to the little horn. This is Antiochus IV Epiphanes. See Appendix C for an outline of key dates in early Jewish history.

At the end of their rule, when the transgressions have reached their full measure, a king of bold countenance shall arise, skilled in intrigue. He shall grow strong in power, shall cause fearful destruction, and shall succeed in what he does. He shall destroy the powerful and the people of the holy ones. By his cunning he shall make deceit prosper under his hand, and in his own mind he shall be great. Without warning he shall destroy many and shall even rise up against the Prince of princes. But he shall be broken, and not by human hands (8:23-25).

He was broken or, at least, Jerusalem (all but the citadel) was liberated by Judas Maccabeus in 164 BCE. Jews still celebrate the rededication of the temple as the Festival of Hanukkah. This had probably not happened by the time Daniel was being written. Here and elsewhere in Daniel we find the faith that God will bring liberation from the oppressor. Exactly how is left open.

This is similar to what we find in the Book of Revelation where there is a similar mood, suggesting its days may be the last days. There are coded references to rulers, most of which we can decipher, but the future solution is left very open. It is rooted in the conviction that the future belongs ultimately to God and God will not abandon his people.

Revelation 12

We shall look briefly at Revelation 12–14. The woman clothed with the sun and moon is an image of Israel, echoing Joseph's dream in Genesis 37:9. The great red dragon also echoes the Old Testament imagery of Leviathan or Rahab, the monster of the deep. Possibly the author is also making connections with the propaganda of the emperor cult which pictured the emperor as Apollo, who in Greek mythology slew the dragon.

The child is the Messiah and refers to Jesus. The emphasis in the vision is not on details of Jesus' life but on its impact. On earth the mother must flee. In heaven Michael expels the dragon (identified as the devil) from heaven. The victory has been won. The dragon then pursues the woman. The images are telling the story of the persecution of God's people (the true Israel, the church).

While the church faces an apparently hopeless situation the author is reminding them that the victory has been won already. Now it is a matter only of time and like Daniel, from whom he borrows much, a rough figure is given of how much longer they must endure (1260 days — three and half years has now become a symbol for: not too long!).

Revelation 13

Next we meet two beasts who are the agents of the dragon. Daniel 7 contains a vision about four beasts coming up out of the sea, a lion, a bear, and a fourth with 10 horns. Revelation combines these elements into one beast and adds that it has 7 heads. 17:9-11 explains these as the seven hills of Rome and also seven emperors, of whom six have come and gone, and an eighth is still to come. This unravels the history in a way that we recognise here as a reference to the Emperor Domitian who ruled 81-96 CE. In addition the wounded 6th head (13:3) must refer to Nero. The fear that he might return some day was widespread and is reflected in 13:3.

We can see Rome's oppression in 13:5-10, including what is probably a reference to the crushing of the Jewish revolt in 70 CE, but also its emperor worship. 13:11-18 brings us a second beast and more concrete detail, probably reflecting the Roman apparatus of emperor worship in Asia Minor on the ground with its temples and priests. People were marked and those without the emperor's mark could not trade (13:16-17). We have also another allusion to Nero who was wounded. The coded allusion, 666, is also most likely to be an allusion to Nero. Letters served as numerals and the Hebrew letters used to write Nero Caesar add up to 666.

Revelation 14

In Revelation 14 the scene changes to one of hope. 144,000 reflects playing with numbers: 12 × 12. It is symbolic of Israel and its 12 tribes, but now refers to Christians. Apparently these are those who remained celibate, if we are meant to take 14:4 literally. They are not, however, alone or superior to others. A multitude of others join them. They gather on Mount Zion. This reflects the prophetic visions which looked to a great gathering and feast of all peoples on Mount Zion, an image which Jesus richly employed and which lies at the base of our Holy Communion, which acts it out in the present. It is an inclusive vision. All peoples come.

The sudden positive turn in Revelation 14 is not without connection to what comes before it in Revelation 12–13. For in 14:7 we hear that the day of judgement has come and 14:8 that Babylon (Rome) is fallen. Later, in Revelation 18 we have a longer version of this celebration of Rome's fall, replete with accounts of its abuses. Revelation 17 pictures Rome as a prostitute sitting on seven hills.

Judgement will fall on those who received the mark of the beast (14:9-11, referring back to 13:16-17). "One like a Son of Man," an allusion to Daniel 7:13-14, will lead in the acts of judgement. Much of what follows describes these judgements. Revelation places great importance on assuring the suffering Christians that their enemies will not only be brought to account but be made to suffer. It is a spirit of vengeance close to hating enemies which jars with the compassion of the gospel and means that we must approach Revelation with a caution informed by the controls and counters of the rest of the New Testament.

Hope in Adversity

From the perspective of people facing Rome's power in Asia Minor hope focused on the demise of Rome. Revelation ends with prospects of that defeat, especially in Revelation 18. Beyond that, however, there is a flood of images which celebrate hope and take us on for a further four chapters.

The celebrations begin in Revelation 19 with scenes of singing in heaven. These meet us first in chapters 4 and 5. The heavenly world is a place of worship and praise. It will doubtless have been seen as a model for praise on earth, so that what we read here may be telling us about how early Christian in Asia Minor worshipped. It is responsive worship, with different voices taking different parts.

19:7 introduces the marriage feast of the lamb. This is a variation on the vision of the great feast for all peoples with Christ as the centre. Christ, the lamb, meets us as an image already in 5:6. Hailed as the Lion of Judah, the Messiah, he appears as a slain lamb, a striking statement about a new kind of power based on vulnerability.

19:11-16 then pictures Christ as the rider of a white horse, faithful and true, the Word of God, who overcomes the enemies. As happens often in Revelation, it is yet another attempt to portray the final victory. The rider and his army destroy the beast and the false prophet (representing Rome and its apparatus in Asia Minor). These are ancient images reaching back to Israel's ancient fears of being surrounded by armies. Visions of hope often included such scenes which then issued in a final victory against the aggressors.

The author recycles these images in a way that speaks to his time, but has the capacity to speak to all situations in which people feel overwhelmed by oppression. This gives to such visions a timeless quality. This is even more so when the author recycles older images of how history might reach its climax. The idea that the Messiah would reign in Jerusalem for a thousand years is one of these. Here only the martyrs take part. It is a first resurrection. This is a special reward. It is also part of the way the author sought to combine traditions of different origin.

Next he envisages a return to conflict and we see another version of the image of Jerusalem as the besieged city (20:7-10). This time the solution is permanent. Satan and his oppressive agents have gone forever. The images come and go swiftly. 20:11-15 describes a final judgement when all will stand before God to be condemned or rewarded. 21 returns to the image of Jerusalem, but now as a city coming down from heaven. 21:9-22 offers a detailed description rich in biblical allusions and symbolism.

The focus is on God's presence, "making all things new" (21:5). The city has no temple and no sun. God and the Lamb are enough (21:22-27). The final chapter enriches the image of the city with echoes of paradise and prophetic images of a fertile stream and miraculously fruitful trees. Almost every verse is an echo of biblical images of hope.

Familiar Strangeness

The Book of Revelation is very strange. For people in churches of the time it would not have seemed quite so strange. Many of them would have known similar writings from the Old Testament, which provides the author with most of his images, especially Daniel and Ezekiel. There were also many other books written in the interim which made extensive use of dreams and visions to address issues of their time. One is probably even earlier than Daniel: 1 Enoch.

Such writings are called "apocalyptic" or revelatory. Usually they take a figure from the past (like Daniel or Enoch) and write either in the person of the ancestor or at least tell that person's story in a way that their dreams and visions relate to much later times. Perhaps the visions and dreams reflected what the authors themselves experienced. Perhaps they reflect careful creativity. Most are reworking images and symbols from previous writers. The use of Daniel in Revelation is a good example. There is an element of poetic licence in this which people would not have seen as fraud or deception. It was an accepted way of writing and inspiring hope.

The Book of Revelation belongs to this category of writing, although it has its own distinctiveness. The author names himself as John of Patmos, not to be confused with the "John" associated with the gospel or the Elder of the epistles. The style and linguistic ability is so different that we need to see John as a person in his own right. It is unusual in this literature to name yourself. John does so and tells us he is on the island of Patmos. He knew the experience of suffering firsthand. It has landed him in exile.

So John is not following the usual pattern of attributing his visions to some ancient figure. They are his own and may reflect actual experiences. Many dreams consist of recycling what we know. John clearly knew biblical material very well. Another peculiarity is the form of the writing. Unlike other such works, it is a letter addressed to concrete communities. It even contains seven mini-letters addressed to individual congregations, addressing local issues which they would have recognised but about which we can largely only guess.

Engaging Revelation

Revelation has been controversial. It nearly did not make it into the New Testament, especially as people realised that the claim it was by the apostle John was not credible. Some churches still do not include it.

Having an apostolic name associated with a writing became an important consideration for those defining what should be treasured, but substance and status as a source of faith also counted highly. This guaranteed Paul's letters, although including some written in his name. The same is true at least for 1 Peter and James. The gospels (and Acts) became linked with leading figures. They also differed significantly in quality from those from later times which were mostly full of legend and speeches reflecting preoccupations of much later times. The combination of assessment and experience (despite some misinformation about authorship) ensured we have the earliest and best selection, at least for the basic core collection of the gospels (Acts), Paul's letters, 1 Peter, and 1 John, which were already beyond dispute by the end of the 2nd century, and of James, Hebrews, and Revelation. The last two failed the criterion of authorship, but content commended them finally.

Revelation is a rich treasury of images and a window on worship. Many hymns have found their inspiration here. It defies oppression and injustice by Rome. In that sense it is very political. It recognises the evil which corrupt and oppressive regimes can perpetrate. Its understanding of salvation includes these larger dimensions and could never be reduced to the hope for individuals to be happy in heaven. God is the one who seeks to make all things new.

While it recycles the cries and creativity of hope from former times, its own contribution has been a source of inspiration for many over the past 2000 years. Attempts to see in it a coded reference to contemporary politics have ended in a succession of embarrassments, but they will persist, especially among people unaware of its original setting and style of writing. 666 is not a reference to credit cards! Babylon is not the European Community, nor Saddam Hussein, nor Russia or China!

Setting such bizarre interpretations aside, Revelation may still alert us to dimensions of oppression in our own time. It may still inspire some to hold out against what seem to be impossible odds. It will still support the defiant belief that there must be change and that love must bring renewal. But usually this is only possible with a good deal of translation.

We can pick off the gems, the wonderful phrases, and take up inspiring scenes of watered trees and cities of hope. But most of it is rather inaccessible and only to be fathomed with informed commentary in hand. Even then the book confronts us with attitudes at times which we cannot reconcile easily with the good news if at all. Critical engagement is essential if we are to take this writing seriously. It is a place for discovery and hope — but its tourists need to be well equipped for its difficult terrain.

Beyond Revelation

The Book of Revelation was neither the last New Testament book to be written — that honour goes to 2 Peter — nor the last book inspired by the new faith. Clement, bishop of Rome, wrote to the Corinthians in the 90's. The letter is known as 1 Clement. From not long after we have sermons such as the so-called Letter of Barnabas and collected teachings, such as The Didache. The 2nd century also saw the production of many new gospels. Of those which have survived, the Gospel of Thomas has attracted most interest, because it contains mainly sayings of Jesus, some of which are not in the four earlier gospels. It reflects the later period and its issues, but it seems to be based on a collection of sayings which many think is as old as those in the earlier gospels.

One of the reasons for the proliferation of gospels and legends about the early church was simply the desire of pious minds to imagine the past and fill in the gaps. They were not beyond extending what was already a technique used by writers of biblical books, namely passing off their works as written by someone long since dead. The outcomes in the 2nd century were often bizarre, such as in the Infancy Gospel of Thomas, which depicts the boy Jesus performing magic and behaving petulantly when crossed.

Gospels of "New Ideas"

Another impulse came from inspirational experiences in which people claimed to have learned new ideas. Many of the new gospels claim to have extensive information about teaching Jesus is said to have given after his resurrection. Some suggest that Jesus had his favourites to whom he communicated secrets. We see the beginning of this trend in the figure of the beloved disciple in John's gospel. Others sought to justify their new slant on Christian faith by claiming that it came to special disciples, whom Jesus especially befriended, and of whom the other disciples then became jealous.

In reality, we are seeing the conflicts of the 2nd century being played out in the stories. These writers and their communities rejected the church which took the old gospels as its authority and sought to preserve what it saw as the apostles' teaching. So we learn in the Gospel of Mary Magdalene, for instance, that she developed a particular liaison with Jesus, from whom in pillow talk, as it were, she learned new teachings which contradicted the beliefs of the other disciples and of the church of the traditional gospels. Similarly the recently discovered Gospel according to Judas claims a unique and positive role for Judas, from whom, then, the 2nd-century movement of its author learned their new ideas.

Such movements are generally known as "gnostic" because they claim to know *(gno)* secrets which will set people free. In the case of these and many other similar gospels, the secret knowledge relates to what it means to be a human being. It teaches that we are sparks of light who belong to another world, but are trapped in a world of material created by a evil god. This turns Genesis on its head. It also entails a very negative attitude towards our humanity as flesh and blood and often leads to disparagement of sexuality, because it is the mechanism that keeps reproducing this evil material.

Thus in the Gospel according to Judas, Jesus can thank Judas because his action will lead to the sacrifice of the man who clothes Jesus. The flesh and blood human Jesus is, according to this view, not the real Jesus, but just a kind of garment for the true light within. In a bizarre twist, this leads to the conclusion that Judas was doing Jesus a favour!

Such views sound strange to modern ears and were considered by most in the church of their time as an aberration. We need to see, however, that they might make sense for people who saw no hope in this world and could contemplate hope only as a kind of escape into another world. They had strong appeal, as do messages of escape in every age. They still live on today within Christianity in less radical forms, but wherever faith sees hope largely as something unrelated to this world.

The seeds of such thought were present from very early in the movement. The church of those days rejected these trends with a mixture of good and bad arguments, but inspired by its tradition, which insisted that Jesus really was human, that creation really is something good, from a good God, and this God was present in a unique way in Jesus. The conflicts seem to lie already behind 1 John, as we have seen. At stake, ultimately, was an affirmation of reality and a refusal to avoid it.

Conclusion

It requires considerable imagination to take oneself back 2000 years into the world of the New Testament. Not only is there the vast difference in time. There is also a vast difference in culture, not to speak of language. Yet more than ever before we live in a world where we meet people of different cultures and religious backgrounds. At worst we may insist that they should all learn our language and change their ways to become just like us. At best we learn their language and open our eyes and ears and our minds to encounter the richness and diversity of different peoples.

Even in meeting people within cultures familiar to us where we all speak the same language, communication can be a challenge. We all know people who never listen properly or only hear what they want to hear. And sometimes we may feel that we have not been met at all. Rather we have simply been used and are left feeling that people have not been taken us seriously or treated us with respect. That can happen where people do not like us. It can also happen when they put us on a pedestal and we want to plead: please accept me as I am! I sometimes imagine New Testament writers saying that.

Our encounter with the New Testament has been an attempt to take its writings seriously. That includes listening as carefully as possible to what is being said and not reading into them our own ideas. It has included taking them seriously in their own terms, in their own cultural and religious world. It has included also treating them with respect, indeed, as holy, which is how, I would argue, we should treat all people. It has also meant, therefore, neither disparaging them nor putting them on a pedestal. We do not have to change the natural sense of what they say to make it fit our ideas. We can listen openly, with our hearts and our minds full engaged in what we are doing.

Strangely and wonderfully it has been the experience of so many that such listening to these writings across the vast chasm of time and culture can have the effect of bringing us into a close encounter which speaks to us today with immediate relevance. Sometimes it is almost as though the more we respect the distance the closer they come. Our shorthand for such experiences is to say that in this way they become God's word to us. In some ways this should not surprise us. People writing from a deep faith and in close proximity to Jesus in the formative days of the church are likely to have produced writings which carry the glow of that fire. The same God, the same Spirit of Christ, which energised them, energised their texts and can be felt 2000 years later.

In its first centuries the church gathered such writings into what we now call the New Testament. The core was established within 150 years, the rest within the next two centuries. They became the authoritative writings. Not that the Spirit of Christ ceased to be active in people's lives, but these were special writings from a special time. They became a reference point for measuring new claims and a valuable tool for showing where such claims cohered with the church's ancient tradition and where they did not.

One response to the power of these writings to evoke encounters with God in the present was to claim them to be God's word in a very literal sense. This threatened to remove them from their rootedness in history and human experience. The Bible then becomes an infallible book, stripped of its humanity and culture and deemed to be valid in all its pronouncements for all time, like a legal document. Even the most ardent proponents of this view find it impossible to sustain. Exceptions are made for things like covering women's heads in church. More moderate exponents compromise the position further by acknowledging cultural factors which have left their trace in the attitudes of New Testament writers to slavery, women, and a number of other features. This makes good sense.

Today there is still a wide range of approaches, but most take some notice of the context within which the New Testament writers lived and wrote. Some prefer to uphold the authority of scripture on a more formal basis of asserting all statements authoritative except those which more obviously reflect cultural values no longer appropriate for out time. Others prefer to focus on core emphases with which they identify and which have spoken to them and to measure the rest on that basis. That allows greater flexibility, and comes close at time to those who prefer the formal approach.

Ultimately, people keep reading New Testament texts primarily because they so often address issues that are at the core of what it means to be a human being and a human community in this world before God. One may define their authority in various ways, but the authority which counts most is when we feel ourselves addressed by God through what we read. That need not mean that we must force these writings into a mould so that we listen to them only selectively, only looking for an authoritative word from God.

We need to listen to them openly, including critically, allowing them to speak in their own terms and to be what they are without our prejudgements and prejudices, positive or negative. That demands discipline but also imagination. It means we need to understand more of their world or at least to make use of resources from people who have made that their area of study. Not all of us will be able to learn the languages, let alone spend the required time to develop an adequate grasp of their culture. Fortunately, we have access to the writings which they treasured as sacred, namely, the Hebrew Scriptures, commonly called the Old Testament. In recent years we have also been able to recover a large body of other writings, some at the Dead Sea, which have enriched our understanding of how people thought in those days and what they hoped for. On pages 194-195 below, there is a list of useful resources for those wishing to find out more about the New Testament, generally, and about the world of its time. For further study of specific New Testament passages see also my weekly on-line commentaries on the Revised Common Lectionary: http://wwwstaff.murdoch.edu.au/~loader/.

Sometimes we meet people for the first time and we know that something profound takes place. That can be the same in reading the New Testament or hearing it read. It is a treasure entrusted to the church, a garden where faith finds nourishment and beauty. If we are to tend the garden and ensure it is open for all to enjoy, we are going to need to know something about its plants, their origins, when they flower, and how they grow. We may even develop the expertise to give every plant its botanical name and explain every last detail at the highest level. But that will mean little if we do not take time to enjoy the garden itself.

Conclusion

Ultimately the joy is the garden, its surprises, its bright colour and its dark places, its gentle blossoms and its hidden thorns. The New Testament writings were written by real people for real people. When we enter their world in their writings, we walk in a garden of life that still carries the seeds of hope for our own world. It is a garden to enjoy and a garden to share. May these ventures in imagining and the samplings of text in this book enrich your experience of the garden.

Appendices

A. The New Testament Writings in Overview

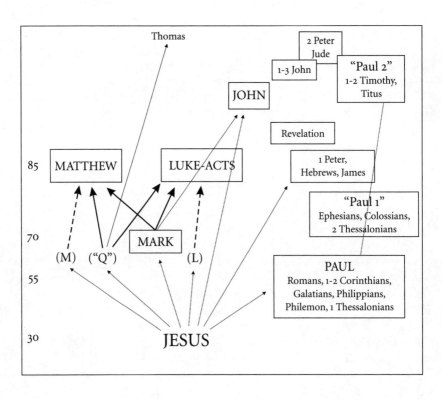

B. Matthew's Use of Mark in Outline

This table is designed to be viewed rather than to be read. It should enable you to see at a glance how the gospels relate and should also provide you a tool for your own exploration.

CAPITALS = from Q
italics = Matthew's independent material
normal = from Mark

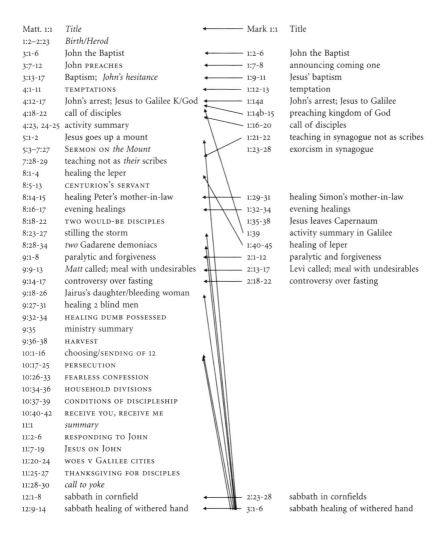

Matt. 1:1	*Title*	←———	Mark 1:1	Title
1:2–2:23	*Birth/Herod*			
3:1-6	John the Baptist	←———	1:2-6	John the Baptist
3:7-12	John PREACHES	←———	1:7-8	announcing coming one
3:13-17	Baptism; *John's hesitance*	←———	1:9-11	Jesus' baptism
4:1-11	TEMPTATIONS	←———	1:12-13	temptation
4:12-17	John's arrest; Jesus to Galilee K/God	←———	1:14a	John's arrest; Jesus to Galilee
4:18-22	call of disciples		1:14b-15	preaching kingdom of God
4:23, 24-25	activity summary		1:16-20	call of disciples
5:1-2	Jesus goes up a mount		1:21-22	teaching in synagogue not as scribes
5:3–7:27	SERMON ON *the Mount*		1:23-28	exorcism in synagogue
7:28-29	teaching not as *their* scribes			
8:1-4	healing the leper			
8:5-13	CENTURION'S SERVANT			
8:14-15	healing Peter's mother-in-law	←———	1:29-31	healing Simon's mother-in-law
8:16-17	evening healings	←———	1:32-34	evening healings
8:18-22	TWO WOULD-BE DISCIPLES		1:35-38	Jesus leaves Capernaum
8:23-27	stilling the storm		1:39	activity summary in Galilee
8:28-34	*two* Gadarene demoniacs		1:40-45	healing of leper
9:1-8	paralytic and forgiveness		2:1-12	paralytic and forgiveness
9:9-13	*Matt* called; meal with undesirables	←———	2:13-17	Levi called; meal with undesirables
9:14-17	controversy over fasting	←———	2:18-22	controversy over fasting
9:18-26	Jairus's daughter/bleeding woman			
9:27-31	healing 2 blind men			
9:32-34	HEALING DUMB POSSESSED			
9:35	ministry summary			
9:36-38	HARVEST			
10:1-16	choosing/SENDING OF 12			
10:17-25	PERSECUTION			
10:26-33	FEARLESS CONFESSION			
10:34-36	HOUSEHOLD DIVISIONS			
10:37-39	CONDITIONS OF DISCIPLESHIP			
10:40-42	RECEIVE YOU, RECEIVE ME			
11:1	*summary*			
11:2-6	RESPONDING TO JOHN			
11:7-19	JESUS ON JOHN			
11:20-24	WOES V GALILEE CITIES			
11:25-27	THANKSGIVING FOR DISCIPLES			
11:28-30	*call to yoke*			
12:1-8	sabbath in cornfield	←———	2:23-28	sabbath in cornfields
12:9-14	sabbath healing of withered hand	←———	3:1-6	sabbath healing of withered hand

12:15-21	*expanded activity*	3:7-12	expanded activity
12:22-30	BEELZEBUB	3:13-19	up a mount choosing the 12
12:31-37	sin AGAINST SPIRIT	3:20-21	family fears mad
12:38-42	SIGN OF JONAH	3:22-30	accused of madness: Beelzebub
12:43-45	SPIRITS' RETURN	3:30-35	Jesus' true family
12:46-50	Jesus and family	4:1-20	parable sower/interpretation
13:1-23	parable sower/interpretation	4:21-25	parabolic sayings
13:24-30	*parable of weeds*	4:26-29	parable secretly growing seed
13:31-32	parable MUSTARD SEED	4:30-32	parable mustard seed
13:33	PARABLE LEAVEN	4:33-34	more about parables
13:34-35	more about parables	4:35-41	stilling the storm
13:36-43	*interpreting weeds*	5:1-20	Gerasene demoniac
13:44-46	*parables treasure and pearl*	5:21-43	Jairus's daughter/ bleeding woman
13:47-50	*parable fishnet*	6:1-6a	Nazareth synagogue
13:51-52	*true scribe*	6:6b-13	sending out the 12
13:53-58	Nazareth synagogue	6:14-16	Herod on Jesus: Elijah, pr. John?
14:1-2	Herod on Jesus: John?	6:17-29	Herod killed John
14:3-12	Herod kills John; *disciples tell Jesus*	6:30-31	disciples return to Jesus
14:13-21	feeding 5000	6:32-44	feeding 5000
14:22-33	Crossing — Jesus + *Peter* on water	6:45-52	crossing; Jesus walks on water
14:34-36	healings at Gennesaret	6:53-56	healings at Gennesaret
15:1-20	Jesus disputes purity interpretations	7:1-23	Jesus disputes purity laws
15:21-28	Canaanite woman	7:24-30	Syrophoenician
15:29-39	healing on mt and feeding 4000	7:31-37	healing deaf/dumb man Decapolis
16:1-4	Pharisees/Sadducees seek a sign	8:1-10	feeding 4000
16:5-12	beware leaven note 5000/4000	8:11-13	Pharisees seek sign
16:13-16	Peter's confession	8:14-21	beware leaven 5000 and 4000
16:17-20	*Peter's authority*	8:22-26	healing Bethsaida blind man
16:21	Son of Man prediction	8:27-30	Peter's confession
16:22-23	Peter's rebuke	8:31-33	Son of Man prediction
16:24-26	disciples to suffer/Son of Man	8:32-33	Peter's rebuke
17:1-9	transfiguration.	8:34–9:1	disciples to suffer/Son of Man
17:10-13	Elijah and John	9:2-10	transfiguration
17:14-21	exorcising boy	9:11-13	John and Elijah
17:22-23	Son of Man prediction	9:14-29	exorcising boy
17:24-27	*temple tax*	9:30-32	Son of Man prediction
18:1-5	dispute over greatest	9:33-37	dispute about greatest
18:6-9	warning AGAINST ABUSE	9:38-41	strange exorcist
18:10	*angels of the little ones*	9:42-50	warnings
18:11-14	PARABLE OF LOST SHEEP		
18:15-18	*community discipline*		
18:19-20	*two or three*		
18:21-22	FORGIVENESS 77×		
18:23-35	*unforgiving servant*		
19:1-2	setting off for Judea	10:1	setting off for Judea
19:3-9	divorce	10:2-9	divorce controversy
19:10-12	*house: eunuchs*	10:10-12	divorce/remarriage
19:13-15	blessing children	10:13-16	blessing children
19:16-29	rich *young* man/dangers of riches	10:17-22	rich man/danger of riches
19:30	first last, last first		
20:1-15	*labourers in vineyard*		
20:16	last first, first last	10:31	first last; last first
20:17-19	Son of Man prediction	10:32-34	Son of Man prediction
20:20-28	James and John's *mother*	10:35-45	James and John
20:29-34	*two* blind men	10:46-52	blind Bartimaeus

21:1-9	entry into Jerusalem	←	11:1-10	entry into Jerusalem
21:10-17	temple expulsion		11:11	entering temple
21:20-22	fig tree cursed/withered		11:12-14	cursing fig tree
21:23-27	Jesus and John's authority		11:15-19	temple expulsion
21:28-32	*parable two sons*		11:20-21	withered fig tree
21:33-46	parable vineyard		11:22-24	faith/prayer
22:1-14	*parable* WEDDING FEAST		11:25	forgiving
22:15-22	tax		11:27-33	Jesus and John's authority
22:23-33	Sadducees/resurrection		12:1-12	vineyard parable
22:34-40	greatest commandment		12:13-17	tax
22:41-46	David's son		12:18-27	Sadducees/resurrection
23:1-36	ATTACKS *on scribes and Pharisees*		12:28-34	greatest commandment
24:1-36	temple and the end		12:35-37	Son of David
24:37-44	. . . AS NOAH . . .		12:38-40	attack on scribes
24:45-51	PARABLE OF SLAVES		12:41-44	widow's offering
25:1-13	*parable of ten girls*		13:1-37	temple and end
25:14-30	PARABLE OF TALENTS			
25:31-46	*parable of judgement*			
26:1-5	plot to kill Jesus	←	14:1-2	plot to kill Jesus
26:6-13	anointing at Bethany	←	14:3-9	Bethany anointing
26:14-16	Judas betrays	←	14:10-11	Judas betrays Jesus
26:17-20	preparing Passover	←	14:12-16	preparing Passover
26:21-25	identifying betrayer	←	14:17-21	warning re betrayer
26:26-29	last meal	←	14:22-25	last meal
26:30-35	predicts denial and scattering	←	14:26-31	predicts denial and scattering
26:36-56	Gethsemane/arrest	←	14:32-52	Gethsemane/arrest
26:57-58	Peter enters	←	14:53-54	Peter enters
26:59-66	Jewish trial	←	14:55-64	Jewish trial
26:67-68	humiliation	←	14:65	humiliation of Jesus
26:69-75	Peter's denial	←	14:66-72	Peter's denial
27:1-2	handover to Pilate	←	15:1	handover to Pilate
27:3-10	*Judas's fate*			
27:11-14	trial before Pilate	←	15:2-5	trial before Pilate
27:15-23	Barabbas + *wife's dream*	←	15:6-14	Barabbas
27:24-26	verdict + *washes hands*	←	15:15	verdict
27:27-31	soldiers mock	←	15:16-20a	soldiers mock
27:31-44	crucifixion	←	15:20b-32	crucifixion
27:45-54	death	←	15:33-39	death
27:55-56	women witnesses	←	15:40-41	women witnesses
27:57-61	burial	←	15:42-61	burial
27:62-66	*setting guards*			
28:1-8	empty tomb	←	16:1-8	empty tomb
28:9-10	*women meet Jesus*			
28:11-15	*lie: body theft*			
28:16-20	*commission*			

C. Luke's Use of Mark in Outline

This table is designed to be viewed rather than to be read. It should enable you to see at a glance how the gospels relate and should also provide you a tool for your own exploration.

CAPITALS = from Q
italics = Luke's independent material
normal = from Mark

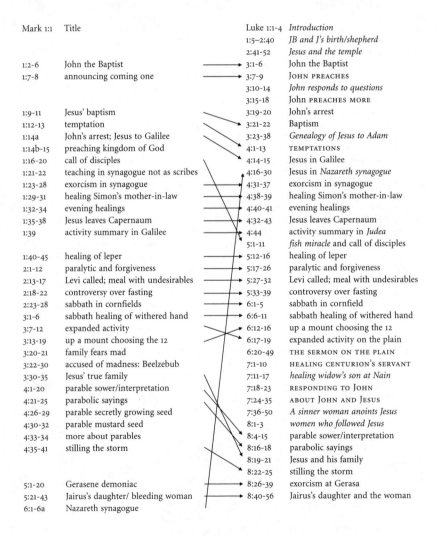

Mark 1:1	Title		Luke 1:1-4	*Introduction*
			1:5–2:40	*JB and J's birth/shepherd*
			2:41-52	*Jesus and the temple*
1:2-6	John the Baptist	→	3:1-6	John the Baptist
1:7-8	announcing coming one	→	3:7-9	JOHN PREACHES
			3:10-14	*John responds to questions*
			3:15-18	John PREACHES MORE
1:9-11	Jesus' baptism		3:19-20	John's arrest
1:12-13	temptation		3:21-22	Baptism
1:14a	John's arrest; Jesus to Galilee		3:23-38	*Genealogy of Jesus to Adam*
1:14b-15	preaching kingdom of God		4:1-13	TEMPTATIONS
1:16-20	call of disciples		4:14-15	Jesus in Galilee
1:21-22	teaching in synagogue not as scribes		4:16-30	Jesus in *Nazareth synagogue*
1:23-28	exorcism in synagogue		4:31-37	exorcism in synagogue
1:29-31	healing Simon's mother-in-law		4:38-39	healing Simon's mother-in-law
1:32-34	evening healings		4:40-41	evening healings
1:35-38	Jesus leaves Capernaum		4:32-43	Jesus leaves Capernaum
1:39	activity summary in Galilee		4:44	activity summary in *Judea*
			5:1-11	*fish miracle* and call of disciples
1:40-45	healing of leper	→	5:12-16	healing of leper
2:1-12	paralytic and forgiveness	→	5:17-26	paralytic and forgiveness
2:13-17	Levi called; meal with undesirables	→	5:27-32	Levi called; meal with undesirables
2:18-22	controversy over fasting	→	5:33-39	controversy over fasting
2:23-28	sabbath in cornfields		6:1-5	sabbath in cornfield
3:1-6	sabbath healing of withered hand		6:6-11	sabbath healing of withered hand
3:7-12	expanded activity		6:12-16	up a mount choosing the 12
3:13-19	up a mount choosing the 12		6:17-19	expanded activity on the plain
3:20-21	family fears mad		6:20-49	THE SERMON ON THE PLAIN
3:22-30	accused of madness: Beelzebub		7:1-10	HEALING CENTURION'S SERVANT
3:30-35	Jesus' true family		7:11-17	*healing widow's son at Nain*
4:1-20	parable sower/interpretation		7:18-23	RESPONDING TO JOHN
4:21-25	parabolic sayings		7:24-35	ABOUT JOHN AND JESUS
4:26-29	parable secretly growing seed		7:36-50	*A sinner woman anoints Jesus*
4:30-32	parable mustard seed		8:1-3	*women who followed Jesus*
4:33-34	more about parables		8:4-15	parable sower/interpretation
4:35-41	stilling the storm		8:16-18	parabolic sayings
			8:19-21	Jesus and his family
			8:22-25	stilling the storm
5:1-20	Gerasene demoniac	→	8:26-39	exorcism at Gerasa
5:21-43	Jairus's daughter/ bleeding woman	→	8:40-56	Jairus's daughter and the woman
6:1-6a	Nazareth synagogue			

Luke's Use of Mark in Outline

6:6b-13	sending out the 12	→	9:1-6	sending out the 12
6:14-16	Herod on Jesus: Elijah, pr. John?	→	9:7-9	Herod about Jesus
6:17-29	Herod killed John		9:10a	return of the apostles
6:30-31	disciples return to Jesus		9:10b-17	feeding the 5000
6:32-44	feeding 5000		9:18-21	Peter's confession
6:45-52	crossing; Jesus walks on water		9:22	Son of Man prediction
6:53-56	healings at Gennesaret		9:23-27	disciples to suffer/Son of Man
7:1-23	Jesus disputes purity laws		9:28-36	transfiguration
7:24-30	Syrophoenician		9:37-43a	exorcising a boy
7:31-37	healing deaf/dumb man Decapolis		9:43b-45	Son of Man prediction
8:1-10	feeding 4000		9:46-48	dispute over greatest
8:11-13	Pharisees seek sign		9:49-50	strange exorcist
8:14-21	beware leaven 5000 and 4000		9:51	setting off for Jerusalem
8:22-26	healing Bethsaida blind man		9:52-56	*rejection in Samaria*
8:27-30	Peter's confession		9:57-62	CHALLENGES TO FOLLOWERS
8:31-33	Son of Man prediction		10:1-12	SENDING OUT 70
8:32-33	Peter's rebuke		10:13-15	WOES V GALILEAN CITIES
8:34–9:1	disciples to suffer/Son of Man		10:16-20	WHO HEARS YOU / RETURN OF 70
9:2-10	transfiguration		10:21-24	JESUS' THANKSGIVIING FOR DISCIPLES
9:11-13	John and Elijah		10:25-28	lawyer's question about life
9:14-29	exorcising boy		10:29-37	*parable of good Samaritan*
9:30-32	Son of Man prediction		10:38-42	*Mary and Martha*
9:33-37	dispute about greatest		11:1-4	PRAYER AND THE LORD'S PRAYER
9:38-41	strange exorcist		11:5-8	*parable of midnight friend*
9:42-50	warnings		11:9-13	*hearing prayer*
10:1	setting off for Judea		11:14-23	BEELZEBUB CONTROVERSY
			11:24-26	WARNING ABOUT SPIRITS
			11:27-28	*not mother but obedient blessed*
			11:29-32	SIGN OF JONAH
			11:33-36	LAMP; EYE AS LIGHT
			11:37-38	*controversy over immersion*
			11:39-54	ATTACK ON PHARISEES AND LAWYERS
			12:1	warning about leaven of Pharisees
			12:2-9	FEARLESS CONFESSION
			12:10-12	SIN V SPIRIT AND HELP
			12:13-15	*anecdote on greed*
			12:16-21	*parable of rich fool*
			12:22-34	ANXIETY/TREASURES
			12:35-53	WATCHFULNESS/ DIVISIONS
			12:54-56	SIGNS OF TIMES
			13:1-9	*parable of unfruitful fig tree*
			13:10-17	*sabbath healing crippled woman*
			13:18-21	PARABLE OF MUSTARD SEED/LEAVEN
			13:22-30	EXCLUSION FROM THE KINGDOM
			13:34-35	LAMENT OVER JERUSALEM
			14:1-6	*sabbath healing of dropsy*
			14:7-14	*seating at meals*
			14:15-24	PARABLE OF GREAT FEAST
			14:25-35	CONDITIONS FOR DISCIPLESHIP/SALT
			15:1-7	PARABLE OF LOST SHEEP
			15:8-10	*parable of lost coin*
			15:11-32	*parable of prodigal son*
			16:1-9	*parable on unjust steward*
			16:10-13	*being faithful/serving* 2 MASTERS
			16:14-15	*attack on Pharisees*

		16:16-17	LAW AND PROPHETS
10:2-9	divorce controversy	16:18	*divorce*
10:10-12	divorce/remarriage	16:19-31	*parable of rich man and Lazarus*
		17:1-3a	AGAINST ABUSE
		17:3b-4	FORGIVENESS 7 TIMES
		17:5-6	faith as grain of mustard seed
		17:7-10	*unprofitable slaves*
		17:11-19	*healing ten lepers*
10:13-16	blessing children	17:20-37	DAY OF THE SON OF MAN
10:17-22	rich man/danger of riches	18:1-8	*parable of unjust judge*
10:31	first last; last first	18:9-14	*parable of Pharisee and publican*
10:32-34	Son of Man prediction	18:15-17	blessing the children
10:35-45	James and John	18:18-30	rich ruler/dangers of riches
10:46-52	blind Bartimaeus	18:31-34	Son of Man prediction
11:1-10	entry into Jerusalem	18:35-43	healing of blind man
11:11	entering temple	19:1-10	*Zacchaeus*
11:12-14	cursing fig tree	19:11-27	PARABLE OF KING'S MONEY
11:15-19	temple expulsion	19:28-40	entry into Jerusalem
11:20-21	withered fig tree	19:41-44	*weeping over Jerusalem*
11:22-24	faith/prayer	19:45-48	temple expulsion
11:25	forgiving	20:1-8	Jesus' and John's authority
11:27-33	Jesus and John's authority	20:9-19	parable of vineyard
12:1-12	vineyard parable	20:20-26	tax
12:13-17	tax	20:27-40	Sadducees on resurrection
12:18-27	Sadducees/resurrection	20:41-44	David's son
12:28-34	greatest commandment	20:45-47	attack on scribes
12:35-37	Son of David	21:1-4	widow's offering
12:38-40	attack on scribes	21:5-33	temple and end
12:41-44	widow's offering	21:34-36	WARNING TO WATCH
13:1-37	temple and end	22:1-2	plan to kill Jesus
14:1-2	plot to kill Jesus	22:3-6	Judas betrays
14:3-9	Bethany anointing	22:7-14	preparing for Passover
14:10-11	Judas betrays Jesus	22:15-20	Passover/last meal
14:12-16	preparing Passover	22:21-23	warning re betrayer
14:17-21	warning re betrayer	22:24-30	dispute over greatest
14:22-25	last meal	22:31-34	prediction and *prayer for Peter*
14:26-31	predicts denial and scattering	22:35-38	*getting swords*
14:32-52	Gethsemane/arrest	22:39-53	Gethsemane/Arrest
14:53-54	Peter enters	22:54-62	Peter follows/denies
14:55-64	Jewish trial	22:63-65	humiliation
14:65	humiliation of Jesus	22:66-71	Jewish trial *morning*
14:66-72	Peter's denial	23:1	delivery to Pilate
15:1	handover to Pilate	23:2-5	trial before Pilate
15:2-5	trial before Pilate	23:6-12	*before Herod Antipas*
15:6-14	Barabbas	23:13-16	"Not guilty" — Pilate
15:15	verdict	23:17-23	Barabbas
15:16-20a	soldiers mock	23:24-25	Pilate's verdict
15:20b-32	crucifixion	23:26-43	crucifixion
15:33-39	death	23:44-48	Jesus' death
15:40-41	women witnesses	23:49	women witnesses
15:42-61	burial	23:50-56	burial
16:1-8	empty tomb	24:1-12	empty tomb
		24:13-35	*Emmaus appearance*
		24:36-43	*Appearance to 11*
		24:44-53	*Last words*

D. Some Significant Dates in Early Jewish History

538   Persians (Cyrus) conquer Babylonia and allow the return of the exiles

520-515 Rebuilding of the temple; 5th-cent. return of Ezra/Nehemiah: walls rebuilt/ Pentateuch settled; early 4th cent. Samaritans alienated/build temple at Gerizim

333   Alexander the Great defeats Persians at Issus, extends empire as far as India, bringing Hellenistic culture/language

323   Alexander dies; by 300 his generals control Egypt and Palestine (Ptolemy) and Syria (Seleucus)

200   Syrian Antiochus III takes Palestine from Egypt; more Hellenisation

175   Rivals (Onias III, Jason, his brother, and Menelaus) claiming high priesthood in Jerusalem appeal to Antiochus IV Epiphanes, who exploits the situation to gain wealth to pay tribute to the conquering Romans, plundering temple wealth in 169

167-164 The Maccabean Revolt. Antiochus acts to suppress Judaism, forbidding circumcision, sabbath observance, enforcing pagan sacrifice, setting up an altar to Zeus in the temple (Dan 11:31); the Hasmonean Mattathias initiates a revolt with success under his son, Judas, called "Maccabeus" (= hammerer) with the support of the anti-Hellenist pious (*hasidim* = holy ones). The story is retold in 1 and 2 Maccabees and is the setting for writing of the Book of Daniel

164   Judas liberates Jerusalem; the temple is rededicated

162   Alcimus, a Zadokite, is appointed high priest

161   Jonathan succeeds Judas (killed in battle), plays politics to keep in power, like his successors till well into the 1st century, by exploiting internal divisions in Syria

152   Jonathan (non-Zadokite) claims high priesthood (a deal with a Seleucid rival, Alexander Balas); some disaffected

143   Jonathan is executed by the Syrians. His brother, Simon (143-134), takes the Jerusalem citadel. Hasmonean dynasty (143-63): John Hyrcanus (134-105) forcibly converts Idumeans, destroys Samaritan temple (128); Aristobulus I (105-103); Alexander Janneus/Jonathan (103-76): his territory was as large as Solomon's, in 88 crucifies 800 Pharisees who collaborated with Seleucid Demetrius III. Succeeded by his widow, Salome Alexandra (76-67), favourable to Pharisees, and Aristobulus II (67-63)

64   Roman general, Pompey, appealed to by Hasmonean rivals (Hyrcanus II and Aristobulus II), enters Jerusalem and temple in 63, with commander Aemilius Scaurus, supports Hyrcanus II as high priest (63-40) with strong man Antipater (Idumean). Jews play politics in supporting rival Romans and win favour for their religion by sending troops to aid the winning side under Julius Caesar

40-37   Parthian invasion puts the rival Hasmonean faction (Antigonus) in power briefly. 37 Romans defeat Parthians and install Antipater's son, Herod (the Great), 37-4B CE, clever, ruthless, noted for building programmes (upgrading temple); Jesus of Nazareth born near the end of his reign

4 BCE   Unrest on Herod's death (especially in Galilee). Herod's sons appointed: Philip, tetrarch of north Transjordan (33 CE); Antipas, tetrarch of Perea and Galilee (39 CE); Archelaus, ethnarch of Judea — deposed 6 CE on complaints to Rome from the populace because of oppression and cruelty

6 CE   Romans install prefects in Judea, hold census; revolts (Judas of Galilee)

26-36   Pilate as prefect, cruel, anti-Jewish, finally recalled; has Jesus crucified on charge of pretensions to kingship and subversion by 41 Herod Agrippa I (grandson of Herod) had been placed over the three territories

44   Agrippa kills James son of Zebedee (Acts 12), dies, is replaced by procurators; his son Agrippa II is set over small territory in the north, then Philip's region

50s & 60s   under Felix, Festus and Gessius Florus: growing Jewish nationalism; Paul falls victim to it; and James, the brother of Jesus, is killed in 62; revolutionary movements sporadically rise and fall

66-70   1st Jewish War: priests cease the sacrifice for the emperor, uprising is successful in Jerusalem and elsewhere

67   Vespasian reconquers Galilee (Josephus, Jewish general, taken, accompanies the Romans, later writes a history of the war)

68   Qumran destroyed (settled since late 2nd century BCE by disaffected religious group related to the Essenes) — library hidden in caves

70   Jerusalem falls, defence by factions in conflict among themselves (Zealots, Sicarii) finally fails before Titus; the temple is destroyed; rebels hold out at fortress Masada till 74

132-135   2nd Jewish War. Simon Bar Kochba. Jerusalem captured and levelled

For Further Reading

Aland, Kurt (ed.). *Synopsis of the Four Gospels: Completely Revised on the Basis of the Greek Text of the Nestle Aland (English-only text)* (26th ed.; New York: United Bible Societies, 1982) (excellent resource for comparing gospels)

General Introductions

Brown, Raymond E. *Introduction to the New Testament* (Anchor Bible; New York: Doubleday, 1997)

Duling, Dennis C. *The New Testament: History, Literature, and Social Context* (4th ed.; Belmont: Wadsworth, 2002)

Harris, Stephen. *The New Testament: A Student's Introduction* (5th ed.; Boston: McGraw-Hill, 2004)

Holladay, Carl R. *A Critical Introduction To The New Testament: Interpreting The Message And Meaning Of Jesus Christ* (Nashville: Abingdon, 2005)

Jesus and the Gospels

Dunn, James D. G. *Jesus Remembered* (Christianity in the Making, Vol. 1; Grand Rapids: Eerdmans, 2003)

Freyne, Sean. *Jesus, a Jewish Galilean: A New Reading of the Jesus-story* (London/ New York: T&T Clark, 2004)

Murphy, Frederick J. *An Introduction to Jesus and the Gospels* (Nashville: Abingdon, 2005)

Powell, Mark Allan. *Jesus as a Figure in History: How Modern Historians View the Man from Galilee* (Louisville: Westminster John Knox, 1998)

Stanton, Graham N. *The Gospels and Jesus* (2d ed.; Oxford Bible Series; New York: Oxford University Press, 2002)

Paul

Dunn, James D. G. *The Cambridge Companion to St Paul* (Cambridge Companions to Religion; Cambridge: Cambridge University Press, 2003)

Horrell, David G. *An Introduction to the Study of Paul* (Approaches to Biblical Studies; London/New York: T&T Clark, 2005)

Sanders, Ed. P. *Paul: A Very Short Introduction* (Very Short Introductions; New York: Oxford University Press, 2001)

Schnelle, Udo. *Apostle Paul: His Life And Theology* (Grand Rapids: Baker, 2005)

The World of the New Testament

Nickelsburg, George W. E. *Ancient Judaism and Christian Origins: Diversity, Continuity and Transformation* (Minneapolis: Fortress, 2003)

Rousseau, John J., and Rami Arav. *Jesus and his World: An Archaeological and Cultural Dictionary* (Minneapolis: Fortress, 1995)

Tiede, David L., and Calvin J. Roetzel (eds.). *The World That Shaped the New Testament* (rev. ed.; Louisville: Westminster John Knox Press, 2002)

Subject Index

Subject Index

Scripture Index

Major discussions are in bold.